The Martin Ukulele

The Little Instrument That Helped Create a Guitar Giant

Tom Walsh & John King

HAL LEONARD BOOKS
AN IMPRINT OF HAL LEONARD CORPORATION

Published in 2013 by Hal Leonard Books
An Imprint of Hal Leonard Corporation
7777 West Bluemound Road
Milwaukee, WI 53213

Trade Book Division Editorial Offices
33 Plymouth St., Montclair, NJ 07042

Photo credits can be found on pages 209–211, which constitute an extension of this copyright page.

Printed in the United States of America

Book design by Tom Walsh

Library of Congress Cataloging-in-Publication Data is available upon request.

ISBN 978-1-4768-6879-0

www.halleonardbooks.com

To Nuni, the love of my life

Contents

Preface

In 1990, my good friend James Heinegg gave me a ukulele for my birthday. James is a wonderful guitar player, and he thought just maybe I'd be interested in learning to play an instrument also. The ukulele was a plywood ukulele made in Japan, probably from the 1960s, that he had found at an antique store. The ukulele was not at all a popular instrument at the time, but I managed to track down a few older books with chords and basic songs. Soon, I was hooked.

As a big fan of antique stores, flea markets, and garage sales, I soon found the opportunity to upgrade to a better quality ukulele, and then another, and then another. I introduced the instrument to a few of my friends and soon I started to run into others who had an interest in this under-appreciated instrument. Whenever anybody talked about the best sounding ukuleles, one name always topped the list—Martin ukuleles. When I looked into buying a new Martin ukulele at the time, I learned they were only made on special order and that even the most basic Style 0 was well in excess of $1000. This led me to look into the vintage market. At the time a clean vintage Style 3K could be had for less than Martin was charging for a new Style 0. I finally saved up my money and purchased a nice 1920s Style 2 soprano with its original hardshell case in New York City at Chelsea Guitars. From that day on, I basically stopped playing any of the dozen or so other ukuleles I had accumulated.

My interest in the general history of the ukulele grew over the years, and my interest in Martin ukuleles grew as I picked up a few more of them. My sister called one day and told me she had found a ukulele that had been left behind in a trash can in the house she had just moved into. The house was a 1950s era home, so I figured it was most likely a plastic ukulele, but I still said I would be happy to take it. The ukulele was very dirty but clearly a nice old instrument labeled Oliver Ditson on the headstock and in the soundhole. I had to call a friend who knew more about ukuleles than I did at the time to find out that it was a rare 1920s Martin-made Ditson Style 3 mini-dreadnought ukulele. Then I lucked into an inexpensive Style 0 at an antique store in Seattle. Next was a Martin-made Wurlitzer Style 1K at a street fair in Rutherford, New Jersey. I suddenly found myself to be a Martin ukulele collector.

In 1996, I agreed to become one of the founders of the Ukulele Hall of Fame Museum, a newly-forming non-profit organization dedicated to the preservation of ukulele history. In September of that year we held our first Ukulele Expo, in Montague, Massachusetts. It was at this Expo that I first met my wife, Nuni. Nuni, the great-granddaughter of early ukulele-maker Manuel Nunes, had flown out from Seattle to come to the Expo. Less than a year later we were married.

I first met John King in 2001, after he had released his first CD on which he played Bach on the unaccompanied ukulele. Later that year he flew in from Florida and played at Ukulele Expo 2001. Nuni and I soon became good friends with John. Within a couple of years John had joined the Board of Directors of the Museum and was soon participating in induction ceremonies. After years of inducting members into the Hall of Fame at our Ukulele Expos between 1996–2004, we began doing inductions at various ukulele events organized by other groups. When the Ukulele Guild of Hawaii held its convention in November of 2006, John, Nuni, Nuni's sister Donelle, and I all flew to Hawaii to participate in that year's Ukulele Hall of Fame inductions. Donelle is a graphic artist and creates beautiful portraits for each Hall of Fame Inductee. The 2006 Hall of Fame inductees were Herb Ohta (Ohta San) and Frank Henry Martin. When it came time to induct someone from Martin into the Ukulele Hall of Fame, Frank Henry was the obvious choice. He had run the company through the period of the ukulele's development and greatest success. John spoke at Martin's induction ceremony, discussing the important place that Frank Henry held in ukulele history. Unfortunately, no Martin representative was able to attend the ceremony.

In April of 2007, John flew in to New Jersey, and Nuni, Donelle, he, and I all drove out to Nazareth, to present the portrait of Frank Henry to a representative at Martin. We were greeted warmly when we arrived by Dick Boak, Director of Artist Relations at Martin. Dick opened the ukulele cases at the beautiful new Martin Museum, posed for pictures with us holding famous ukuleles like the Daisy and the Konter ukuleles, and led us around the factory on a personal tour. Dick had heard that John was working on a book about the general history of the ukulele, and when we were returning from lunch he casually suggested that someone should really write a book specifically about Martin ukuleles. John and I immediately agreed, and this project was born.

Between 2007 and 2009 John and I made numerous trips out to Nazareth, searching for and photographing every bit of ukulele-related information we could find. Nuni often accompanied us and helped with the research and photography. When in Nazareth we always got to hear from Dick about new ukulele models they were working on at Martin. I even had the honor of lending them two of my vintage Martin Style 3 ukuleles, which they used as they were planning their new Style 3 ukuleles. John and I scanned and photographed many thousands of documents, so that we could do the work on the book from our homes, using our photo archive to piece together the Martin Ukulele story. By early 2009 I was working on tabulating ukulele production totals and John had written the first chapter of the book. It seemed the book would progress quickly. Then came the day that I received a phone call from another good friend, Byron Yasui. Byron had spoken to John's brother Paul, who had told him that John had died suddenly of a heart attack. Nuni and I were crushed. We had lost our best friend.

It was difficult for me to get back to work on the book later that year. John and I had put too much into the book already for me to just drop it, but I hardly knew where to start after he was gone. For the last four years I have worked on the book primarily on my own, although Nuni has been invaluable as my proofreader. I am happy and relieved to finally complete the work, and I hope it will be enjoyed by Martin ukulele fans the world over for many years to come.

Tom Walsh

**John King, at the Martin Museum, in a photo
taken on the day that this book project was born.**

Acknowledgments

I would like to thank the following people for their help in creating this book.

Dick Boak, the man in charge of the Museum, Archives, and Special Projects at C. F. Martin & Co. Dick was helpful in so many ways it would be difficult to list all he has done to help with preparation of this book. From initially suggesting the topic to carefully going through the final proofs, Dick has played an important role every step of the way. His efforts in preserving and organizing the Martin Archives and his willingness to repeatedly open the Archives to us made this work possible. I'd like to also thank Chris Martin and everyone at C. F. Martin & Co. for allowing us to do what we needed to do to complete this project.

Frederik Goossens, who helped in many ways, including supplying beautiful photographs of his rare ukuleles, sharing his vast knowledge of Martin ukuleles, and helping me to go through the section on Martin ukulele specifications, offering suggestions and corrections.

Donelle Nunes Sawyer for helping me to understand Adobe InDesign, and for setting up the templates that I have used in preparing the book. Also for her constant encouragement over the last six years.

Greig Hutton, who supplied many pieces of useful information from the Martin Archives that John and I somehow missed during our many visits.

My good friend and fellow ukulele historian Jim Tranquada, for his constant encouragement, even as he was working diligently to finish his own book, *The Ukulele, A History.*

Everyone who contributed historical photographs, photographs of their own instruments, and those who graciously allowed me to photograph and include instruments from their personal collections, including Mark Brown, William Bunch, Leo Coulson, Warren Dovel, Steve Farr, Frederik Goossens, The Mountain Apple Company, Jerry Murbach, Dave Pasant, Roger Phillips, Andy Roth, Billy Voiers, Dave Wasser, Bill Watson, Paul Weber, and Stan Werbin. Note: Full photo credits are listed in the back of the book immediately before the index.

All the contributors at The Four-String Farmhouse forum of the Unofficial Martin Guitar Forum, who have not only shared their passion for Martin ukuleles, but have openly shared information about instrument specifications and dating. Special thanks to Terry Chapman, Frederik Goossens, Mike Halloran, Remco Houtman-Janssen, and Jeff Mercer.

Brian and Paul Majeski of the *Music Trades,* who allowed me to research the archives of their magazine, which has served the music community since 1890.

Everyone at Hal Leonard who has helped bring this project to completion, especially Clare Cerullo, John Cerullo, Carol Flannery, and Brad Smith.

All of my fellow ukulele enthusiasts who have shared their interest in this wonderful little instrument, including those already mentioned as well as Jim and Liz Beloff, Benny Chong, Tony Coleman, Chris Davis, Jay Dougherty, Joel Eckhaus, Tom Favilla, James Hill, Chris, Casey, Sam, Fred, and the entire Kamaka ohana, Bret Klesk, Ken Murray, Geoff Rezek, Lyle Ritz, Hisako and Kazuyuki Sekiguchi, Ralph Shaw, Jake Shimabukuro, Paul Syphers, Bryan Tolentino, Byron Yasui, and Asa Young.

Richard Long, for his help with historical information used in the first chapter.

To my fellow Martin researchers who have written about the company, shared information, and helped organize the Martin Archives, including John Woodland, Richard Johnson, Philip Gura, and especially the first person to explore the history of the Martin Company—Mike Longworth. Mike's book was the first careful look at Martin instruments, including their unsurpassed ukuleles. Mike was always willing to share his vast knowledge of the Martin company. He was a ukulele enthusiast who attended a number of our Ukulele Expos, and was always a pleasure to share stories with. Mike has been sorely missed since his death in 2003.

Debi King, Paul and Joan King, and the entire King family, for allowing John the freedom to spend so much time on this project and for their encouragement even after suffering their devastating loss.

My wife Nuni, who has helped me get this book done in every way possible. She has had to suffer my sitting in front of the computer for large stretches of the last six years, yet she has constantly offered encouragement. At times when I was ready to scrap the whole project she convinced me to persevere. She has been an excellent proofreader, and has helped me to make the book clearer and more interesting. I never could have done this without her.

And, of course, my coauthor John King. By far the most enjoyable parts of this whole project were the times when John stayed with me and Nuni, making daily pilgrimages to Nazareth to unearth more of the wonderful ukulele history contained in the Martin Archives. John was quite simply our best friend. His shocking death in 2009 at the age of just 55 was devastating to us. His remarkable knowledge of music in general and ukulele history in particular as well as his unsurpassed playing technique will always be a source of inspiration. To us, his absence is profound, but he will always be in our hearts.

Tom Walsh

John King 1953–2009

C. F. Martin in Europe

WHO IS SO STUPID THAT HE CANNOT SEE AT A GLANCE THAT A GRANDFATHER'S ARMCHAIR OR A STOOL IS NO GUITAR, AND SUCH AN ARTICLE APPEARING AMONG OUR INSTRUMENTS MUST LOOK LIKE SAUL AMONG THE PROPHETS.

— Memorandum of the Worshipful Guild of Violin-Makers of Neukirchen, 1826.

On a chilly and damp Monday in April, 1933, Nazareth, Pennsylvania service club members assembled in the Milchsack Auditorium of the Nazareth YMCA to celebrate the centennial of "one of the oldest industries of the entire community"—C.F. Martin & Co., manufacturers of the world-renowned Martin guitar. Among the capacity crowd gathered to pay homage to the House of Martin were Rotarians and Lions, Nazareth Chamber of Commerce and Building & Loan Association members, and friends and guests from neighboring towns and cities. Tables were decorated and a luncheon was served befitting the occasion; an invocation was offered up and familiar songs were sung to the accompaniment of a piano. Then, as described in the *Nazareth Item*, came the introduction "or rather the treat, as no introduction was necessary," of Frank Henry Martin, who rose to his feet "to relate the experience of a concern operating continuously for a period of one hundred years."

With the aid of hand-written notes, Frank Henry delivered a straight-forward, craftsman-like meditation on the history of the Martin guitar as reflected in the lives of his forebears, particularly that of his grandfather, Christian Frederick Martin, Sr.:

One hundred years ago, in the Fall of 1833, Christian Frederick Martin landed in New York with his wife, one son Christian Frederick Jr., and an infant daughter. What moved him to leave his home in Germany we can only gather from records of what transpired there... It is a fair assumption that he, in common with many others of his time, felt dissatisfied with Old World surroundings and longed for the freedom of a new country.

Christian Friedrich Martin, son of the carpenter and musical instrument maker Johann Georg Martin (1765-1832), was born January 31, 1796 at Neukirchen in Vogtland, a Germanic province of the Kingdom of Saxony. Little is known of Martin's early life and education in Neukirchen a small town named for the "new church" built there in the thirteenth century and renowned for its community of instrument makers. Martin was the second of five children, only three of whom survived infancy and was well educated, as his many existing letters and business records attest. A small manuscript volume of keyboard music preserved in the C. F. Martin & Co. Archives also implies he was musically trained. Dated 1809, the Clavier Büch von Christian Friedrich Martin recalls the collections of music Johann Sebastian Bach lovingly prepared for his wife and eldest son in the neighboring principality of Anhalt-Köthen in the 1720s. Presumably he learned to work wood from his father who saw promise in the boy, for Christian Friedrich would one day find himself employed in the Vienna workshop of the noted guitar maker, J. G. Stauffer.

Martin was married in Vienna in 1824, but it is not known when he arrived there from Saxony. He grew up in the era of the Napoleonic Wars, when Europe was in a state of social and political turmoil. In 1815, following Napoleon's defeat at Waterloo, the map of Europe was redrawn at the Congress of Vienna. Saxony then became part of a coalition of sovereign principalities and free cities known as the German Confederation. Did Martin travel to Vienna during the tumultuous years of the Napoleonic Wars or later, during the relatively stable period after the Congress of Vienna?

In 1815, Vienna was a city of narrow streets, magnificent houses and a few old buildings that recalled the Middle Ages. It was the third largest metropolis in Europe, after London and Paris, with a population of a quarter-million people. Auguste La Garde-Chambonas, a French noble present at the time of the Congress, described Vienna as having a comfortable and prosperous population. "The families of the trades people and artisans," La Garde-Chambonas observed, "testify at once, by the expense in which they indulge, their own industry."

Among these industrious artisans was Johann Georg Stauffer, the guitar maker Martin would ultimately work for in Vienna. A native Viennese, Stauffer was the pupil of Franz Geissenhof, a Bavarian violin maker, and Ignaz Christian Partl, taking over the latter's shop when Partl died in 1819. Stauffer built his early guitars in the Italian style, after the Neapolitan Giovanni Battista Fabricatore, whose instruments were characterized by a loud sound that died out rapidly, a fingerboard flush with the table, the higher frets inlaid into the soundboard, and a top of spruce or pine with maple back and sides like a violin. Stauffer's guitars took on an even stronger resemblance to

The Baptismal Certificate of Christian Friedrich Martin, over 200 years old yet still very colorful.

instruments of the violin family with the arrival in Vienna of the guitarist Luigi Legnani in 1822. Legnani, a virtuoso performer and, more importantly, an instrument maker, designed and played a guitar with a fingerboard like a violin or cello, which projected over the table of the instrument. The "Legnani Model" as it came to be known, with a stylized, scroll-like peghead and fitted with an adjustable neck, soon epitomized the Austro-Italian guitar and was openly copied and manufactured by Stauffer, Stauffer's son, Johann Anton, and Martin.

As Stauffer's pupil, Martin may have had interactions with a host of guitarists in Vienna, both amateur

and professional. Guitar heroes with names like Heinrich Gründler, an amateur who organized a benefit concert for soldiers blinded in the Napoleonic wars, Anton Diabelli, a music publisher who contributed the theme for Beethoven's "Diabelli" Variations, and Vincenz Schuster, for whom Stauffer created the cello-like arpegionne, or bowed guitar. Prior to Legnani's arrival, the great Italian guitar virtuoso and composer Mauro Giuliani lived and performed in Vienna from 1806 to 1819, moving in the same artistic circles as Beethoven, Franz Schubert, and Johann Nepomuk Hummel. Whether Martin had any contact with Giuliani, or even Legnani, is not known. Undoubtedly, exposure to such first-rate performers, if it occurred, would have had a profound affect on Martin's understanding of guitar construction and its relation to tone and playability, both hallmarks of his later production.

Martin returned to Neukirchen sometime between the births of his first two children: Christian Friedrich, Jr., born in Vienna on October 2, 1825, and Rosalie Ottilie, born in Neukirchen on May 4, 1832. A little-known biography of Martin written in 1913 by his granddaughter relates that, after their marriage, Christian Friedrich and his wife, Ottilie Kühle Martin, remained in Vienna "for four years returning thence to his birthplace in Saxony," about 1828. In a narrative taken from a 1927 German publication, *The Historical Review for the Joint Celebration of the Musical Instrument Makers' Guild*, Martin supposedly returned to Neukirchen about 1826, just in time to come into conflict with the Worshipful Guild of Violin Makers over his guitar-making activities there. However, recent research has shown that the original Guild documents—consisting of repeated petitions to regional authorities for a directive restricting the manufacture of guitars to guildsmen—do not mention Christian Friedrich Martin, calling into question whether he was really living and working in Neukirchen at the time.

Exactly why Martin left Europe may never be known. Alban Voigt, who brought the Historical Review account to the attention of Frank Henry Martin when it was first published, remarked that Christian Friedrich emigrated because he "got tired of having always to fight against [the] narrow-mindedness and jealousy" of the Guild of Violin Makers. Though conjectural, this view has merit considering the disparaging comments directed at Martin's father in the Guild petitions. Frank Henry seconded and effectively immortalized Voigt's opinion in his 1933 centennial address; ever since it has been an immutable component of Martin lore.

Statistically, Christian Friedrich Martin was one among tens of thousands of German-speaking immigrants who fled Europe in the 1830s because of misgovernment, over-population, over-crowding, and taxation. Additionally, reports from America were idealistic and left the impression that America offered refuge from the economic, social, and political issues in Germany. On November 2, 1832, nearly four years to the day after his mother's death, Martin's father passed away. Less than a year later, apparently dissatisfied with Old World surroundings, Christian Friedrich gathered up his family, made his way north through Leipzig to the port of Bremen, and left Europe for the freedom of a new country.

Christian Frederick Martin

From the Old World to the New

THIS WAS THE SECRET OF AMERICA: A NATION OF PEOPLE WITH THE FRESH MEMORY OF OLD TRADITIONS WHO DARED TO EXPLORE NEW FRONTIERS, PEOPLE EAGER TO BUILD LIVES FOR THEMSELVES IN A SPACIOUS SOCIETY THAT DID NOT RESTRICT THEIR FREEDOM OF CHOICE AND ACTION.

— John F. Kennedy, *A Nation of Immigrants*

Saxony to Nazareth

C. F. Martin Sr. arrived in New York City in 1833, apparently with enough money to get both his business and his family firmly established. He opened a store at 196 Hudson Street that sold a full line of musical merchandise, much of which Martin imported from his homeland in Germany. He also sold guitars of his own manufacture. Heinrich (Henry) Schatz, a fellow luthier and a friend of Martin from Neukirchen, had come to New York City two years prior and may have played a part in Martin's decision to immigrate. Schatz formed a partnership with Martin in 1835, then moved to eastern Pennsylvania where he continued to work with Martin, sometimes sending guitars to be finished that he had started. By all accounts Martin's New York business was a successful one. At the least, Martin did well enough to allow him to move his business and family to Pennsyl-

The Martin archives contains an incredible collection of ledgers dating all the way back to the company's New York City days in the 1830s.

C. F. Martin and his friend Henry Schatz formed a partnership in 1835, when Martin was located in New York City. Labels like this one were used in guitar cases of the day.

vania at the end of the decade. He sold off his musical merchandise stock and purchased an eight-acre plot just outside of Nazareth, at Cherry Hill in Bushkill Township, not far from where Schatz had settled in Millgrove. The Pennsylvania countryside has been described as looking quite similar to the landscape they had left in Germany, and the Moravian community there had strong ties to the homeland. Frank Henry, in his speech at the company's 100th anniversary celebration, noted that after the move "Fredrick Martin and Henry Schatz could work at their beloved trade in quiet, surrounded by the hills of Pennsylvania just as they once lived among the hills of Saxony." Without the extra responsibilities of running a full-line musical merchandise store, C. F. Sr. was able to concentrate on his specialty, building high quality guitars. Age fifteen at the time of the move, his son C. F. Jr. was likely in the early years of learning his father's trade.

The Martins made the short move from Cherry Hill to Nazareth in 1859, and in 1867 C. F. Sr. officially went into business with his son and nephew, forming C. F. Martin & Co. When C. F. Sr. died in early 1873, the company was left in good hands. Both C. F. Jr. and C. F. Hartmann had been working for the company for over thirty years. In the mid-1880s, C. F. Jr. became the sole owner of the company. His reign as company leader was brief, however; he died after a short illness in 1888 at the age of just sixty-three. Along with seven daughters, C. F. Jr. had fathered only one son, Frank Henry Martin, born in October of 1866. Upon his father's death, Frank Henry would take control of the company at the age of just twenty-two. His youth may have been a factor in his willingness to try new ideas; a willingness that would open up his company to unprecedented growth over the next sixty years.

Frank Henry Martin

Madeira to Honolulu

The idea of a cabinetmaker branching out into musical instrument construction was certainly not unique to Germany. In 1879 on the small island of Madeira, a Portuguese possession about 600 miles southwest of Lisbon, lived three such woodworkers with shared dreams of a better life in a new land. In April of that year, Augusto Dias, Manuel Nunes, and Jose do Espirito Santo left for the islands of Hawaii along with 417 other Madeirans. In exchange for their passage, these three men accepted contracts as agricultural laborers. Like C. F. Sr., they had left their European homeland and relocated their families to a new world in hopes of establishing a better life. As with Martin, they settled in a land that had physical similarities with the native country. Madeira and Hawaii, due to their volcanic origins, have many physical characteristics in common and also share in their geographic remoteness from any mainland.

After completing their contract work, most likely in the sugarcane fields on other Hawaiian islands, Dias, Nunes, and Santo all returned to Honolulu to get back in the woodworking business.

Right: An example of what a machete looked like in Madeira around the time the first Madeirans came to Hawaii. Luthier Dave Means built this meticulous reproduction of an original machete made in Madeira by Octavianno Nunes around the middle of the 1800s.

It is not documented that any of these three cabinet-makers had experience making musical instruments in their native Madeira, but it is clear from their existing early instruments that they all had solid knowledge of the design and building techniques required to make the typical Madeiran stringed instruments. Along with other woodworking, each was building instruments in Hawaii by the middle of the 1880s. They built stringed instruments of various sizes, most similar to those of their native Madeira.

The popularity of two Madeiran instruments, the rajão and the machete, grew quickly in Hawaii. The machete was a small instrument with four strings tuned DGBD in order from lowest to highest. The rajão was a larger instrument with five strings, similar in size to a modern tenor ukulele. The rajão used a re-entrant tuning, DGCEA, with the C of the third string being the lowest note. The modern re-entrant GCEA tuning of the four-string ukulele seems clearly to have come from the tuning of the rajão, simply by leaving out the fifth string. There is even indication that it may not have been an uncommon practice in Hawaii at the time for some players to leave the

fifth string off the rajão. There are a number of photographs and illustrations from Hawaii in the 1880s and 1890s where a five-string rajão is strung with just four strings, and in each case it is the D string that is omitted. Strung like this, the rajão has the exact tuning that was applied to the four-string machete. Thus the instrument that would eventually be known in Hawaii as the ukulele was actually a cross of two Madeiran instruments; it was the size of the machete, but tuned like first four strings of a rajão.

By the late 1880s and early 1890s the machete began to be referred to as the ukulele, and the rajão became commonly known as the taropatch fiddle (or taropatch guitar). The Hawaiian word 'ukulele predates the arrival of the Madeirans; before it was applied to the machete the word meant simply a flea. Exactly when and who first applied the name to the instrument is not known, but by the late 1880s the word was being used as the name for the Madeiran machete. The term taropatch fiddle was sometimes used to describe both the machete and the rajão, but eventually came to be applied specifically to the larger instrument. By adapting the rajão tuning to the

Postcard of a young girl in traditional Madeiran attire, holding a machete.

Photo of a woman holding an early ukulele, taken in Honolulu by photographer J. A. Gonsalves, who, in 1879, arrived in Hawaii on the same ship as ukulele makers Dias, Nunes, and Santo. Circa 1890.

ukulele, the two could be played with very similar chordings, making it easier for a player of one to play the other, especially with the rajão's fifth string removed.

Generally made almost completely from Hawaiian koa wood (acacia koa), the ukulele came to be thought of as a Hawaiian instrument and its Portuguese origins began to fade. Bolstered by King David Kalākaua's endorsement as part of his widespread patronage of native music and dance, the ukulele had been embraced early on by the Hawaiian people. Despite the popularity of the instrument in Hawaii, it remained little known outside of the islands as the new century approached.

Left: Diagram from *One Summer In Hawaii*, written by Helen Mather and published in 1891. Along with a guitar and other instruments, the illustration features a ukulele and a five-string taropatch. Note that the taropatch, despite having five tuning pegs, appears to be strung with just four strings. Strung this way a taropatch would be tuned GCEA, just like a ukulele.

Right: A five-string taropatch made in Hawaii circa 1890.

Above: A postcard view of Funchal, Madeira, the hometown of Augusto Dias, Manuel Nunes, and Jose do Espirito Santo.

Changing Tastes

NOW I HEAR SOMEONE SAY 'PRAY TELL WHAT IS A 'UKELELE' FOR THERE ARE PERHAPS MANY, WHO LIKE MYSELF HAD NEVER HEARD OF THE INSTRUMENT BEFORE. THE NAME TRANSLATED MEANS "HOPPING FLEA." IT IS A SMALL INSTRU-MENT, IN APPEARANCE LIKE A GUITAR, BUT SMALLER THAN A MANDOLIN AND IS MADE OF A PECULIAR WOOD GROWN ONLY IN THE HAWAIIAN ISLANDS. IT IS AN INSTRUMENT OF THE HAWAIIANS, BUT VERY POPULAR AMONG CALIFORNIANS.

— Edward R. Day, "My Visit In California, 1913." The *Crescendo*

Hawaii Comes to the Mainland

The late 1880s and early 1890s in Hawaii were a period of political turmoil. In 1887, King David Kalākaua was forced under the threat of violence by white business leaders to sign a new constitution that greatly reduced his authority. When Kalākaua died in 1891, he was succeeded by his sister, Lili'uokalani, who intended to restore some of the power the monarchy had lost. Instead, however, the Queen was overthrown in 1893 and replaced by the Provisional Government of Hawaii, which was replaced in turn the following year by the Republic of Hawaii. In 1898, the islands were annexed by the United States to become the Territory of Hawaii. This momentous series of events brought Hawaii into the eye of the American public as it never had been before. As control of the islands moved into the hands of white businessmen, efforts to promote Hawaii's products on the mainland and to stimulate tourism led to Hawaii's increased presence at World's Fairs in the U.S., showcasing island goods and featuring native musicians and exotic hula dancers.

The first known appearance in the U.S. of Hawaiian musicians with ukuleles was a group of men billed as the Volcano Singers, who sang and played native instruments at the Hawaiian Pavilion on the midway of the 1893 World's Columbian Exposition in Chicago. The pavilion featured the Cyclorama, a colossal painting intended to give visitors a view of what it would be like to visit the great volcano of Kilauea. The Volcano Singers played two gui-

Frank Henry Martin became President of C. F. Martin & Co. in 1888 at just 22 years of age. Between that time and his death the Martin Company grew from a small maker of high quality guitars to a major manufacturer of fine fretted instruments.

Left: Anthony Zablan, in a colorized version of a photograph taken at the 1901 Pan-American Exposition in Buffalo, New York, in 1901.

Below: The Cyclorama building on the midway at the 1893 World's Columbian Exposition in Chicago.

tars, a five-string taro-patch, and a ukulele. Hawaiian musicians were seen and heard at many other fairs and expositions over the next fifteen years, including the 1894 Midwinter International Exposition in San Francisco, the 1899 Greater American Exposition in Omaha, the 1901 Pan-American Exposition in Buffalo, the 1905 Lewis and Clark Centennial Exposition in Portland Oregon, and the 1909 Alaska-Yukon Pacific Exposition in Seattle. The varied groups of Hawaiian performers from each of these appearances often stayed on the mainland touring the country. In this way, those parts of the country that were not near one of the big expositions often had Hawaiian music come to them. It was during this first decade of the 1900s that Hawaiian music started to creep into the American consciousness. Little did anyone know how completely infatuated Americans would become with it during the second decade. The strange sounds of instruments from an exotic land were about to capture a nation's heart as well.

An important moment in the spread of Hawaiian music on the mainland was the production of Richard Walton Tully's play *The Bird of Paradise*. Opening in 1911 in Los Angeles and on Broadway in 1912, the play featured the music of native Hawaiian musicians playing ukuleles and Hawaiian guitars. Although its Broadway run lasted only three months, the play was very popular as a road show. It toured many cities across the country in the years following its Broadway run, and eventually had successful runs in Europe and Australia. Many contemporary accounts give a great deal of credit to the play in popularizing Hawaiian music and the instruments needed to play it.

Back in Nazareth

*W*hen Frank Henry took control of the Martin company in 1888, the company was well established as the maker of some of the highest quality guitars available anywhere. Still, the company had seen little growth in many years, and Frank Henry looked to new markets hoping to widen his customer base.

In 1880 a group of touring European musicians came to the United States and caused quite a sensation. The group, referred to in the U.S. as the "Figaro Spanish Students," played music primarily on guitars and bandurrias, which were small twelve-string instruments with six doubled strings. The group spawned a number of touring imitators, many of whom replaced the bandurrias with another small double-coursed instrument, the mandolin. By the late 1880s, the growing fascination with the mandolin had caused American instrument manufacturers to enter the market and compete with the instruments that were being imported, primarily from Italy. Mandolin orchestras started to appear all over the U.S. and the demand for this newly popular instrument continued to grow. Hoping to capitalize on the surge, Frank Henry decided to enter the market. Martin's first mandolins, bowl-backed models similar to those produced by other manufacturers, were introduced around 1896. In the first twenty years of mandolin production Martin sold roughly as many mandolins as it did guitars, but the new instrument did little to substantially help Martin's bottom line. The company's slow growth could not nearly match the rapid expansion that much of its competition was enjoying. Companies like Lyon & Healy in Chicago were selling thousands of instruments per year—something that the much older Martin company had never been able to achieve.

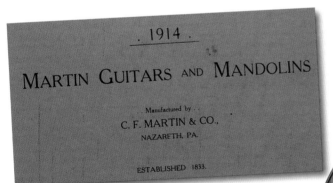

. 1914 .

MARTIN GUITARS AND MANDOLINS

Manufactured by
C. F. MARTIN & CO.,
NAZARETH, PA.

ESTABLISHED 1833.

Above: By 1914 Martin was regularly selling more mandolins each year than it was guitars. This title page from the 1914 catalog gives the two instruments equal billing.

Right: This harp guitar, made in 1902, is one example of Frank Henry's willingness to experiment with new instruments in an effort to grow the company.

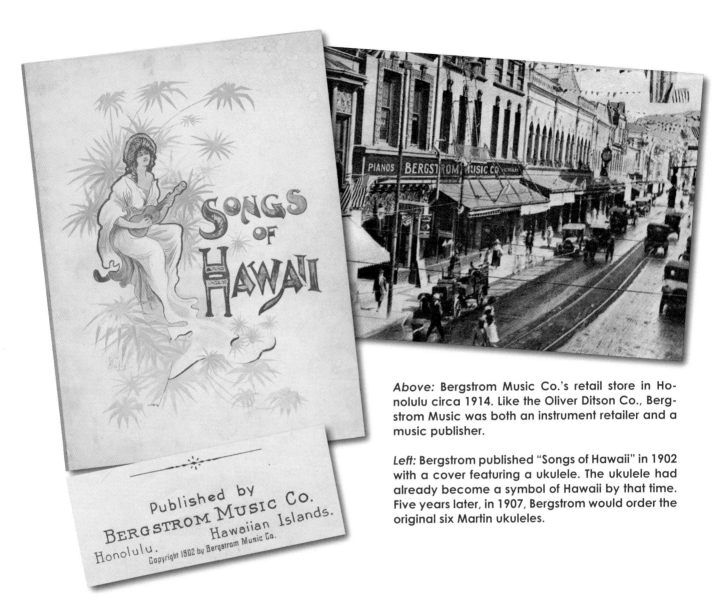

Above: Bergstrom Music Co.'s retail store in Honolulu circa 1914. Like the Oliver Ditson Co., Bergstrom Music was both an instrument retailer and a music publisher.

Left: Bergstrom published "Songs of Hawaii" in 1902 with a cover featuring a ukulele. The ukulele had already become a symbol of Hawaii by that time. Five years later, in 1907, Bergstrom would order the original six Martin ukuleles.

In a 1906 article written for the *Music Trades*, Charles Bobzin summarized Martin's difficulties in a few short sentences:

> Thirty years ago the guitar sought most was manufactured by a family named Martin, in the little town of Nazareth, Pa. How long this factory was in existence before that the writer does not know, but the output was limited and the prices asked for the instruments were practically prohibitive in those days, making it necessary for jobbers, dealers and retail buyers to look for similar goods in a cheaper market.

It seems Bobzin did not even realize that Martin was still in the instrument business. However, Frank Henry had been investing himself in maintaining Martin as a premiere instrument manufacturer, with a willingness to move the company into new markets to meet the changing needs of American musicians. Along with the new mandolin line, Martin tested other potential instrument markets. Experimental models of harp guitars, harp mandolins, and even bandurrias were built on special order. Still, nothing caught on strongly enough to warrant any major expansion in production.

In 1907 Bergstrom Music Co., a major Hawaiian music retailer, requested Martin make up a sample lot of six ukuleles. Martin made the ukuleles and established a selling price of $6.50 each. The sale was noted in December of that year, but no further orders were received. For a time it seemed the ukulele would join the harp guitar, harp mandolin, and bandurria as instruments with which the company experimented and then dropped. It would be another eight years before Martin would again get into ukulele manufacture.

The Original Six Martin Ukuleles of 1907

When a Hawaiian music store looked to Martin as a possible ukulele manufacturer, Frank Henry Martin was open to the possibility. In October of 1907, J. W. Bergstrom, of the Bergstrom Music Co., Honolulu, visited the East Coast. As Mike Longworth first reported in his classic *Martin Guitars: A History*, the first record of Martin ukulele production is a note in the sales ledger dated December 10, 1907. The sale was made to the Bergstrom Music Co. Ltd., of Honolulu, Hawaii. "6 Hawaiian Ukeleles made to sample as trial lot to calculate price." Martin arrived at a price of $6.50 each, charging Bergstrom a total of $39 for the six of them. It certainly seems possible that the J. W. Bergstrom trip and the ukulele order were related. Bergstrom Music had sold Martin guitars at least since 1900, so it would not be surprising if J. W. had visited the Martin factory on his trip east. Longworth makes the following statement about the ukuleles:

> The first Martin ukuleles were not well received. They were made much like a guitar, with too much bracing in the top. Spruce was used for the tops of these experimental models, and this material did not produce the light bouncy tone that is wanted in the uke. Since the tone was not acceptable, the matter rested.

It is unclear where the details of this account came from. There is no remaining correspondence from this time period, although some may have existed at the time Longworth was doing his research. It is also possible that he was passing along first hand information that he had heard from C. F. Martin III,

who would have been thirteen years old in 1907 and may have recalled that original trial lot. Still, some of the details in this description are curious.

It would be redundant to say both "to sample" and "as trial" if they were just trying to state that these first attempts were simply samples. It is much more likely that the words "made to sample" in the sales ledger denote that the ukuleles that Martin made in 1907 were to be patterned after a sample instrument, presumably supplied by Bergstrom. If a sample was supplied by Bergstrom, it certainly would have been a Hawaiian-made instrument most likely made by Manuel Nunes or Augusto Dias, who were the two prominent builders in Honolulu at the time. If this were the case, the sample instrument would have been a lightly-braced instrument made almost entirely from Hawaiian koa wood. Why Martin would have used guitar-like bracing on the top instead of the simple ladder bracing found on the Hawaiian ukulele is an interesting question.

The mention of the spruce top also raises some

Ukulele Method published by Bergstrom Music circa 1907, at around the same time Bergstrom ordered the first Martin ukuleles.

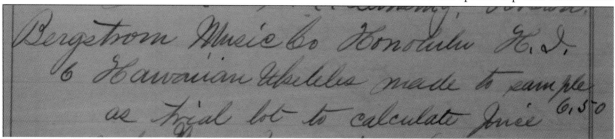

Ledger entry marking the sale of the original six ukuleles made in 1907 for Bergstrom Music of Honolulu.

questions. The Hawaiian instrument would have had a koa wood top, made from the same wood as the rest of the body. Was spruce unquestionably used on these trial instruments? Other evidence from the Martin archives suggests that it was the experimentation in the first batches of production ukuleles made in 1915 and early 1916 that indicated spruce for ukulele tops was inappropriate. In the first ten ukuleles recorded in the sales book, most are listed simply as "plain style" or "style 1," except one (serial no. 8) with a "plain mahogany top," another (no. 9) with a "veneered mahogany top," and a third (no. 6), with a "spruce top" sold to J. A. Handley of Lowell, Massachusetts, on November 18, 1915. At least one other spruce-topped ukulele was made during the first few months of production. In 1927, in correspondence with the Chicago Musical Instrument Co., C. F. III discussed their early ukulele production. Martin was responding to a request that they make a special model of ukulele bearing the name of Jennie Durkee, a well-known ukulele player and teacher of the 1920s. CMI proposed a spruce-topped "Martin-Durkee" model. C. F. III's response reads in part:

> We feel, however, that she would not want her name used on a Ukulele which was not fully up to the Martin standard of tone and we must say that we would hardly know how to make up an instrument sufficiently different in model and design from our present line and equally good in tone. When we began making ukuleles, more than ten years ago, we experimented considerably with different models and different woods, among them Spruce which we abandoned because it did not produce as free a tone as Mahogany.

If the original six ukuleles had failed in part due to their spruce tops, why would spruce have again been tested in 1915? None of the original six Martin ukuleles is known to exist, so it is hard to say for certain what doomed the first trial run of ukuleles. Because the lot was done "as trial to set price," one reasonable conclusion would be that the price was simply too high. At $6.50 each plus shipping to Hawaii, it would be tough for a distributor to make a profit. Adding on the standard 100 percent dealer mark-up would result in an instrument too expensive to sell in the islands where the competition was selling ukuleles for well under $10. A Bergstrom Ukulele Method book from this time period lists Hawaiian koa wood ukuleles at $5 and $7.50, retail. Martin shipped the six ukuleles to Hawaii and Bergstrom paid the bill, but they didn't place another ukulele order with Martin until ten years later, when the ukulele craze was in full swing.

Three ukuleles sold by Bergstrom Music of Honolulu at about the time they ordered the first six Martin ukuleles. If Martin patterned its first ukuleles after a "sample," the sample supplied by Bergstrom would likely have looked something like one of these.

From Coast to Coast

During the first decade of the 1900s, the popularity of Hawaii as a tourist destination was steadily increasing. With ukuleles popular as souvenirs being brought home by island visitors, the instrument's popularity on the mainland slowly began. As tourist travel to and from the islands was done almost exclusively from San Francisco and Los Angeles, the ukulele first gained popularity on the U.S. mainland along the West Coast. As demand grew, West Coast music retailers began to import and sell Hawaiian ukuleles. As early as 1907, the Los Angeles music retailer George J. Birkel Co. was running newspaper ads promoting the "Bouncing Flea."

When Bergstrom Music Co. in Honolulu ordered six ukuleles from Martin in 1907, it was looking for options in filling the huge demand in Hawaii. The Oliver Ditson Co., with branches in Philadelphia, New York City, and Boston, is the first East Coast retailer known to have sold ukuleles. Ditson advertised ukuleles at least as early as 1910 but, based on some early ukuleles with Ditson labels, they likely were selling them soon after the turn of the century. The instruments were standard Hawaiian koa wood instruments, at least some of which were made by Manuel Nunes. It is possible that Ditson was getting their instruments through Bergstrom Music in Honolulu, as Bergstrom likely was selling Ditson's goods in Hawaii. It is interesting to think that at the same time Ditson was importing Hawaiian ukuleles and distributing them from the East Coast, Bergstrom was reaching east to Martin looking for another possible ukulele supplier. Martin and Ditson would establish a direct East Coast ukulele connection eight years later.

In 1909 Ditson published the first mainland-made "Method for the Ukulele," edited by T. H. Rollinson. In 1910 Ditson's New York City branch, Chas. H. Ditson & Co., advertised a display of "Musical Instruments You Don't See Every Day" that included the ukulele along side Chinese crash cymbals, bandurria, Aeolian Harp, and other unusual instruments. It would be just a few short years before the ukulele would move from the ranks of the exotic and into the mainstream. Just months after The Broadway run of *The Bird of Paradise*'s Broadway run in 1912, the popularity of the ukulele in New York was evident. An article in October in the *Music Trade Review* noted that the Chas. Ditson store in New York was doing good business. "This house sold a great many Ukuleles the past few months. Many of these instruments go to the leading young ladies' schools in this country."

In 1916 when the first ukulele craze was in full thrust, the *Music Trades* magazine wrote a "History of the Hawaiian Ukulele" in which they looked for the root of the instrument's surging popularity and put *The Bird of Paradise* first in line for credit: "Five years ago very few Americans knew that there was such an instrument as the ukulele. Then it was that *The Bird of Paradise* began to tour the country, and those who were charmed and moved by its Hawaiian love-tragedy began to ask what were those little guitar-like instruments, whose haunting strains went far to create the atmosphere for Tully's poignant drama."

The play also introduced audiences to the sounds of the steel guitar. Joseph Kekuku, who claimed to have invented the method of playing a guitar using a piece of steel, was among the musicians who toured with the show. This new method of guitar playing soon also would play a major role at Martin, but not as big a role as the ukulele would play.

Right: Hawaiian-made ukulele sold by Ditson, circa 1910. Ditson's called this a no. 3, and that is what is written in pencil on its label. Strangely, the paper label (*above*) reads "Empire Mandolin."

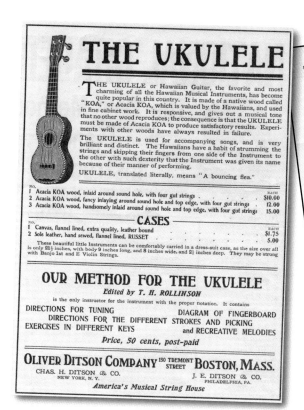

Above: This Ditson advertisement from 1910 shows that Ditson was carrying three styles of ukuleles and two styles of cases, as well as their own ukulele method book. The ukuleles were imported from Hawaii, quite likely purchased through Bergstrom Music.

Above: Joseph Kekuku, one of the early pioneers of Hawaiian steel guitar, toured for years with *The Bird of Paradise*. The play helped to popularize both Hawaiian music and the instruments needed to play it—the ukulele and the steel guitar. This pamphlet from the late 1920s advertised Kekuku's services as a teacher.

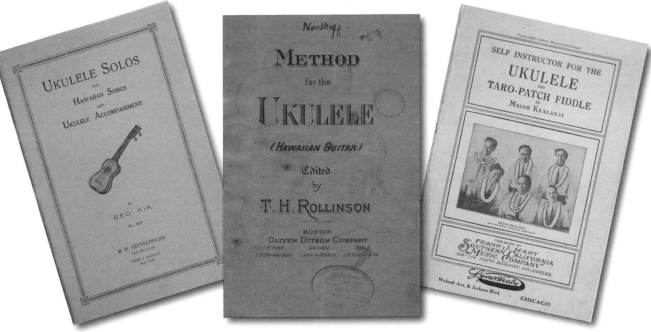

Although the popularity of the ukulele on the mainland grew faster on the West Coast than in the East, the Oliver Ditson Co. of Boston was the first to publish a ukulele method. In 1909 Ditson published their *Method for the Ukulele*, edited by T. H. Rollinson. It wasn't until 1914 that the California publishers started releasing their own ukulele methods, including *Ukulele Solos* by George Kia and the *Self Instructor for the Ukulele* by Major Kealakai.

Sudden Success

A FEATURE OF THE BOOK IS A CUT OF C. F. MARTIN, SR., WHO ESTABLISHED THE FIRM IN 1833 AND WHO WAS CONSIDERED THE FOREMOST GUITAR MAKER OF THE LAST CENTURY. UNDER THE DIRECTION OF HIS GRANDSON, F. H. MARTIN, THE HIGH STANDARDS OF TONE AND WORKMANSHIP WHICH HE ESTABLISHED ARE BEING MAINTAINED, AND AT THE SAME TIME THE LINE OF STYLES HAS BEEN BROADENED TO MEET THE NEEDS OF THE MODERN DEALER.

— The *Music Trades,* describing Martin's latest catalog, 1917

Martin Enters the Market

*I*n 1915 the already growing interest in Hawaiian music, and the ukulele in particular, was greatly accelerated by the opening of the Panama Pacific International Exposition in San Francisco. Although Hawaiian musicians had performed at numerous previous mainland fairs and expositions, never before had they been featured so prominently as they were at the PPIE. The Hawaiian Building featured a quintet led by Henry Kailimai, who was the composer of

No single song deserves more credit for helping to create the Hawaiian music craze than "On the Beach at Waikiki." Written by Henry Kailimai and performed regularly at the PPIE in 1915, it was a smash hit and became popular across the nation.

"On the Beach at Waikiki," one of the first Hawaiian songs to capture the attention of the nation. Many varied Hawaiian music performances were staged at the exposition. While the ukulele had become familiar to many Californians even before the PPIE, with over eighteen million fair-goers coming from across the country, a huge number of attendees had their first exposure to Hawaiian music, steel guitars, and particularly, the ukulele.

The Hawaiian music craze was sweeping across America by the time the exposition closed in December of 1915. While the steel guitar also surged in popularity, the ukulele was the more accessible instrument for Americans who wanted to participate first hand in the new trend. Both in Hawaii and on the mainland, new ukulele manufacturers jumped on the bandwagon. When musical instrument retailers along the East Coast looked for a more local source for the newly popular instrument, Martin was a logical choice.

No Martin company correspondence exists from the time they began full scale ukulele production, other than just a few letters. A single letter from the Southern California Music Co. discussing its area of sole agency is the only piece of correspondence remaining from the year 1915. The reply from Frank Henry, dated July 14, 1915, and carbon-copied on the back of the SoCal original, contains two sentences at the end that say quite a bit: "We note your ukulele enclosure; have you a market for the American made article? We are starting on them for the New York trade."

These two short sentences offer a surprising wealth of information about the early days of Martin's ukulele production. It is unclear exactly what is meant when Frank Henry mentions the "ukulele enclosure." The term enclosure was often used by the company when a borrowed or repaired instrument was included in a shipment. In this case the enclosure may have been an actual instrument, or it may refer to a ukulele pamphlet or other info that SoCal may have enclosed. The question about SoCal's market for the American-made article is interesting—it shows that Martin was not going into ukulele making due to the demand that had grown strongly along the Pacific Coast. Instead, they had been influenced by the "New York trade." Martin had a number of ties to the New York trade, but the particular men who would have been most familiar with the ukulele would

have been two employees of Chas. H. Ditson & Co., William J. Smith and Harry L. Hunt.

The Chas. H. Ditson store on East Thirty-fourth St. in New York City was technically a branch of the parent Oliver Ditson Co. of Boston, but the businesses were run separately. As early as 1910, Chas. Ditson & Co. had included a Hawaiian guitar and ukulele in a display of "Musical Instruments You Don't See Every Day." The display was put together by William J. Smith, who was Ditson's floor salesman in the small goods department. In an article from the *Music Trades* in May of 1915, Harry Hunt talks about Smith: "Our Mr. Smith, who ranks among the first guitar players of the country, has given particular study to Hawaiian music and other instruments. He has become very

Hawaiian music took the nation by storm beginning in 1915, and the ukulele soared in popularity along with it. New York City's Tin Pan Alley began putting out pseudo-Hawaiian titles, many of which were ukulele-themed. These eight pieces of sheet music all came out in 1915 or 1916. This was obviously before some of the songwriters even knew how to spell ukulele, and before some of the cover artists knew much about what one looked like.

expert at playing the ukulele and also the Hawaiian guitar."

"Mr. Smith" must have seen the growing interest in Hawaiian music as a career-changing opportunity. By October of 1915, Smith had left Ditson where he had worked for ten years and went into business for himself. On October 9th, Smith placed his first order with Martin for nine guitars and ten mandolins, which was noted in the Martin sales ledger as "stock for beginning business." The store opening was announced in the *Music Trades* in November, with the headline: "New Firm In Small Goods Trade. Wm. J. Smith & Co., New York, Will Specialize in Hawaiian Instruments." The article notes that "Mr. Smith stated that they would specialize in Hawaiian ukuleles, handling only the genuine native instruments."

Bursting onto the Scene

Despite Smith's claim that he would only carry "genuine native" instruments, he was near the head of the line when Martin finished its first ukuleles. George Stannard, a music teacher in Trenton, New Jersey, purchased the first two ukuleles recorded in the Martin sales ledger on October 29, 1915. However, it was the Ditson and Smith stores that bought the bulk of Martin's early ukulele production. Ukulele no. 5 was sold to Smith on November 13th, just weeks before the publication of the article quoted above. Ditson bought ukuleles no. 8 and no. 9 on November 18th. It is obvious from the sales records that the Martin ukulele changed Smith's opinion on the superiority of Hawaiian-made ukuleles. Of the 310 ukuleles in which Martin put serial numbers, 170 were made for Chas. H. Ditson and 61 were made for Wm. J. Smith. After purchasing just three Martin ukuleles, Chas. Ditson had Martin begin marking its ukuleles with the

Left: **This ukulele was sold by Martin to William J. Smith in May of 1916. Its serial number, 105, can be seen on the neck block (*above*). Smith (*below*), a talented player of the Hawaiian guitar and ukulele, left his job in the small goods department at Chas. H. Ditson's New York City store in 1915. Within months he opened his own music store specializing in Hawaiian instruments and was soon one of Martin's biggest customers.**

Ditson stamp and numbering them with their own distinct set of serial numbers. These earliest Ditson ukuleles were in the standard Martin body shape, as the wide-waisted Ditson models would not appear for a few more months.

Martin initiated ukulele production with three models, Styles 1, 2, and 3. The retail prices were $10, $15, and $25, respectively, with most retailers receiving a fifty percent discount. The bottom-of-the-line Style 1 cost more than many of the fancier looking Hawaiian-made ukuleles of the time. The fact that demand for Martin ukuleles developed so quickly is truly a testament to the quality of the ukulele Martin was producing. The first Style 2 ukulele sold on January 1, 1916 to Wm. J. Smith, and the first Style 3 sold to Chas. H. Ditson on March 3rd. Of the 143 serial-numbered Martin ukuleles, ninety-nine were Style 1s, forty were Style 2s, and only four were Style 3s. Of the 167 Ditson serial-numbered ukuleles, there were ninety-four Style 1s, sixty-three Style 2s, and ten Style 3s.

By 1915, the five-string taropatch fiddle or taropatch guitar that had developed in Hawaii out of the Madeiran rajão had been reinterpreted. A new instrument with eight strings in four courses was being made in the islands by the first decade of the 1900s, and by the early teens it had nearly completely displaced the five-string instrument. Tuned and played like a ukulele, this larger instrument took on the name of its predecessor and became known as a taropatch fiddle, or simply a taropatch. The taropatch was added to the Martin lineup in August of 1916, with a sale of two instruments to the Chas. H. Ditson Co. of New York. The sales ledger notes "1 Taropatch 8 stg."

The Style 3 was Martin's top-of-the-line ukulele from 1915–1921. These two examples are from 1916 or 1917. By 1918 Martin had added position markers to the fretboards. The ukulele on the right is the special wide-waisted model made for Chas. H. Ditson Co., while the ukulele on the left is a standard Martin model.

Regular model No. 1 style" and "1 Taropatch 8 stg. Spanish model No. 1 style." The Regular vs. Spanish styling very likely referred to the standard Martin ukulele body shape and the wide-waisted mini-Dreadnought body shape produced only for Chas. H. Ditson. The fact that Martin specified these were eight-string models shows that they already were contemplating a four-string version of the taropatch. It was two months before the next taropatch sale was made, as Ditson came back for more and other retailers began to request them. In October of 1916 Ditson ordered a total of fifty-six taropatches. These included the first made in Styles 2 and 3 (in both the regular and Ditson Spanish models), as well as the first four-string taropatch. The four-string instrument was really just a larger-bodied ukulele, quite similar to what Martin officially added to its catalog as the Concert Ukulele in 1925. Martin was the first manufacturer known to make a four-string ukulele with a larger body size—an idea that would prove quite popular in years to come, as demonstrated by the eventual production of concert, tenor, and baritone size ukuleles. By the end of its first full year of ukulele production Martin had nine model choices: three styles of taropatch, available in four- or eight-string configurations, and three styles of soprano. They were also able to make any of these models in their special Ditson body shape, so there were actually eighteen different configurations of the new small Hawaiian instruments.

Many minor changes were made to the ukulele models in the first few years of production. Construction details were refined, position markers were added

to the fingerboards, and the body was deepened slightly.

According to serial number records, Martin built 152 guitars in 1915 and 181 guitars in 1916. By the time they stopped putting serial numbers on their ukuleles in July of 1916, they had sold 310 ukuleles in under nine months. It is unlikely that Frank Henry yet understood that this was the beginning of a new era for the company. In the last six months of 1916, the sales ledger records sales of over 1,000 ukuleles.

By early 1917, Martin began to have trouble keeping up with the demand for its instruments. Although no correspondence from this time period is known to exist, there is evidence that the company had reached its limits—unable, perhaps for the first time, to keep up with the orders that were coming in. In March, the *Music Trades* reported on the first of many factory expansions stimulated by the new interest in Hawaiian instruments:

Work on the new building at C. F. Martin & Co.'s factory is practically completed and the firm expects to occupy the additional quarters at once, making every effort to meet the tremendous demand for Martin instruments, especially for the popular Hawaiian ukuleles. The additional men required by the demand for this new instrument were at first accommodated in the old buildings by means of the strictest economy of space, but as the Hawaiian music grew in popularity, it became necessary to provide additional floor space.

The Hawaiian style of guitar playing has been responsible for a very remarkable increase in the volume of Martin guitar sales, especially in the grade used for professional playing. The fact that these guitars are now being used by many of the well-known Hawaiian artists, as they have been used by leading soloists in the regular style of playing for more than eighty years, is an indication of the fine tone quality and satisfactory workmanship found in them.

The Hawaiian music craze sweeping the U.S. was directly responsible for the greatest period of growth that the Martin company had ever experienced. Martin produced 598 guitars in 1917, more than triple the amount it had made in each of the previous two years. Coupling that with 745 mandolins and 2060 ukuleles, Martin produced nearly 3500 instruments in the year. That total is over seven times the number of instruments it had made just two years earlier in 1915!

Original paper pattern for Ditson model taropatches (*above***), like this early Style 3 Ditson taropatch (***left***).**

Martin Standards Prevail

There were quite a few companies manufacturing ukuleles in the U.S. by 1917. Trying to capitalize on the popularity of genuine Hawaiian ukuleles, most companies produced models to compete with those being imported from the islands. Leonardo Nunes, who began producing ukuleles in Los Angeles in 1913, made instruments that were virtually identical in materials and construction to those being made in Hawaii. Of course, Nunes had learned the craft first-hand working with his father, Manuel, in Honolulu in the years before moving to California. Other mainland makers made ukuleles that looked similar to those coming from the islands, often labeling them deceptively and sometimes lying outright as to their place of origin. For example, Sherman Clay & Co. manufactured the "Hanalei Royal Hawaiian Ukulele" in Berkeley. The Hawaiian Ukulele Co. went into business in 1916 in Chicago. The Brooklyn company, Gretsch, after distributing Leonardo Nunes ukuleles for some time, sold ukuleles under its own brand name Kaholas with a paper label reading "Ukulele O Hawaii," remarkably similar to the label used by Nunes. Many companies used ambiguous phrases like "Genuine Hawaiian Koa Wood Ukuleles" or "Genuine Imported Hawaiian Koa Wood Ukuleles."

Yes, the koa wood was Hawaiian, but the ukuleles were not. A number of questionable ukulele brands with labels claiming Honolulu manufacture have no mention in any of the Honolulu directories or records of the time.

The Hawaiian makers were unhappy to be losing business to imitators. In a *New York Times* article from September 1915 with the headline "Hawaiians Are Angry," Hawaiian ukulele makers were said to be upset "because certain manufacturers of musical instruments in the United States are making ukuleles and stamping them with the legend 'Made in Hawaii.'" The article goes on to report that "the Hawaiians are devising a distinct trademark which they will ask to have protected by legislation." This trademark was filed for by the Honolulu Ad Club in May of 1916 and granted in July of 1917. The "Tabu Made in Hawaii" mark was used by numerous island manufacturers for many years to come to distinguish their ukuleles from mainland-made imitations.

When it came to ukulele production, Martin had a very different marketing plan than nearly every other mainland manufacturer. Whereas other manufacturers tried to compete with the Hawaiian makers by making slightly less expensive imitations of Hawaiian instruments or very inexpensive mass-produced models, Martin planned to compete by making a

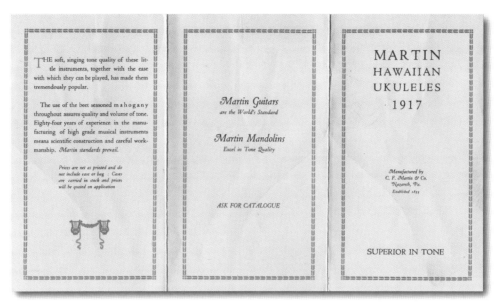

The very first pamphlet featuring Martin's new ukuleles, 1917.

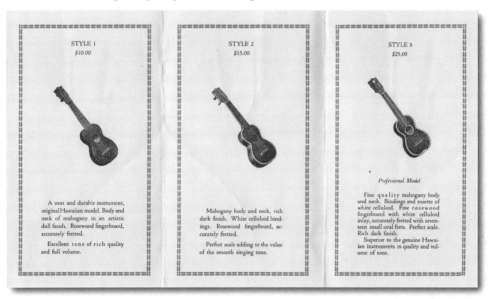

higher quality ukulele than any currently on the market. When Martin came out with its 1917 catalog, they included their first ukulele pamphlet. The *Music Trades* noted "a supplementary folder descriptive of the three ukulele styles which have been so popular among the trade is included." This little tri-fold was the first time Martin had advertised its ukuleles to the public. That it is titled "Martin Hawaiian Ukuleles" is misleading—Martin was by no means trying to associate its instruments with the genuine Hawaiian-made product. They made it quite clear that they felt their ukuleles were a cut above the rest. The description of the $25 Style 3 ukulele states right out "Superior to the genuine Hawaiian instruments in quality and volume of tone." Unlike so many of the other mainland manufacturers, Martin did not want to claim that their ukuleles were as good as the genuine Hawaiian product. Instead, they confidently stated that they were better. On the back of the folder the copy reads:

The soft, singing tone quality of these little instruments, together with the ease with which they can be played, has made them tremendously popular.

The use of the beet seasoned mahogany throughout assures quality and volume of tone. Eighty-four years of experience in the manufacturing of high grade musical instruments means scientific construction and

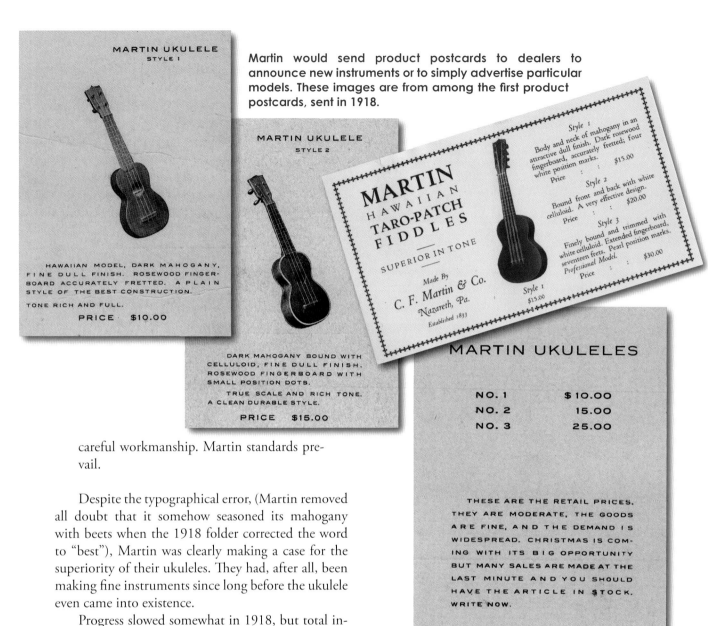

Martin would send product postcards to dealers to announce new instruments or to simply advertise particular models. These images are from among the first product postcards, sent in 1918.

MARTIN UKULELE
STYLE 1

HAWAIIAN MODEL, DARK MAHOGANY, FINE DULL FINISH. ROSEWOOD FINGERBOARD ACCURATELY FRETTED. A PLAIN STYLE OF THE BEST CONSTRUCTION.

TONE RICH AND FULL.

PRICE $10.00

MARTIN UKULELE
STYLE 2

DARK MAHOGANY BOUND WITH CELLULOID, FINE DULL FINISH. ROSEWOOD FINGERBOARD WITH SMALL POSITION DOTS.

TRUE SCALE AND RICH TONE. A CLEAN DURABLE STYLE.

PRICE $15.00

MARTIN
HAWAIIAN
TARO-PATCH FIDDLES
SUPERIOR IN TONE

Made By
C. F. Martin & Co.
Nazareth, Pa.
Established 1833

Style 1
$15.00

Style 1
Body and neck of mahogany in an attractive dull finish. Dark rosewood fingerboard, accurately fretted; four white position marks.
Price : $15.00

Style 2
Bound front and back with white celluloid. A very effective design.
Price : $20.00

Style 3
Finely bound and trimmed with white celluloid. Extended fingerboard, seventeen frets. Pearl position marks. Professional Model.
Price : $30.00

MARTIN UKULELES

NO. 1	$10.00
NO. 2	15.00
NO. 3	25.00

THESE ARE THE RETAIL PRICES. THEY ARE MODERATE, THE GOODS ARE FINE, AND THE DEMAND IS WIDESPREAD. CHRISTMAS IS COMING WITH ITS BIG OPPORTUNITY BUT MANY SALES ARE MADE AT THE LAST MINUTE AND YOU SHOULD HAVE THE ARTICLE IN STOCK. WRITE NOW.

careful workmanship. Martin standards prevail.

Despite the typographical error, (Martin removed all doubt that it somehow seasoned its mahogany with beets when the 1918 folder corrected the word to "best"), Martin was clearly making a case for the superiority of their ukuleles. They had, after all, been making fine instruments since long before the ukulele even came into existence.

Progress slowed somewhat in 1918, but total instrument sales still were at levels much higher than the company had known just a few years before. Ukulele sales dropped from over 2000 in 1917 to just under 1500 in 1918, and some people in the music business thought the fad was fading. Even as early as January of 1918, a report in the *Music Trades*, discussing the opinion of the proprietor of the small goods department at the Hauschildt music store in San Francisco, stated: "As far as strong demand is concerned, Mr. Hanson considers the ukulele a thing of the past." Hanson, like many, seemed to expect that the rapid growth of the ukulele would surely be followed by a rapid decline. That decline, however, was still about a decade away.

The dip in ukulele sales in 1918 was more likely a result of the First World War and the Spanish flu pandemic, and not due to any decline in the instrument's

popularity. By the time the war ended in November of 1918, the flu pandemic was also fading in the U.S., and ukulele sales began to reach even higher levels. In 1919, Martin's ukulele production soared to over 3500 instruments.

Ukulele pamphlets were printed in 1917 and 1918 as a supplement to the Martin catalog, but the 1919 catalog featured ukuleles in the main catalog alongside the company's guitars and mandolins. Their description:

The soft, singing quality and the easy action of these little instruments have made them very popular. They are built of mahogany stained dark, finished dull or semi-gloss.

Eighty-six years' experience in making

These are the earliest photographs of ukuleles in the Martin archives. Dating to 1919 or 1920, photographs of a Style 1 (*left*) and a Style 2 (*right*) were used to produce the engravings (*below*) which could be used by dealers to prepare their own catalogs.

high grade instruments tells on them. They were a success from the start and they challenge the world today.

The great demand for ukuleles and Hawaiian guitars continued to cause many changes at the factory, and weighed heavily on Frank Henry. In April of 1919 he is quoted in the *Music Trades* as saying:

My days and nights are filled with a great deal of worry trying to get out some of our goods, for which there is a big demand. Labor is again to be had, though material for the making of our goods is scarce in some lines. We are trying our utmost to keep our plant running at full capacity, and it may not be long before this occurs. Our factory has been enlarged and much improved.

It seems every quote from Martin during the last years of the teens has to do with the factory expan-

sion. In October of 1919, the *Music Trades* mentions that Frank Henry visited Wm. J. Smith & Co. in New York and stated that "demand for his line of instruments is so great that he plans to still further enlarge his factories." However, a slow decline began for a couple of years. As early as April of 1920, an article in the *Music Trades* asked "Is The Ukulele Losing In Popular Favor?" The article discusses the Indianapolis ukulele factory of Frank Bremmerman, and how his factory is gearing up to make mandolins and guitars. Worried about "fickle public taste," Bremmerman was "taking no chances." The article attempts to answer its title question in an ominous final sentence: "But consider how long it has been since you have heard a band of Hawaiians in a vaudeville theater or seen them in a café and judge for yourself." By this time, Martin had to be wondering if the ukulele and Hawaiian guitars were no more than a passing fad. It wouldn't be long before they discovered that the interest in their new instruments was not only far from over, but in many ways was just beginning.

K is For Koa

In 1913 the Southern California Music Company (SoCal) was granted Martin's Sole Agency for Los Angeles, when it purchased over $500 in guitars and mandolins. It bought over $1,400 of instruments in 1914, and in 1915 it was granted Sole Agency for "all of California south of Bakersfield, including same," as noted in Martin's dealer ledger. At this time, SoCal had a deal for purchasing ukuleles with Manuel Nunes, the Honolulu manufacturer who's company was by far the best known name in these instruments. Although Nunes' earliest ukuleles included a label that read "Guitar Maker and Repairer," it is unlikely he ever made guitars for SoCal. In fact, it is not well known exactly when his company ceased it's guitar production. Before Nunes renamed his company in 1909 as M. Nunes and Sons, he had advertised himself in the city directories as a guitar maker. Afterwards, he generally advertised as a maker of "musical instruments." Also after 1909, he used a label that proclaimed he was the "Inventor of the Ukulele and Taro Patch Fiddles in Honolulu in 1879" and that no longer made mention of guitars. As the Hawaiian music craze swept the Pacific Coast in the early teens, SoCal was one of the premiere places to go for Hawaiian guitars and ukuleles. SoCal could get its supply of ukuleles from M. Nunes and Sons in Honolulu, but looked to expand its Hawaiian guitar sales by handling Martin instruments.

In 1916 SoCal supplied a shipment of koa wood to Martin to build a sample lot of guitars, six each in Styles 0-18, 0-21, and 00-28. The guitars received were koa on the back and sides, with spruce tops. SoCal wrote back saying "Workmanship, tone, correct-ness of scale, are perfect on these instruments" but also requested some changes. They wanted their guitars made with koa tops as well, and they requested that they conform more nearly to the specifications of three M. Nunes and Sons ukuleles that they had enclosed. In this way, Southern Cal could market the guitars as products of M. Nunes. This they did for a time— selling Martin-made koa guitars marked only with the "Southern California Music Company Los Angeles" stamp on the back and a paper label inside reading "M. Nunes & Sons Royal Hawaiian Hand-Made Steel-Guitars Made from thoroughly seasoned KOA-WOOD Expressly for Frank J. Hart Southern California Music Company." On the front of the headstock there was an M. Nunes decal applied, complete with the Hawaiian crest.

SoCal ordered the first koa wood ukuleles from Martin in October of 1917. Six instruments were made, three corresponding to Martin's standard Styles 1, 2, and 3, and three others in "Special Styles." The three special styles were priced the same as the three made in Martin's standard styles. There was no extra charge for koa wood, probably because it was SoCal's koa wood Martin was using. Martin did not again make koa wood ukuleles until the middle of 1919, probably because it had difficulty in securing the wood during the years of the First World War.

In 1919 Martin began building substantial quantities of koa wood ukuleles, which were sold on special order. SoCal placed the first big or-

Left: **An early Martin Style 1K made for the Southern California Music Company around 1919.**

Opposite page: **Stamp on the back of the headstock of the Style 1K. These models did not carry the Martin name at all.**

der for koa wood ukuleles in May of 1919. They ordered fifty Style 1s, fifty Style 2s, and twenty-five Style 3s, along with Martin's very first koa wood taro-patches—one each in Styles 1, 2, and 3. Other sellers soon followed. In July, Buegeleisen & Jacobson (B&J) ordered 100 Style 1 koa ukuleles for January, 1920 shipment. The price was to be equal to the price of their mahogany ukuleles plus seventy-five cents, each, for the use of koa wood.

In 1920 Martin first publicly offered koa wood as an option in both the guitar and ukulele sections of its catalog. In the Martin catalog of September 1920, the same description is used for the ukuleles as in the 1919 catalog, with the exception of one additional sentence: "The same styles can be had in koa wood, built to order, prices quoted on application." The koa used on these early ukuleles was generally rather plain, even on the high-end model of the time, the Style 3K. Soon they would become much more choosy about the "curliness" of the koa they were using. Martin koa wood ukuleles were an instant hit. Of the 3,000 plus ukuleles sold in 1920, nearly one quarter were made from koa wood.

By 1922 Martin had started to obtain its koa wood mainly from the Bergstrom Music Co., Ltd. of Honolulu, the same company that had ordered the original trial lot of six ukuleles from Martin back in 1907. Letters went back and forth regularly between the two companies. Late in 1921 Martin had written Bergstrom requesting help in locating quality koa wood in large-sized logs. Bergstrom wrote back to say they had located "a man in the district of Kona, Island of Hawaii, who will furnish Koa lumber in large sizes." Martin's reply let Bergstrom know exactly what they were looking for: "What we want is clean, live wood, with a figure, and as to size we want nothing less than 12" x 12" and will prefer a piece of up to 20" square, or something like that, and ten feet long." They also specified the shipping that should be arranged. "Shipment

should be by water all the way to New York, either direct through the canal or transshipment at San Francisco or Los Angeles, but not in any case by railroad." The first sample log of koa arrived by May of 1922 and Martin wrote to say it was "highly satisfactory for quality, only it is so small." They paid thirty cents a board-foot for the sixty-three board foot log—a total of $18.90 plus the shipping fees.

Martin immediately asked Bergstrom to send more koa wood, this time "the cheaper, straight-grained kind." Bergstrom arranged for the shipment of six straight-grained logs but, before they had even arrived in New York, Martin's increasing business caused them to write to Bergstrom again:

We wrote you May 24th asking for some more Koa logs. Our trade in this wood has been growing ever since so we would appreciate the favor of having some more sent than we first asked for.

At that time we thought the small proportion of the finest curly stock and the greater part plain wood might be the right proportion. As it develops now we would like more of the extra fine wood, say about one thousand feet all told.

Bergstrom replied that they could get Martin the curly wood they were seeking, and apologized for the delay in sending out the six logs. "Considerable delay was experienced at this end getting the logs shipped, due to the fact that the Steamship lines leaving Honolulu at this time of year are so loaded up with sugar and pineapples that other miscellaneous freight must wait." The relative ease with which Martin was able to procure quality koa wood in 1922 would not last much longer.

Martin was able to keep its koa ukulele and guitar models pretty well stocked throughout 1924, thanks to regular shipments of koa wood purchased through The Bergstrom Music Co. of Honolulu. Martin had been able to obtain seemingly unlimited amounts of fine koa wood in 1922, but this condition changed in 1923. Quality koa wood became harder to come by and Martin wrote Bergstrom more than once requesting more curly koa. At the beginning of 1924 Martin was quite happy to receive a shipment of logs from Bergstrom as well as a letter saying there was more available if Martin wanted it. In January Frank Henry wrote to Bergstrom: "You wrote November 24th that there were some more logs available, of very good quality, and since our sales keep up well we will be thankful if you send several, say equal in amount to the last four or a little over." This shipment was made, but the incredible pace of orders in 1924 must have been using up the wood almost as fast as it could be readied. In September C. F. III wrote Bergstrom requesting another thousand feet of curly koa. Growing more desperate, Martin sent Bergstrom a telegram on November 6th: "PLEASE RUSH KOA URGENT NEED ADVISE BY MAIL THANKS."

Moving into 1925 Martin continued to have great trouble finding high quality koa wood for its Style 3 and 5 ukuleles and its 0-28K guitars. Dozens of letters can be found in the correspondence files documenting Martin's desperate search for curly koa. Martin sent a telegram to Bergstrom at the beginning of May: "DOUBLE QUANTITY KOA ORDERED RUSH THANKS." The last shipment of koa that Martin had received did not contain any of the curly

koa needed for its fanciest ukuleles and guitars. When Bergstrom wrote back they included the name of their "man in the forest" Allen Wall of Kealakekua, Hawaii. Martin wrote to Wall in late June pleading for a shipment of curly koa wood, and Wall replied discussing the difficulty of obtaining such wood: "I can get you all the koa you want but curley koa is extremely scarce and hard to get as there is not one on a hundred trees that are curley." Wall sent off two shipments of koa through Bergstrom. Bergstrom explained in their letter about this wood that, according to their lumberman at Kona: "the delay was caused by heavy rains which washed out the mountain roads, and before the koa logs could be brought down the roads had to be repaired and in some places rebuilt."

In October Martin wrote to Wall again, not

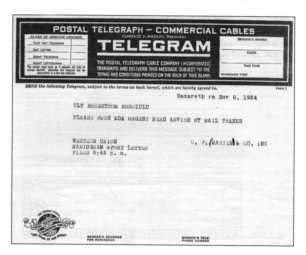

Above: At times Martin was in such dire need of koa wood that it would send a telegram to the islands looking to rush a delivery.

Left: Postcard showing a koa forest in the town of Volcano, on the Big Island of Hawaii.

completely satisfied with the shipment that had arrived. Referring to the wood, C. F. III wrote: "The first lot was unusually good in quality and gave us a very fair proportion of the curly stock which we need for our high priced instruments. The second lot was not so good and will give us considerable waste." Martin made it clear to Wall that they were willing to pay for what they wanted. "We are quite willing to give you the time necessary, and to pay a higher price, to assemble the curly wood as you are able to get it." Martin's strong need for koa wood also caused them to send out inquiries to a number of different suppliers, including White Brothers in San Francisco and I. T. Williams and Sons in New York, with Williams supplying a number of the logs used later in the year.

After 1926 the great demand for koa in quantity subsided. In the 1930s Martin slowly started to phase out koa wood models. The Style 2K ukulele was last made in regular production in 1931, and by 1938 the Style 1K was the only instrument still being made by Martin in koa. The last of the Style 1Ks were made in 1944, and koa wood fans would need to wait another 60 years before a koa Martin ukulele was built again in regular production.

When Martin first began making instruments from Hawaiian koa wood, they were not particularly choosy when it came to the curliness of the koa. The Style 3K (*left*) was built around 1920 and features rather straight-grained koa, despite the fact that it was Martin's top-of-the-line ukulele. Within just a couple of years Martin became much more demanding about the style of the wood used on their high-end instruments. The wood on this mid-1920s Style 3K (*right*) shows much more of the desired curliness.

A New Era Dawns

AN UNEXPECTED, AND IN SOME MEASURES AN UNACCOUNTED FOR, DEMAND FOR UKULE-LES HAS DEVELOPED THROUGHOUT THE COUNTRY SO THAT JOBBERS AND DEALERS, AND TO SOME EXTENT MANUFACTURERS, PARTICULARLY IN THE EAST, ARE UNABLE TO FILL ORDERS.

— The *Music Trades,* July, 1922

Making Changes

In 1919 Martin had sent a note to its dealers explaining its need to increase prices, saying "this is so because of advances in labor and material," and warned "these advances are still going on and it may become necessary to raise prices further." It is likely the price increases were also in response to the fact that the factory, despite multiple expansions, simply was not able to keep up with the increased demand for its instruments and Martin was willing to adjust its prices to correspond with demand. Their ukulele prices would go up and down over the next twenty years in accordance with the number being sold.

In 1920 Martin's ukulele sales dropped a bit to just over 3,000, and in 1921 they were barely half that, at under 1,700. This time it really did appear that the fad had passed. Some of the decline, however, may have been due to large increases in ukulele prices. The price of a Style 1 jumped from $10 to $13.20, a Style 2 from $15 to $17.60, and a Style 3 from $25 to $27.50. These were announced in the October 1919 price list, and sales were being completed at the new prices by Christmas of that year. Prices went up again on April 1st of 1920. The Style 1 increased to $14,

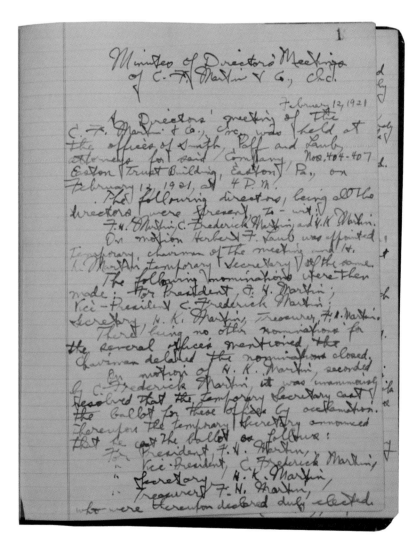

The minutes from the very first meeting of the Board of Directors of C. F. Martin & Co., Inc., February 12, 1921.

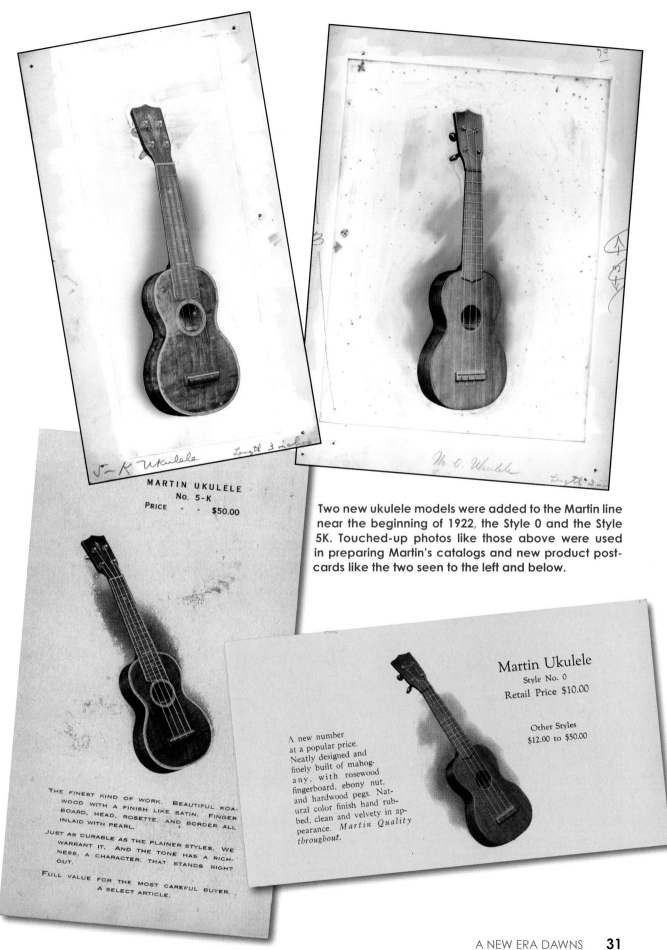

MARTIN UKULELE
No. 5-K
PRICE - - $50.00

Two new ukulele models were added to the Martin line near the beginning of 1922, the Style 0 and the Style 5K. Touched-up photos like those above were used in preparing Martin's catalogs and new product postcards like the two seen to the left and below.

THE FINEST KIND OF WORK. BEAUTIFUL KOA-WOOD WITH A FINISH LIKE SATIN. FINGER-BOARD, HEAD, ROSETTE, AND BORDER ALL INLAID WITH PEARL.

JUST AS DURABLE AS THE PLAINER STYLES. WE WARRANT IT. AND THE TONE HAS A RICH-NESS, A CHARACTER. THAT STANDS RIGHT OUT.

FULL VALUE FOR THE MOST CAREFUL BUYER. A SELECT ARTICLE.

Martin Ukulele
Style No. 0
Retail Price $10.00

Other Styles
$12.00 to $50.00

A new number at a popular price. Neatly designed and finely built of mahogany, with rosewood fingerboard, ebony nut, and hardwood pegs. Natural color finish hand rubbed, clean and velvety in appearance. *Martin Quality throughout.*

The Tiple

On May 8, 1918, Wm. J. Smith ordered six miniature guitars, listed in Martin's order book as "three Gtrs ¼ size, Style 18 and three Gtrs. ⅛ Size Style 18." Shop order listings and the sales record show that these were actually three ¼ size and three ½ size Style 18 guitars. It is possible that Smith was starting to think about a new instrument when he ordered these small guitars. The sale was recorded on June 14th. On August 9th Smith made another unusual order. The order book entry reads:

> 6 Gtrs. ¼ size Style 18. Trial order of new South American instrument. Four strings triple, tuned like ukulele. Six string machine head. Bridge according to judgment. Build the six then finish one to test bridge. Brace extremely light. Price not set.

When the first sale is marked in the sales book, the price Smith was charged was $12.50, meaning a standard twenty-five dollar retail price with the usual fifty percent discount.

The Smith order of Dec. 19, 1918 includes the simple line "6 Tiple Gtrs," so it appears he had settled on his ten-string design, although no specifications are mentioned in the order book. Smith continued to order tiples periodically for the next few years. The tiples that Smith was having Martin build were quite different from their South American namesake. The tiple played in Colombia and other South American countries is a much larger instrument closer in size to a guitar. The Colombian tiple has twelve or ten strings in four courses. It is tuned D G B E, with paired strings in unison and tripled strings each usually with a middle string tuned an octave below the other two.

In August of 1919 Martin received an order for one tiple from the Robert L. White Music Company of Cleveland, Ohio—the first tiple ordered by anyone other than Smith. Two more were sent to White later in the year. The next tiple ordered elsewhere wasn't until December of 1921 when Southern California Music Company ordered one, noted in the order book "as sample." It does not appear that Martin had ever made any agreement with Smith that they would not sell tiples to other dealers. In January of 1922, H. L. Hunt of the Chas. H. Ditson New York store wrote to Martin requesting "a sample of each 'tipple' that you make as we wish to catalogue this." Martin obliged, mentioning in his reply that "this instrument is at present made in one style only and there is possibility of a change in the design." It is possible he was considering additional models so as not to upset Smith—who had originated the design.

As it turns out, Smith was indeed upset. In February of 1922 Smith sent a letter to Martin expressing his anger: "If I remember rightly you promised that you wouldn't sell at least to any New York firm." Ditson was

1920s studio photo of a T-18 tiple

Smith's biggest competitor in small instruments, and Smith was upset at the prospect of losing business. He goes on to complain "the time that I have put in on the instrument has been a waste, and I don't mind telling you that I feel pretty sore." Smith felt his long-standing relationship with the Martin company was being ignored and closes his letter with "there may come a day when you will think this matter over and see that you have not done just the right thing by me."

The tone of the Smith letter is very unusual for correspondence in the Martin archives. The Martin company was run with such consistency and integrity that it is very rare to see a customer write with harsh sentiment. There are many letters of disagreement in philosophy or disappointment when goods could not be delivered promptly, but nearly none accusing Martin of any sort of wrong-doing. Two days after sending the letter, Smith ordered six eight-string tiples, apparently looking to find a different arrangement that he could call his own. In the same letter he requested one eight-string tiple in Style 28 and another in Style 42. Frank Henry, clearly upset by Smith's accusations, replied:

> I feel too much grieved over your letter to make a full reply today.
>
> I showed my esteem when I agreed to supply you Martin goods just the same as Ditsons when you started in business, and again last year when I made the arrangement that our retail outlet in New York should only be two firms, Ditsons and Smith…
>
> This being so, I think we should stand together and consider that in such an arrangement there are mutual benefits. We have both had so much experience in the instrument line that we ought to be able to handle a new instrument together.
>
> Why can we not make the Tiple in two lines, differing perhaps in model, perhaps in some other things. Before your last order came I had an idea to develop it with eight strings and call it a Guitar-Ukulele, but if you are now experimenting with eight strings then this would not make a point of difference.
>
> Further than that I can suggest nothing today."

On February 16th Smith ordered another new model, "1 Gtr ¼-18, Tiple Neck, Gtr. Head, 6 strings in 4 groups." On February 22 he ordered three more tiples, presumably with the standard ten string arrangement, one in Style 28, one in Style 42, and the third in Style 45—all koa. This was at a time that Martin had just introduced its 5K ukulele, perhaps it was an inspiration for the pearl inlaid koa tiple. As far as Martin records show, only this one Style 45K tiple was ever produced.

Smith was again soon ordering tiples in the standard ten string configuration. For a time the name "Ukalua" became synonymous with the name tiple. In June of 1922 correspondence, he mentions a ¼ size guitar "tuned like a

1930s T-28 tiple

U ka lu a." When Dick Konter (of later polar exploration and Konter-Uke fame) published his first ukulele method book in 1923, it was titled "Dick's Ukulele Method Showing How To Apply Chords on the Ukulele, Ukalua, Ukulele-Banjo, Taro Patch and Tenor Banjo." It doesn't appear the Ukalua name lasted long though, for the following year Dick's improved method came out, titled "Dick's Improved Ukulele Method Showing How to Apply Chords On The Ukulele, Banjo-Ukulele, Taropatch, Tiple, Bari-Uke, and Tenor Banjo (Uke Tuning)." The original name "tiple" had become well-established and won out over newer names "ukalua" or even "guitar-ukulele."

The tiple rose in popularity over the next few years. Martin settled on two standard models, the T-18 and the T-28, with ornamentation similar to their Style 18 and Style 28 guitars. Soon, other manufacturers added tiples to their lines, and requests started to come in from many retailers and distributors. In July of 1924 Carl Fischer asked about ¼ size "triple" guitars in koa or mahogany, and asked if they could be played "as an Hawaiian Steel Guitar by applying attachments." Herbert Keller responded that koa was not an option due to the "increasing difficulty to keep up with the demand on the Style T-18." He also adds: "This instrument cannot be used as an Hawaiian Steel Guitar, but we believe you will find it to be a

MARTIN
TIPLE — STYLE T-17

MAHOGANY—NATURAL FINISH—FINE RICH TONE
Price $30.00
C. F. MARTIN & CO., INC.
Established 1833
NAZARETH, PA.
MAKERS OF MARTIN GUITARS

Postcard sent out to dealers by Martin announcing the new T-17 model tiple, 1927.

very active seller as a ukulele novelty."

A letter from Herbert Keller to his father in February of 1925 mentions that Harmony and Regal are making tiples to wholesale at seven dollars. Writing again later that week from Chicago, he adds that "there seem to be several cheaper tiples on the market, but dealers say tiples, as also taros, do not sell in this section. Lyon & Healy are making a tiple somewhat different in design, not yet completed." It is likely that the Lyon & Healy tiple he mentions is the bell-shaped tiple first shown in the 1925 Lyon & Healy catalog. Martin tiple sales peaked in 1926 when over 650 were produced.

The Martin tiple became a favorite instrument of a number of ukulele performers in the 1920s. This is because it could be played in a fashion similar to a ukulele, but it was considerably louder than a ukulele or a taropatch. This made it popular for both stage use and recording. Johnny Marvin, a Vaudeville performer in the early 1920s and a major ukulele-playing recording artist later in the decade, was an early adopter of the new instrument. Another performer, Doyle Davis, wrote to Martin in February of 1922 inquiring about a "catalogue regarding your Triple Ukes" mentioning that he had "seen Mr. John Marvin who recommended your company to me." Marvin had visited the Martin factory the previous winter, so it is possible that was when

T-18 and T-28 tiples, as shown in the 1970 Martin guitar catalog.

he was introduced to the instrument. In April, Marvin himself wrote to Martin, sending along the "card of a store that haven't got your Tipole yet." He continued: "Now they saw me use it here in the theatre and liked it very much and asked me the price…" In his reply, Frank Henry pays Marvin a nice compliment: "Your playing must take hold to have people fall in love with the instrument as they do," and assures Marvin that they would write to the store he had mentioned.

Another performer who was known to perform with a tiple is Wendell Hall. Hall had become quite well known with the release of his hugely popular 1923 recording "It Ain't Gonna Rain No Mo'." On the sheet music for the song, Hall holds a tiple, quite probably a Martin. Hall wrote to Martin in 1924 asking about a Style 3 taropatch, and mentions that he had been playing "taro patch and a ten stringed ukulua" on the radio and in recordings for the last two and a half years. Martin lets him know that "several times it has been brought to our attention that you have been using the Ukalua, or Tiple, and that some of your publications contained photographs of yourself playing this instrument." Another early ukulele performer who used the tiple was the singer and songwriter Frank Crumit. Wm. J. Smith sent Crumit's tiple back to Martin in March of 1922 in need of a new top. Smith asked Martin to speed up the repair if possible, saying "I loaned him an instrument while this is being fixed and in as much as these fellows are pretty rough on instruments, I don't want him to have my instrument too long."

By the time Martin added the more affordable all-mahogany T-17 to the tiple line-up in 1927, interest in the instrument was beginning to wane. Sales soon dropped off quite quickly and by 1929 only fifty tiples were produced. The decline of the tiple was evident through sales records, and was occasionally also a topic of correspondence. In 1932 a letter came in from a tiple owner upset that he was having trouble trading in his instrument. He had taken his thirty-five dollar tiple in to a Wurlitzer store, where he was told "it was in good shape but that it was an obsolete instrument or in other words just a troublesome ukulele which took a lot of time to tune." The writer goes on to ask that Martin send a "Martin Ukulele gratis." Upon receiving the ukulele the writer would return the tiple. He went on to say "now the Gibson people would do that much, for the dealer told me so. They stand behind all their goods regardless of dealer." Martin's reply tells much about the state of the tiple at the time:

> Your proposal to exchange your Martin Tiple for a Ukulele has had our careful consideration. We would like to do something for you but the fact is, as the Louisville dealers told you, that there is practically no call for Tiples. We have discontinued the Style T-18, the one you have, and are closing out our remaining stock at a reduction. We also have a surplus stock of parts so your instrument would have no value whatever to us…It is simply a case of a change in fashion which has made this type of instrument less valuable than it was when you bought it."

The tiple was not quite dead yet, however. Martin made between 25 and 100 tiples nearly every year from the early 1930s through the late 1950s, except during the World War II years when metal shortages stopped tiple production altogether. In 1949 the T-15 was first made. Small numbers of tiples continued to be made most years until 1993 when they were dropped from the catalog.

the Style 2 to $18, and the Style 3 to $30. The Martin Style 1 was by far its biggest selling uku-lele model—nearly three out of every four ukuleles sold were Style 1s—and raising its price by forty percent in just under six months was destined to cause more than a few customers to look elsewhere for more affordable goods.

C. F. Martin & Co. officially incorporated in 1921. At the first Board of Directors meeting on February 12th, F. H. Martin was elected President of the corporation, C. F. Martin Vice President, and H. K. Martin Secretary. Two weeks later at the second Board meeting, it was agreed that the President should act as General Manager, the Vice President as Assistant Production Manager, and the Secretary as Assistant Sales Manager. At this same meeting it was resolved that the corporation "lease the factory building hitherto occupied by F. H. Martin." The factory is described in the lease as "a frame building twenty four by seventy six feet with brick wing eighteen by sixty feet." The brick "wing" was the oldest part of the factory and the newer "frame building" had been added in the 1880s. It was this frame building that was being expanded in the teens to make room to keep up with the increased demand for ukuleles.

Within months of the incorporation, sales had dropped substantially from the levels reached in the two previous years. At the third Board of Directors meeting in April, just two months after first establishing their own salaries, the salaries of all three company officers were reduced by twenty percent, citing "the present depression in business." At the next Board meeting in July, it was noted that "for the first half of the year 1921 expenses have exceeded sales" and that "this deficiency appears to be caused by dullness in trade." The minutes do end on a hopeful note though, stating that "present orders and prospects make it possible that this deficiency can be made up by the end of the year." Yet, the President's report presented at the January 1922 Board of Directors meeting opened with: "The year 1921, the first year of the corporation, was unsuccessful for making money." However, by the time that Frank Henry made this report, the corporation already had initiated a number of ideas that would help ensure unprecedented profits for years to come. The year 1922 would be hugely important for the Martin company. Fortunately, a great deal of Martin's correspondence for the year has been preserved, allowing for a closer look into the company's business and a better understanding of its philosophy.

Widening the range: Styles 0 and 5K

*J*n May of 1921, barely a year after the last price increase, uku-lele prices were reduced. The Style 1 dropped to $12, and the Style 2 and 3 prices returned to their original 1916 levels of $15 and $25, respectively. Koa was an option on all models at an additional cost of $2. Reducing the Style 1 to $12 instead of its original $10 price left room for a new $10 ukulele model at the bottom of the Martin line. The Style 0 ukulele was added to the Martin ukulele lineup in January of 1922 and quickly became Martin's best selling instrument.

The Style 0 ukulele allowed Martin to sell an instrument of uncompromised quality at a popular price. At about the same time, Martin added a ukulele at the other end of the spectrum. The Style 5K would be the instrument that would cement Martin's place as the maker of the finest ukulele in the world. The new product postcard sent to dealers in 1922 described the

Martin's new top-of-the-line ukulele, the Style 5K.

Above: This photo from the Martin archives was used in a 1929 ukulele method published by the U. S. School of Music in New York City. Many method books of the time used illustrations featuring Martin ukuleles, and the Style 5K was a particularly popular choice.

Right: Other Illustrations from the method book.

CORRECT PLAYING POSITION

D-String Tuning Peg

F-sharp String Tuning Peg

B-String Tuning Peg

A-String Tuning Peg

Nut

"A" String as tuned

"A" as written in the Music

4th (A) String — as tuned

3rd (D) String — as tuned

2nd (F#) String — as tuned

1st (B) String

Frets

UKULELE Tuning Pipes

Fingerboard

Sound Hole

Bridge

Tail piece

THE UKULELE AND THE TUNING DIAGRAM

new model as follows: "The finest kind of work. Beautiful koa-wood finish like satin. Finger board, head, rosette, and border all inlaid with pearl. Just as durable as the plainer styles. We warrant it. And the tone has a richness, a character, that stands right out. Full value for the most careful buyer. A select article."

Martin advertised its newest ukulele to the trade with an ad in the August *Crescendo*: "The Martin Ukulele No. 5-K: An instrument to satisfy the most exacting demands that can be made upon the ukulele. Selected Koawood body. Ebony Fingerboard. Seventeen Frets. Patent Pegs. Richly Ornamented. A Martin Instrument."

The success of the new models, especially the Style 0, is evident in an interesting correspondence between Frank Henry and Mr. A. C. Huff of the Huff Music Store in nearby Bethlehem in October of 1922. In response to Huff's request to exchange two bowl-back mandolins for "$10.00 ukuleles which are much more popular in Bethlehem," Frank Henry wrote:

It is very much to our interest to have dealers carry fast-moving styles; they are then able to run along with little investment; they will feel like handling our goods more than any others; and the quick turnover enables them to pay us promptly so that we are in shape to push manufacturing.

You are quite right in guessing that we are busy. The reduction in our prices last winter gives us a popular line, at the lowest prices in the market, I believe, for like quality. At any rate orders have come every month throughout the year so far and on the first of October we had unfilled orders for a thousand instruments.

The No. 0 ukulele, retailing at ten dollars, is naturally the leader for big sales and my son, Frederick, tells me all of that style are promised up to the sixth of November. The right thing then is that you make up an order for a number of Style 0 ukuleles and whatever else you wish to put in at this time, and send the mandolins for credit either at once or when you receive the new goods.

I would further suggest that if you have more than these two mandolins we may as well take them as we have customers here and there who always take a few. I am not sorry that they have almost dropped out of the market, because it reduces the number of our styles, and they are indeed hard to build. They are good and they are handsome but it does us no good to look in the past, we must make money today and in the future."

Style 0 made for New York City retailer Chas. H Ditson. Soon after Martin introduced the Style 0 in 1922, Ditson was ordering them in their unique mini-dreadnought shape. Ditson bought more of these Style 0s in 1922 than all other Ditson model ukuleles combined.

Sole Agencies and Customer Models

One of the big changes Martin made in 1922 was coming up with a way to circumvent its own long-standing policy of granting sole agencies to some customers. This policy granted exclusive rights to a retailer or distributor as sole agent to sell Martin instruments in a specified geographic region. In exchange, the agent promised to purchase a certain minimum dollar amount of instruments each year, commensurate with the population in the region. The concept is explained well in a 1922 letter sent to L. F. Collin of Melbourne, Australia. Frank Henry explains:

> "We come back directly to our general system of placing agencies, which is the outgrowth of years of trial; namely, to agree, with the placing of a first order, that we will not sell to any other person in a certain territory as long as the return of business is satisfactory. The agent by this plan is free to push the goods or not, and we never withdraw an agency without giving ample time. In your case we consider that the two orders already placed, taken together with the assurance of the advertising and other selling effort you intend to give, are enough for us to promise that we will not sell to anyone else in the continent of Australia until July of next year, should there be no further offers.

Sole agencies were granted to various stores in all parts of the country and around the world. Agencies could be huge regions like L. F. Collin's sole agency in Australia and Southern California Music Company's sole agency in all of California south of Bakersfield, or could be much smaller like Peate's Music

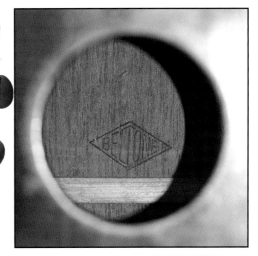

Beltone was a registered brand name of Perlberg and Halpin, a New York City based musical retailer. Martin made 154 Beltone branded ukuleles for P&H all in 1922. Shown is a Beltone Style 0. Notice the minor differences to Martin's standard Style 0, the larger position dots and the maple nut and saddle.

Martin's Customer Model instruments were similar to Martin's existing models, but had small differences to distinguish them. The ukulele on the left is a Wurlitzer Model 837, on the right is a standard Martin 1K. The Wurlitzer model had a maple nut and bridge saddle while the Martin used ebony. The rosette on the Wurlitzer is different than the standard Martin rosette and the fingerboard markers on the Wurlitzer were slightly larger.

House and its sole agency in Utica, New York. Some areas might not get a sole agency, but could be limited to two agencies. For example, at the beginning of 1922 Chas. H. Ditson and Wm. J. Smith were the only two retailers in New York City who could order instruments directly from Martin. By 1922 Martin felt that the sole agency policy was not helping its business as it was intended. Their first strategy was to initiate Customer Models.

Martin did not intend to abruptly terminate the long-standing policy, for fear of upsetting many of its oldest and largest customers. Instead, they first looked for a way to circumvent it. In December of 1921, H. & A. Selmer, Inc. wrote to Martin requesting a direct agency in New York City. Frank Henry replied that "we wished to supply you direct" but went on to say that "it will hardly do for us to add to our present customers – Chas. H. Ditson & Co. and the Wm. J. Smith Co." He suggested to Selmer that they could obtain instruments from the Ditson house and said "I hope you will sell quite a number of Martin Instruments, getting your supply from them." But then in the last paragraph Martin first made mention of a new plan that was being considered. He was not ready to fully extend an offer as yet, so instead he wrote: "There is one chance remaining, but that can not be offered now; it is that we may do more in the way of dealers' own name on special styles. If it comes to that, we will be sure to remember you."

Frank Henry could not offer a Customer Model yet because he felt the need to hear from his biggest customer before implementing such a change. On the very same day that he wrote the letter to Selmer, he also wrote to Chas. H. Ditson. His letter asks the simple question:

Can we furnish stenciled goods to any number of dealers, either special styles or regular styles with dealer's name and no other change, without doing a moral wrong to our local agents and thereby hurt our goodwill?

It should be noted that by "stenciled goods" Martin was referring to the metal stamps used to imprint the company logos on the ukulele, which were supplied by a firm called the New York Stencil Works. By no means should this term be confused with the inexpensive guitars and ukuleles sold by other companies with painted designs stenciled on the tops. Frank Henry goes on to repeat himself, asking the same question in a more specific way:

To make the most direct illustration, considering the effort you are putting into the sale of Martin goods, could we make an own-make line for Wurlitzer and another for Selmer, goods that will perhaps be different in style but easily recognized by an expert as coming from the Martin factory, without hurting your trade?

He ends the letter with a sentence that says a lot about the Martin philosophy: "Of course, we are after our own benefit to increase our business, but benefit in business comes to more than one person in every transaction and that is why I ask about the effect on you."

In his reply, Ditson's small-goods manager H. L. Hunt basically gave Martin the go-ahead, if somewhat conditionally. "If you wish to preserve the precedent of Martin Trade Marks," wrote Hunt, "viz.: C. F. Martin & Co., Nazareth, Penna. We would advise you to not stencil your regular styles." He continues, "Our suggestion would be to make up a separate line different from the regular Martin styles and stencil this for the firms that wish them." He goes on to take a bit of a jab at Martin: "When we approached you on this ourselves many years ago, you turned us down cold. Times do change."

This last statement is somewhat puzzling considering that Martin had been producing a special line of instruments for Ditson for over five years. Actually, Martin had been making a few special lines of ukuleles, as well as marking its standard ukuleles with the names of other firms, since the very beginning. Ukuleles marked "Oliver Ditson, Boston, New York" were sold to both the parent Oliver Ditson Co. of Boston and the agency of Chas. H. Ditson in New York. The ukuleles with the mini-dreadnought body shape had been made for Chas. H. Ditson since 1916, while standard shape ukuleles with the Ditson stamp had been sold to the Boston store. There are numerous cases where the sales book notes sales of instruments to Wm. J. Smith marked with the "Smith stamp." Martin's first koa wood ukuleles and guitars were marked "Southern California Music Co." for the company that ordered them and supplied the koa wood. What was different now was that Martin was pushing the Customer Line specifically to increase sales in areas they had not been able to fully supply due to the sole agency policy.

Apparently, the response from Ditson was the last piece Martin needed to put its Customer Model plan into rapid action. In a letter written just ten days after Martin had received Hunt's reply, plans were already well under way to create a model line for the Rudolph Wurlitzer Co. of Cincinnati. Within weeks, Martin had sent solicitations to

John Wanamaker opened one of the nation's first department stores in Philadelphia and later another in New York City. In 1922 the New York store ordered twenty-seven Customer Model ukuleles from Martin, one of which is shown here.

Many of the metal stamps
Martin used on its ukuleles
in the 1920s are still in
the Martin archives.

C. F. Martin & Co. Ukuleles
Made by America's Foremost Ukulele Maker

The new line of Wurlitzer Ukuleles was created with a view of perfect workmanship and the soft deep singing quality of tone. These instruments are built to meet with the demands of the most discriminating purchasers. Fingerboard and scale are guaranteed to be absolutely accurate.

No. 835

No. 835—Body and neck made of mahogany natural finish, nickel silver frets, guaranteed perfectly adjusted. Price $11.00

Nos. 836-837

No. 836—Body and neck made of mahogany, top and back bound with dark colored mahogany, strip of white purfling around outer edge of top and sound hole, nickel silver frets, guaranteed perfectly adjusted. Price....**$13.50**
No. 837—Same description as No. 836 with the exception that the body is made of genuine Koa wood. Price **$16.00**

No. 838

No. 838—Body made of genuine Koa wood, top and back bound with white celluloid, black and white strip of purfling inlaid around top edge and sound hole. Nickel silver frets, guaranteed perfectly adjusted. Price....**$20.00**

No. 839

No. 839—Body and neck made of solid Koa wood, dull finish. Top and back bound with white celluloid. Top edge and sound hole inlaid with black and white celluloid purfling. Ebony fingerboard inlaid with fancy pearl ornaments. Patent pegs with white buttons. Price...**$30.00**

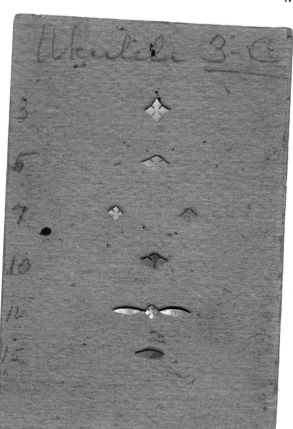

Above: Wurlitzer catalog page featuring Martin-made Wurlitzer Customer Models. The instrument on the bottom right in the ad is Wurlitzer's model no. 839, its special version of the Martin 3K.

Right: A Style no. 839 made by Martin in 1922, the only year of production with these special features.

Left: Although Martin made special models for Wurlitzer for less than a year in 1922, the original card that specified their inlays for the model No. 839 is still in the Martin archive. The "3-C" was Martin's designation for a Style 3 Customer's model.

a number of different businesses. Some, like Wurlitzer, were new ukulele contacts, others were current customers whom Martin was hoping to get to increase their orders by offering them their own line of instruments. Most, however, were businesses that Martin had been unable to sell to in the past, at least in part due to the restrictions of its sole agencies.

At the end of January, one month after their initial correspondence, Henry Keller sent Selmer a letter explaining the new option: "We are getting out a Customers' Line of goods, similar in price but differing somewhat in design from our regular line. On these goods we can put your name, leaving the Martin name off entirely." He closed the letter specifying the conditions under which they were willing to make such a line: "The making of these goods will be possible only on quantity orders, placed quite far in advance of your needs."

Similar offers were made to many other firms, including retail establishments, instrument manufacturers, and wholesale "jobbers." The fact that jobbers were solicited was the biggest change in policy. Jobbers were instrument distributors who sold to the trade rather than retailers selling directly to the consumer. Jobbers generally bought large lots of instruments from a manufacturer, and expected a bigger discount than was being given to a retailer. Jobbers, including two large New York City jobbing firms, C. Bruno & Son and Buegeleisen and Jacobson (B&J), had done business with Martin in the past, but by 1921 Martin had discontinued the practice of selling to jobbers. This was because the jobbers could sell Martin instruments in any market, thus interfering with Martin's practice of sole agencies. The adoption of a Customer Line offered Martin a chance to re-establish its ties with the bulk-purchasing jobbers. In a letter to Bruno in January 1922, Frank Henry wrote:

Above: **Martin sold ukuleles to both the Boston and New York City Ditson stores, and the same stamp was used on each. However, the special Ditson baby dreadnought body shape was made specifically for the New York store, Chas. H. Ditson.** *Right:* **The Ditson model 5K is a very rare example.**

A year ago we withdrew our goods from jobbing channels because of interference with our local agencies. It is only fair we tell you now of a new move meant to overcome this handicap as much as possible.

We are starting a line of goods which will be furnished to dealers, both wholesale and retail, with their own stamp. It will be a genuine Martin product, guaranteed to the buyer, made of the same grade of materials as our catalogue line, differing more or less in appearance. The prices will be the same as the catalogue styles, our equivalent, according to the ornamentation.

If there is room for such a line in your sales system, we are at your service.

Martin's margins on most of its lines were so small that they did not offer jobbers a bigger discount. Instead, they were offered goods at the same price any large retailer would pay—fifty percent of the suggested retail price. This was not always satisfactory to the jobbers, who expected deeper discounts for their larger orders. Frank Henry explained in a February 1922 letter to B&J that they were not putting out a typical deep-discount jobbing line:

So long as we stamp goods with customers' name we cannot see that it makes any difference whether it is their own name or a trade name controlled by them. We can therefore, furnish as many styles as you may need stamped 'S. S. Stewart', made to your order. …We do not put this out as a jobbing line because the price cannot be low but if the goods satisfy well enough to bring the high prices needed, then, of course, they can be used for that purpose.

Among the firms that Martin offered a Customer Line were The Bacon Banjo Company of Groton, Connecticut.

Bacon made banjos, banjo-ukuleles, and standard wooden ukuleles, but they were looking for a way to concentrate on their banjo products. They had spoken to Martin about making a special line of Martin-Bacon ukuleles, but Martin suggested they take up the Customer Line instead, "stamped with your name only."

In addition to Wurlitzer, Selmer, Bruno, B&J, and Bacon, other retailers and jobbers who were offered a Customer Line included Grinnell Brothers of Detroit, W. J. Dyer & Bro. of St. Paul, and the New York City firms of John Wanamaker and Perlberg & Halpin. Most of these firms took Martin up on their offer and had Martin stencil their ukuleles as their own. Some opted for their brand name, others for their company name. Michigan-based Grinnell chose to sell instruments under its "Wolverine" brand name, but included "Made for Grinnell Brothers at Nazareth, PA" on the stamps inside the instruments— likely as a way to prove that they actually were made by Martin. Dyer had Martin make up a sample set of instruments stamped with the Dyer brand "Stetson," but then decided to just continue carrying the standard Martin models. B&J had Martin mark their instruments with the trade name they had purchased in 1915—"S. S. Stewart." Perlberg & Halpin used their "Beltone" trademark. Stamps with company names included "Wurlitzer," "H. & A. Selmer, Inc.," and "John Wanamaker New York." In the case of Wurlitzer, Martin also would use the customer's own model numbers. Martin denoted Customer Models in its sales book by adding a "-C" to the style, such as "1 Uke 3K-C" to denote a single soprano koa wood Style 3 Customer Model ukulele (starting in 1925, Martin used the C notation without the dash to denote concert-sized ukuleles).

Production of Customer Models would last for only about a year before being discontinued. As sales soared throughout 1922, Martin seems to have pulled back a bit on the Customer Model restrictions. At first Martin, in agreement

S.S. Stewart was a trade name used by Buegeleisen & Jacobson (B&J) on their better instruments, like this Customer model made by Martin. Martin made 325 S.S. Stewart Customer Model ukuleles between 1922 and 1926.

THE WAIKIKI TRIO

The Waikiki Trio was a Hawaiian music trio based out of Lincoln, Nebraska. The ukulele player is holding a Martin Style 3 made within a year or two of 1920. The standing guitarist is also playing a Martin, a Style 42 guitar.

with (or deferring to) the suggestion from Ditson, seemed to feel that the Customer Models needed to be distinctively different than their regular line. It is impossible to now tell exactly what all of these differences were, but small pieces of information do show up in the correspondence. Perlberg & Halpin were told that their Beltone ukuleles would have maple nuts and saddles instead of ebony, but eventually P&H requested the nuts be stained dark to match the rest of the instrument. Martin also suggested that they "consider the advisability of adopting the natural finish regularly because it will distinguish your instruments more completely from ours and the natural finish seems to be gaining in popularity."

The one case where Martin spells out major changes from its standard ukulele line was in an exchange with the Wurlitzer Co. In a letter discussing catalog illustrations, Frank Henry writes:

> We have decided to change our regular Style 3 design in making up your special line and will ask you to retouch the photographs accordingly. The change will consist of the omission of the white piece in the lower end of the body and of the centre strip in the fingerboard, and the addition of several fine pearl ornaments as position marks in the fingerboard. These changes will make this number look a little different from our regular No. 3, which is rather distinctive in appearance.

In subsequent correspondence, Wurlitzer made it clear that they want Style 3K ukuleles and not mahogany Style 3s, and elaborated on the changes they needed to make in their catalog illustration from the illustration Martin had supplied of a regular Martin Style 3:

> The changes that have been made are as follows – the white piece on the bottom of the top and the strip in the center of the fingerboard have been eliminated and we have used the same style of fancy position marks like used on the 5-K. That will give the instrument a very attractive appearance."

Examination of Customer Model ukuleles still in existence reveals some of the other very minor changes made for these instruments. For example, some

Martin ukuleles marked Wurlitzer and Beltone feature rosette inlays that are a little different from those used on the Martin-marked instruments.

The original concept of the Customer Model did not last long. As sales picked up in 1922, it likely became a burden for Martin to supply special models for particular customers, even if ordered in large lots and well in advance. By the end of 1922, Martin had moved toward selling only its standard line of instruments, but still was willing to stamp them with other names. They wrote to Wurlitzer in December about a damaged Customer model 3K-C ukulele (Wurlitzer's no. 839) that had been sent for replacement. Martin sent a standard 3K as a replacement:

> Since the 3K will be supplied on all your future orders in place of this special 3K-C which we have been making for your No. 839, we presume that the substitution we have made will be satisfactory.

Martin sold a total of 62 3K-C ukuleles to Wurlitzer in 1922, presumably all with no stripe on the fretboard, no ornament at the bottom of the body, and fancy Style 5 type inlays on the fretboard. These are likely the most distinctive Customer Model ukuleles Martin made during its short-lived experiment.

Wolverine model ukuleles were made for Grinnell Brothers, a Michigan music retailer based in Detroit.

Unable to Meet Demand

*I*n 1922 ukulele sales soared to levels even greater than those during the Hawaiian craze just a few years earlier. While still popular, the interest in Hawaiian music had unquestionably declined. However, the ukulele was moving into an era of unprecedented popularity. As Americans began to use the ukulele as accompaniment to all sorts of popular music, the demand became incredible. In July of 1922, the *Music Trades* gave a detailed account of the situation in an article titled "Unable To Meet Demand For Ukuleles":

> An unexpected, and in some measures an unaccounted for, demand for ukuleles has developed throughout the country so that jobbers and dealers, and to some extent manufacturers, particularly in the East, are unable to fill orders.
>
> The ukulele always has a spurt of sales in summer, as this instrument is particularly adapted for camping. However, the present demand is said to be far greater than that at any previous year, with the possible exception of the year when these instruments first gained popularity.
>
> Small goods dealers are urgently in need of these unique and novel Hawaiian string musical instruments. Records show that for the last two weeks the demand and actual sales of ukuleles locally far exceeded the days when there was a wild craze for Hawaiian music by the public.
>
> So great is the demand at the time of writing for ukuleles that many jobbers and even retailers have offered to pay higher prices to manufacturers in order to get prompt deliveries. The *Music Trades* has made a thorough investigation by inquiring of manufacturers, jobbers and dealers in the East. The representative learned that 'summer time' is really ukulele time. For manufacturers, jobbers and dealers have sold out their ukulele stock this season.
>
> Large orders for future deliveries have been placed by big jobbing firms, requesting shipments be made in part monthly. Many of these manufacturers cannot see their way clear at this time to supply the immediate needs of the trade, because the rush for 'uks' came suddenly. However, the manufacturers are trying their hardest to please their many customers. Many have ordered the machinery and skilled operatives to work overtime, so that orders might be caught up with. Others are devoting their entire factory to making ukuleles only.
>
> The summer resorts are crowded with young folks playing the ukulele. At camping, yachting and motoring parties Hawaiian ukuleles can be heard.
>
> There is a movement on foot to have publishers of sheet music provide notes of harmony for the ukulele to accompany the piano in each number printed. Such a move will not only increase the demand for ukuleles and sheet music, but will make the instrument a standard one.

It seems certain that Martin was one of the manufacturers contacted for information for this story. There were not many other large manufacturers "in the East," so it would not be surprising if Martin had supplied information about its ukulele demand. Various company correspondence from 1922 confirms that Martin was having difficulty keeping up with the orders coming in.

One of the many symbols used by sheet music publishers to attract customers. In 1922, ukulele manufacturers were already having difficulty in meeting the demand for their instruments. Around this time, popular sheet music publishers began including ukulele arrangements on their music sheets, and demand for ukuleles became even greater.

By 1923 Americans were beginning to hear the ukulele used outside of the world of Hawaiian music. Wendell Hall (*top right*), Cliff "Ukulele Ike" Edwards (*above*), and Johnny Marvin (*bottom right*) were three of the first recording artists to accompany themselves on ukulele. Not surprisingly, they all played Martin instruments, as did so many of the other performers who would soon begin releasing ukulele recordings.

Ukuleles Surpass Guitars

*T*he year 1922 was a great one for the C. F. Martin Co. Although their guitar sales only increased slightly from 1921 levels, and mandolin numbers actually declined, ukulele sales increased enough to change the company's fortunes. Ukulele sales nearly tripled, going from 1,672 in 1921 to an unprecedented 4,770 in 1922. At the first Board of Directors meeting of 1923, President Frank Henry opened his annual report as follows:

> The report of the second year of the corporation is very different from the report of the first year. It is a record of success, but perhaps the success was greater because of the difficulties that had to be met the first year. They were met and overcome; every part of the business was willing to do its share and did it. New styles were made, new customers hunted up, and prices reduced enough to keep orders coming steadily. Every month in the year was busy, and every month except one showed an amount of sales greater than the amount of expenses. The great danger now is that we might become overconfident and do wrong or needless things. That is the task before the management.

The Martin ukulele reached an important milestone in 1922. From 1833 to 1897 Martin did not use serial numbers on their guitars. When serial numbers first were used in 1898 they started with the number 8,000, as this was Martin's estimate of the number of guitars made to that point. Sometime near the end of 1922, Martin completed a batch of ukuleles that put the little instruments in the numerical forefront. By this time, total Martin ukulele production was 18,095. The last guitar serial number from that year was 17,839. In just its seventh full year of ukulele production, Martin had built more ukuleles than it had produced guitars in its celebrated ninety-year history.

In 1922 Martin had its biggest production year yet, but 1923 would prove to be even bigger. Although ukulele sales stayed at about the same level as in 1922, with over 4,700 total instruments, mandolin sales climbed somewhat, and guitar output nearly doubled from the previous year. The factory was reaching its maximum capacity with greater sales than the company had ever before known. Two of their newest instruments, the Style 0 ukulele and the Style 2-17 guitar, were leading the way. The question of price increases was discussed at the April 1923 Board of Directors meeting, due to "increasing costs in labor and material" but the report of Vice-President C. F. III notes that it was decided "the present time was too soon for this to be done, because a raise would affect too much the immense benefit we were getting, in both production and sales departments, from popular priced styles."

As the popularity of the ukulele moved into the 1920s pop culture mainstream, its association with Hawaiian music was fading. Many Vaudeville performers began using ukuleles in their acts and record companies were beginning to issue non-Hawaiian recordings featuring the ukulele. Wendell Hall's 1923 Victor recording "It Ain't Gonna Rain No Mo'" featured "ukulele accompaniment" and became a smash hit. This was likely the first time most Ameri-

Martin Guitar, Mandolin, and Ukulele Running Totals 1898 - 1930

This graph shows the total number of guitars, ukuleles, and mandolins sold by Martin with the lines representing the all-time running totals. Ukuleles only needed seven years to pass guitars in all-time total production. By 1924 Martin had made more ukuleles than mandolins and guitars combined.

The Players: Wendell Hall

Wendell Hall, a long-time vaudeville performer who had performed as "The Singing Xylophonist" and promoted the Ludwig song whistle, took up the ukulele as it became popular in the early 1920s. Calling himself "The Red-Headed Music Maker," Hall was one of the early stars of radio and became known across the country after his song "It Ain't Gonna Rain No Mo' " became a big hit. He was also one of the many performers to inquire about a special arrangement with Martin.

Hall wrote to Martin in 1924 telling them of his many musical accomplishments: "I have been playing an eight stringed taro patch and a ten stringed ukulua for the last two and a half years on radio, from fifty-three different stations throughout the country." He goes on to discuss his recording with Victor records and mentions that he has never endorsed a particular brand of instruments. He continues, "Of late I have become a bit partial to that good looking taro patch you make. I think it is a number three."

He then jokingly mentions that he doesn't believe he has been influenced at all by "Miss Marion Martin, 'the little girl in Chicago', who will be the bride at my radio wedding, June 4th, at station WEAF, New York City, and re-broadcast through Providence, Washington and Chicago." Hall continues, hoping that there might be some sort of "mutual connection that we could make."

(It is interesting to note that Wendell Hall was married on the air. Could this be where Herbert Khaury, who was quite familiar with the radio stars of the 1920s, got his idea? Fifty-five years later Khaury, better known by his stage name Tiny Tim, married Miss Vicki on television's The Tonight Show in front of an estimated forty million viewers.)

Herbert Keller responded:

It is a pleasure to hear from you and to learn from you direct of the various activities in which you are engaged. Several times it has been brought to our attention that you have been using the Ukulua, or Tiple, and that some of your publications contained photographs of yourself playing this instrument. In regard to supplying you with a Taro Patch, we will be pleased to do this at the regular professional discount of 20% from the list. It is against our policy to allow more than this in any case. However, we have this particular proposition to make, which we believe will be agreeable to you, several times lately we have inlaid the names of prominent people on the head of their instruments in pearl letters. Would you like to have this done?

There is no sign in the archives of a response from Hall, and no record of a ukulele being made especially for him. By 1926, Hall had made a deal with the Regal Musical Instrument Co. of Chicago, who mass-produced the "Red-Head" ukulele with Hall's photo on the red-painted headstock.

Wendell Hall

cans had heard the ukulele used in a recording that was not related even remotely to Hawaii. "Ukulele Ike" (Cliff Edwards) also began to record tracks with ukulele accompaniment in 1922. Hall and Edwards were two of the first, but soon many other recordings could be found featuring the ukulele. And the ukulele of choice for both Hall and Edwards was a Martin. Martin's ukuleles were the instrument of choice for many performers—leading more than a few to write to Martin looking to work out some sort of endorsement deal.

As 1923 progressed, Martin became overwhelmed with orders. The April decision to not raise prices was reversed, and Frank Henry noted in his President's report to the Board of Directors that "prices were raised 10% flat, wages about the same, including salaries except officers'. It was not possible to increase production without raising wages and prices both." The raise in prices did not seem to slow orders, and the company worked hard to increase production. The report of C. F. III noted "an hour has been added to the working day (making a 55 hour week), beginning October 15th, and new workers will be engaged as fast as suitable applicants appear, up to the limit of factory space. Several new workers have been hired making a total working force of 32; which leaves room for 4 or 5 more." Even with the new hires, it would soon become evident that the company was not nearly able to keep up with orders. More drastic measures would be needed.

The Hawaiian music craze of the teens had introduced the ukulele to a wide audience, but in the 1920s the instrument itself was a sensation. No longer limited by its Hawaiian association, ukulele sales across the country soared. The pieces of sheet music above all came out between 1923 and 1926, the peak years of the ukulele craze.

The Tenor Banjo

The year 1922 was a time of innovation at Martin with new models and new methods of selling both contributing to the tremendous growth in sales. However, further ideas for new models also arose, not all of which ever got fully off the ground. In April of 1922 C. F. III wrote to Joseph Rogers, Jr., a supplier of fine quality banjo heads. In a request for prices, he announced the company's latest plan: "We are about to make a beginning in the manufacture of Banjos, particularly the Banjo-Mandolin and the Tenor Banjo." Oddly, just eight days later he wrote to the Waverly Novelty Company, maker of metal musical instrument accessories including pegs and banjo hardware. Perhaps he had changed his plan: "We have decided to start our Banjo line with a Ukulele-Banjo. May we ask you the favor of starting us right in the matter of hardware, by making up and sending us all the necessary hardware parts for six instruments?"

A. K. Trout, Waverly's Vice-President, was excited at the prospect. He replied, saying: "We assure you that what is needed in the Banjo and the manufacturing end of the small goods industry is more high grade people like your goodselves."

Martin soon settled on the Tenor Banjo as the first banjo-related instrument the company would produce. Various correspondence makes it clear that they planned to add banjo-mandolins and banjo-ukuleles at a later date. C. F. III began to ask around about where he might find a man to come to the company to work on the new instruments. He wrote to a few nearby clients, in one letter mentioning "we want a good man, of course, and could not use a man trained to cheap work." When Martin eventually found a man who was interested in the position, they wrote him a letter showing that their high standards extended to those they employ: "What opportunity have you had to keep in touch with recent improvements in Banjo making? We understand the modern instruments are different in many respects from the old ones." They then make clear the company philosophy: "Our reputation as Guitar makers is such that we must produce a very high grade Banjo, strictly up-to-date, or none at all."

Martin was still looking for a banjo man in May, when Waverly's A. K. Trout wrote a letter suggesting Martin speak with Fred Bacon, of the Bacon Banjo Co. He began: "Mr. Fred Bacon, whom you no doubt know personally and if you don't know his reputation as a Banjo player and maker, is unequal." Apparently Bacon was interested in the prospect of joining up with Martin. Trout continues: "I am lead to believe from my conversation with Mr. Bacon that his services could be had by your goodselves if you cared to take up the matter with him."

Bacon was a well-respected five-string banjo player who had only gone into the banjo manufacturing business the year before. His company was not yet the banjo powerhouse that it would soon become. From Trout's report, it seems Bacon may have seen the chance to join up with the well-established C. F. Martin Co. as an excellent business opportunity. Martin replied: "The subject under discussion is a big one, and the light you throw on it an entirely new one, so we will take a little extra time to consider all phases of

THE BANJO CLUB

WIGTON MARTIN FURMAN MAXFIELD
WILLIAMS STARBUCK WOLFF RIDDLE FLEMING
PITNEY QUINBY KILNER DYCKMAN WHITE

C. F. Martin III (*top row, second from left*) in the 1914 Princeton yearbook posing with the Banjo Club.

the matter as carefully as possible."

Martin apparently decided against trying to lure Fred Bacon to the company, or at least if they did no record of any conversations could be found in the archives. It is intriguing to think about what might have been, had Bacon come to Martin. Instead, Bacon teamed up with veteran banjo designer David L. Day. Bacon and Day went on to produce what are considered by many to be the best tenor banjos ever made.

Martin began banjo production by early 1923, using metal parts supplied by A. D. Grover, the same Company that supplied the tuners used on their high-end ukulele models.

At the October 1923 Board of Directors meeting, Vice President C. F. III reported: "On account of the large number of orders for guitars, mandolins, and ukuleles the tenor banjo has not been pushed." Looking forward, he continued: "As the working force increases this work will be resumed and developed for large production next year."

Similar statements are found in the minutes of meetings for the next few years. Factory expansion was expected to open up space for banjo production. Then suddenly there is no more mention of the banjo. However, as late as the beginning of 1925 the possibility of adding a banjo ukulele to the Martin line was still a consideration. Herbert Keller wrote to his father in February: "The banjo-uke is growing, from reports, tenor banjo slightly losing." He added in his next letter: "Everyone on whom I called remarked about the growth of the banjo-ukulele…. Several asked when we were going to make one." Less than a week later he adds: "Banjo-uke is still popular." But in one of his final letters from the trip his enthusiasm has declined: "I have had some second thoughts on banjo-ukes... if we figure that they may help us when the uke itself slumps we may

Martin
Tenor Banjo
No. 1

Retail Price $66.00

New product postcard for the Martin tenor banjo, 1924.

be confronted by the fact that the banjo-uke is just as likely to slump at the same time."

Martin produced a total of only 96 banjos, ending production in 1925—their biggest year for ukulele orders. It may seem somewhat ironic that the eventual "failure" of the Martin tenor banjo might appear to be related to the success of one of their competitors—the Bacon Banjo Co., considering how close Fred Bacon may have come to joining Martin. In reality, the eventual failure of the Martin banjo to ever reach substantial production was much more a result of competition from within the company. The huge success of their ukulele and guitar lines dominated all aspects of the company, and left little chance for Martin to concentrate on other products. In September of 1925 when Martin was getting ready to have new price lists printed, they requested the printers make one final change to the old price list: "Strike out Tenor Banjos and insert instead Concert Ukulele No. 1, $18.00."

It is interesting to note that the ukulele may have helped Martin survive the depression years of the 1930s, even if slumping ukulele sales were not directly helping the bottom line at that time. The ukulele boom of the mid-1920s had left Martin no choice but to abandon its plan to become a major producer of tenor banjos. Many of the major banjo manufacturers were hit hard by the depression. The combination of an economic downturn and the changing instrument tastes of the American public proved lethal to a number of manufacturers. The fact that Martin had not invested heavily in banjo production equipment helped it through a trying time. Martin was well prepared to help supply the market when the popularity of the guitar grew in the 1930s as interest in the banjo and ukulele faded.

The Boom

NINETEEN HUNDRED AND TWENTY-FIVE AGAIN SHOWED AN INCREASE, DUE TO THE UKULELE. IT IS WORTH NOT-ING THAT THE FIRST FULL YEAR OF UKULELE MANUFACTURE, 1916, AND THE TENTH YEAR, 1925, ARE THE BEST YEARS ON RECORD FOR INCREASE IN EVERY WAY – ORDERS, SALES, PROFIT, SIZE OF PLANT, AND CASH BALANCE.

— F. H. Martin in his annual President and Treasurer's Report to the Board of Directors, January 18, 1926

Growing Pains

By the end of 1923, it was clear that orders were coming in faster than instruments could be built, and the company had to consider expanding the factory. In the joint report of the President and Treasurer presented at the January 1924 Board of Directors meeting, Frank Henry states: "The only failure of the year is that we could not get many banjos out. That business is still promising and should be developed; if for any reason other orders fall off we will push it and if they do not fall off the factory should be enlarged." By the time of the April 1924 meeting Frank Henry had asked for bids on an addition to the building. The President's report was filled with good news:

Business for the second quarter kept up so well that there is no doubt but that production should be increased. Demand is general,

C. F. MARTIN & CO. MANDOLIN AND GUITAR PLANT, NAZARETH, PA.

D 2504

Postcard featuring the Martin factory circa 1930. The far right end of the building is the original brick structure. The large two story addition on the left side was built in 1924 and 1925, during the peak of the ukulele craze. Ironically, the postcard refers to the building as the "C. F. Martin & Co. Mandolin and Guitar Plant."

profits are steady, so that there is no need of any changes, only to increase volume of production for the need of present customers. Collections are reasonably good and the cash position is strong.

On the fourth of July The President made a general distribution of $5 to every person on the payroll, with the idea that this might be continued every year. The President decided to erect a building at his own expense for the use of the corporation, this being now in building operation.

At the same meeting, C. F. III noted that "production as a whole will have to be considerably greater during the fall. This might be obtained in part by greater efficiency encouraged by an advance in the wage rate." In July of 1924 a special meeting of the Board of Directors was called to do just that, and wages were raised. In an August meeting, instrument prices were raised slightly "to make round figures."

The unprecedented number of instrument sales in 1924 caused Martin to change certain business practices. One such change occurred in the way that Martin kept track of its instrument sales. The Martin sales ledgers had always included full information about every instrument sold. The specific Style was listed, as was the serial number of each instrument—except, of course, ukuleles, which had no serial numbers. Other details were noted for special order instruments, such as in the sale in April of 1924 of one Style 3 taropatch to the Southern California Music Co. where the sales book notes: "Extra chg for inlaying 'Buster Keaton' in Pearl Letters on head." Unfortunately, it appears the unprecedented volume of business due to surging ukulele sales made keeping track of each individual instrument impossible. Beginning in May of 1924 the sales were marked in this book simply stating the total number of guitars, mandolins, ukuleles, and banjos in each sale, as well as the total selling price. From this point on it becomes impossible to tell from the sales record exactly how many of each individual model of ukulele were actually sold in any given year.

In 1922 and 1923 Martin fell behind somewhat and often left customers waiting for goods for much longer than they were used to waiting. By the end of November in 1923, Martin could not supply any more Style 0 ukuleles for the Christmas season, promising only a January 15th shipping date. By the early months of 1924, generally the slow season in the instrument business, the situation had not gotten any better, with long delays continuing on orders of

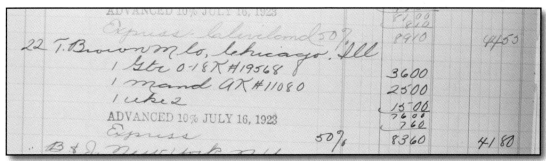

A typical listing from the Martin sales ledger, like the one above from March of 1924, listed the specific instruments that were sold including serial numbers of all guitars, mandolins, banjos, and tiples. Beginning in May of 1924 the sales listings were simplified, as shown below, and only included the total number of guitars, mandolins, ukuleles, and banjos but no serial numbers and no breakdown of the specific number of each model in the sale.

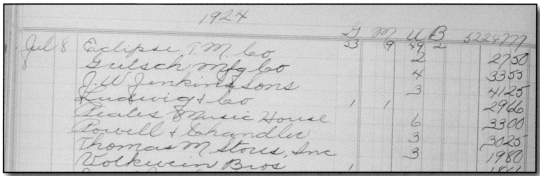

their lower-priced ukuleles. On February 21, C. F. III wrote to Wm. J. Smith and mentioned that they were sold ahead through April 1st on Style 0 and Style 1 ukuleles, as well as Style 2-17 and 0-28 guitars.

Though never trying to pull any underhanded sort of bait-and-switch, Martin would often mention in correspondence to those ordering Style 0 and Style 1 ukuleles that they had other pricier models more readily available. When the inexpensive ukulele models were back-ordered for a full two months, Herbert Keller wrote to Carl Fischer noting "we have available either at once or within the next two or three weeks

ANNOUNCEMENT

🙚 ✳ 🙚

November 13, 1924

A change has been made in the price of No. 0 and No. 1 Ukeleles, making

No. 0 . . . . . $12.00
No. 1 . . . . . $14.00

Effective, November 13th.

Orders now on file will be filled at the old prices.

C. F. MARTIN & CO., INC.

Late in 1924, even with the large new addition to the factory, orders were coming in much faster than instruments could be produced. The two most popular Martin instruments, the Style 0 and Style 1 ukuleles, were the main cause of the backlogs. Martin raised the price of these models in November, but orders continued to pour in.

Styles 2, 2K, 3, 3K and 5K. Perhaps these would help you." Similar letters were sent to other customers, especially as Christmas approached.

Many letters were sent by Martin to customers apologizing for the delays. In October, Herbert Keller sent a letter to R. S. Williams & Sons, a Toronto retailer, explaining the delays: "The situation with us seems to get worse month by month. Usually during the summer months we can build ahead so that when the Fall rush comes we have at least some styles to count on for prompt delivery." He closed the letter saying: "We hope that next year, with the help of the factory addition which will then be in use, we will be able to do better."

Prices of the Style 0 and Style 1 ukulele were raised in November, but the price change was only for new orders and so did not go into effect until around the middle of February in 1925. The Style 0 ukulele, which Martin had introduced just three years earlier as its ten-dollar model, moved to $12 and the Style 1 went to $14. But sales continued their unprecedented climb.

Death of the Sole Agency

The year 1924 brought big changes for the Martin company. A large new building was added to the factory and production greatly rearranged. It was the last year of production for the bowl-back mandolin—a product that had helped keep the company going during some difficult years in the first two decades of the century, and the concept of the sole agency was slowly starting to be eliminated. With many companies opening branches in various cities, the sole agency concept no longer served the same purpose as it had previously. When Sherman Clay, Martin's sole agent for San Francisco, opened a branch in Los Angeles, where the Southern California Music Company was Martin's sole agent, Martin had to make a decision. At first they would not ship direct to the Sherman Clay branch in Los Angeles but, of course, Sherman Clay's main branch could purchase Martin goods and ship them on to the Los Angeles store. Martin could not control where its instruments wound up after they were sold. In a letter to SoCal in March of 1924, Frank Henry explains the changes that he felt were inevitable:

A change has been coming over our trade for

some time, a change which has worried me greatly and must now be faced. It is the extension of branch houses as affecting our sole agencies.

Perhaps you too are contemplating branches, but at any rate we have already Wurlitzer, Selmer, Fischer, and Sherman, Clay, perhaps other who do not occur to me at once. Sooner or later they all ask direct shipment to some point where we have an agency. This we always refused to do but since they could always ship from the home office it followed that competition actually existed. This has been pretty well known and I now feel it is time for us to recognize the changed condition.

The simplest way would be to discontinue the systems of agencies entirely, but I believe it is better to go only as far as necessary and have divided agencies instead of sole agencies to the extent that branch houses are added.

You will now see why I have worried over the change. It is not easy to give up the old for the new, but the march of time is merciless.

Herbert Keller summarizes the reason for the change nicely in this May 1924 letter to The Chicago Musical Instrument Co.:

We have gradually been drawing away from sole agencies and at present have standing very few such agreements; the parties in question being the most reliable agents in past years. The main reason for the discontinuance of the agency system was the realization that the quality and prices of Martin Instruments were such as to make it possible for a dealer to sell them without the special advertising going along with a sole agency arrangement.

Sherman Clay's expanding business helped prompt the policy change, partly because they claimed they could give Martin bigger business on the Pacific Coast. In a March 1924 letter to Martin, Sherman Clay's F. A. Norton explains some of the reasons why Martin ukuleles were a little slow to catch on out west: "The koa instruments, made by Kumalae in Honolulu, and Nunes in Los Angeles, were in the field before you were putting out instruments and had a thoroughly established demand at prices very much lower that you asked for your goods." He continues: "Furthermore, in the better grade of ukuleles, there has always been an inclination on the part of the Pacific Coast trade to give preference to, what they regard as genuine Hawaiian Ukuleles, over those of mainland make."

Later that month, Martin made it official and let Sherman Clay know that they would be able to ship directly to their Los Angeles branch. In the same letter Frank Henry explained to them about the company's ongoing practice of supplying Customer Lines of goods not marked with the Martin name, even offering Sherman Clay such a line. Sherman Clay replied,

Jonah Kumalae (*seated, far right*) in the 1917 Pan-Pacific Carnival Parade in Honolulu, on a float titled "The Invention of the Ukulele". Kumalae owned the largest ukulele manufacturing plant in Hawaii in the late teens and 1920s. Most of the West Coast music stores got their ukuleles from Kumalae or from Leonardo Nunes in Los Angeles. It took Martin ukuleles some time to gain popularity in the West competing against what were often advertised as superior "Genuine Hawaiian" instruments.

seemingly quite surprised by the policy: "I do not quite understand the application of the last paragraph of your letter. Am I to infer that you are manufacturing the Stewart line of instruments for Buegeleisen and Jacobson?" He knew Martin made ukuleles for a few musical retailers but was surprised to find they were making instruments for large jobbing firms like B&J. He ends his letter with: "However, the world moves and times change and where money and wide distribution is sought perhaps one can't be too particular as to methods."

Frank Henry's reply makes it clear that the company had put quite a bit of thought into the policy:

We are not making the regular Stewart line; we give Buegeleisen and Jacobson the choice of our name or their own on Martin goods, at catalogue price, requiring that orders with their name be large and be placed well in advance. This is the standing offer to all customers whose business is large enough to warrant it. It was well considered when we first put on the Ditson name and the results have been good so we feel satisfied. Personally, I would prefer to make goods without any name, depending only on the quality to bring a sufficient price. I never carried out this preference neither is it likely that the present corporation will ever do so, for the reason that buyers in general prefer a brand. My mention of it is merely to illustrate the guiding policy, vis., to give a buyer value for his money in the merchandise and leave everything possible in his choice.

This is the only known photo of ukulele production in the Martin factory in the 1920s. Taken in 1925 in the new wing of the Martin factory, Earl Hartzell is the worker at the sander.

Still Unable to Meet Demand

As the popularity of Martin ukuleles increased and the factory reached its production limit, the need to advertise Martin instruments disappeared. Even before this point, Martin had made it a policy to not advertise with any particular customer, and would only run general ads in magazines like the *Crescendo* or the *Music Trades*. For example, many times a retailer would plan a newspaper ad featuring the Martin ukuleles available at their store, and request that Martin help pay for the ad, as it would be of mutual benefit. When Lyon & Healy wrote suggesting such an arrangement, Frank Henry replied:

> We can not give advertising aid for the reason that our prices are figured without that as a matter of fundamental policy. That precludes extending it to all customers, and if we should do it in a few select cases we would feel uncomfortable.

Frank Henry explained the company's philosophy more fully in response to an advertising request from Sedgwick and Casey. The Hartford, Connecticut retailer had requested Martin advertising in a new ukulele method book by Dan Nolan that they were publishing. Frank Henry wrote:

> The objection to our granting aid in advertising lies in the system on which the factory is conducted; it is not a matter of volume. Years ago, as a result of personal contact with dealers, I concluded that our future lay in the right use of our advantage in a small town, low overhead and substantial character of labor. Following the idea through I figured closely and that is the reason we can sell styles of high quality at popular prices. No allowance is made in the prices for advertising aid and I believe you will see that any exception would put me in an uncertain position, perhaps a dangerous one.

1924 marked the third straight year that Martin reached new levels of sales in both number of instruments and dollar amount. They sold slightly more guitars than they had in 1923 and slightly fewer mandolins. The real growth, however, was in what were often referred to simply as "small instruments" at the Board of Directors meetings, namely ukuleles and taropatches. Ukulele sales soared from just under 4,800 in 1923 to over 7,000 in 1924, an increase of more than forty-five percent. Some of the production increase can be attributed to the opening of the new building during the final months of the year. C. F. III's Vice President's report from January of 1925 explained some of the details of the move and the new assignments:

> The fourth quarter of 1924 was featured by the moving of the machine department into the new

Despite being unable to keep up with the demand for its soprano ukuleles, Martin introduced a new larger model ukulele in 1925. Eventually they settled on the name "Concert Ukulele."

The Parks Sisters, Frances and June, were a popular Vaudeville act in the 1920s. The sisters apparently had different tastes in ukuleles. Frances (*left*) is playing a Martin Style 3 taropatch, while June plays a Washburn Deluxe Tenor, manufactured by Lyon & Healy.

Left: The first advertising cut of the new Martin Concert Ukulele, introduced in 1925. Note the wooden pegs. *Right:* Just two years later when patent pegs became standard equipment on the concert ukulele, Martin needed a new photograph for their catalogs.

building, with little loss of productive time. The new arrangement, which uses individual motor power and includes a new sanding machine in place of the old one, seems to work well particularly in respect to the effect on the workers.

The old machine-room, which has been enlarged by removing the partition at the south end, in now being repainted and will be occupied by a new department to handle all ukulele work after binding and before finishing, and fretting on all lines. This change involves the rearrangement of the finishing room, and will permit the addition of three or four workers in each department.

Production continued in good volume during the quarter, with no changes in personnel. As new workers are added ukulele production will be increased and banjo production will be started on a quantity basis.

At that same January meeting the President's report mentioned that "the coming year will not call for much equipment unless the buildings are again enlarged, which may prove advisable. The new wing erected this year is now in use and promises to pay well because of its better lighting and more convenient arrangement of machinery." The company had not yet fully moved into its expansive new wing, but Frank Henry was already looking ahead to further expansion. By the April 1925 Board of Directors meeting Martin was falling even further behind in orders, despite a marked increase in production. Frank Henry's President's report included the following: "unfilled orders April 1st: 4,151. This excess of orders is so great that it marks only one plain course, to expand as much as possible before September so as to hold customers through the winter season." In the summer of 1925, a second story and attic was added on top of the new wing that had been completed just a year earlier. By the time the October meeting was held, C. F. III's Vice-President's report discusses the occupation of the new addition:

> The feature of the third quarter was the completion and occupation of the new building. The construction department moved into this room in September; and the room vacated, after repainting, was occupied by a new department in which all instruments will be hand-sanded for the varnish room. Guitars and mandolins will also be fitted with necks in this new department. This relieves the fretting room of the ukulele sanding and gives room there for expansion of the finishing room.

He goes on to mention the other strategies that had been employed in the third quarter to increase production. Five new workers were added to the force, a ten hour workday went into effect for the fall season, and an increase in wages made the standard rate seventy cents an hour. He noted that the wage increase "seems to have stimulated both the trained men and the learners to closer application and greater activity." Despite all of these measures and the resulting greatly increased production, it seemed no matter what the company did the orders came in faster than they could produce the instruments.

In 1924 the backlog of orders seemed to present the company with a welcomed challenge. However, by 1925 the delays had grown to the point that they became a more serious concern. Martin began to lose customers who could just not wait any longer. The company worked hard to try to satisfy as many of their current customers as possible, but had to turn away all new customer accounts. At least the success did allow the company some leverage in collecting

Spray Finish

One way that Martin was able to increase production was by improvements in the manufacturing process. One important change that occurred in 1926, noted by C. F. III in the July meeting, was the "change from brushed varnish to sprayed lacquer finish on all goods except the styles bound with celluloid." Martin had been considering a new finishing process at least as far back as 1924 when they wrote to the DuPont company asking about their Viscolac finish. DuPont informed them their Viscolac finish "could only be applied by spraying" and asked if Martin was equipped with a pneumatic spraying machine. Martin explained they had no such equipment and the topic was temporarily dropped. In June of 1925 Martin sent DuPont two ukuleles to have treated with DuPont's finish Duco Clear. In July two more were sent to the Murphy Varnish Co. of Newark, New Jersey. DuPont won out, and by the end of 1925 Martin was planning the necessary changes to the factory to allow for spray finishing.

The change to spray finishing would not be a simple one, as evidenced in a letter from Martin's Lumber Insurance Company. The insurance man wrote to Martin with extensive warnings about the dangers involved in setting up a spraying room: "If you do this, it will necessitate an increase in rate, and it will also be necessary to operate the spraying machine in a room entirely cut off from the rest of your building." He continues, "The material you intend using is one of the most hazardous materials now used for finishing purposes. It is practically liquid T.N.T. and the vapor from same is highly explosive."

Eventually Martin worked out the difficulties of setting up the room, and began spraying its finishes in the spring of 1926. C. F. III noted in July that "this change enabled the finishing room to produce more work with one man less than before."

on accounts, as Frank Henry mentioned in the July Board of Directors meeting: "The course indicated is to give preference in shipment to prompt paying customers and point out to others the need of caution." Looking through the 1925 correspondence files it is remarkable just how many letters exist where a new customer account is declined. For a company that had worked hard for many years to bring in new customers, it must have been quite difficult to have to now turn so many away.

B&J, the biggest jobber of Martin instruments at the time, was one of the many customers who could not get Martin ukuleles in fast enough to supply their demand. Small retailers, unable to get their Martin goods from the usual jobbing line, turned to Martin looking for direct sales. Martin, however, was forced to decline all new accounts. The sometimes desperate sounding customer letters received apologetic replies that were at least hopeful that the further factory expansion could cause a change in the situation in the coming months. It is clear from the replies that Martin was quite uncomfortable disappointing potential customers. One example of such an exchange went on between Martin and the Adams Music Company of Fort Worth, TX. In August of 1925 Adams wrote: "We are the only dealers handling Martin instruments in Fort Worth and now that we have built up a very nice business, especially in the Uke line, we are unable to secure Martin Merchandise from any of the jobbers." Concerned about losing sales, he continues: "Please advise if you will sell us a few Ukes and the price and types of same. We are trying to get lined up for the Holidays and will appreciate any help that you can give us."

The company's reply, written by Herbert Keller, reads:

> We are at a loss for a suitable reply to your letter. Your position is unfortunate in that you have worked up a trade for Martin Ukuleles and Guitars and now find yourselves short of stock; but we are quite unable to help you. For some time past we have been running three to four months behind orders and cannot consider taking on any new accounts before Christmas.
>
> If you are in the market after that time, we will appreciate hearing from you and have no doubt but that we will be able to supply instruments.

In an apology to the Rudolph Wurlitzer Company over delays, C. F. III summarizes the situation well:

> In regard to Ukulele deliveries we must admit that we are making poor showing in living up to our promises. We hope you will believe, however, that it is not a matter of bad faith on our part but merely a mistake in judgement; and perhaps we might say, misplaced optimism in anticipating an increase in production which we are not able to realize, due to the great difficulty of training new men to our standards of workmanship.

With the Martin factory producing instruments as fast as they could, other ways of increasing revenue were explored. It seems there may still have been some

The second issue of Frets magazine, April 1925. Frets was published by the William J. Smith Music Co. of New York City. Smith had been one of Martin's biggest customers since going into business in 1915. Still, Martin had little interest in advertising in Frets or anywhere else, when they were already overwhelmed with business.

The Players: May Singhi Breen

May Singhi Breen was an important part of the ukulele world for decades beginning in the 1920s. Known as "The Ukulele Lady," Breen partnered with songwriter Peter DeRose on the radio from 1923-1939. Known as the "Sweethearts of the Air" they were among the biggest radio stars of the day. Breen did much to promote the ukulele, including writing method books, recording a two-sided 78 rpm Ukulele Lesson, and doing countless ukulele arrangements for popular sheet music. Breen took the instrument seriously, and her choice in ukuleles was always a Martin.

Breen was a regular customer at the New York City store of Wm. J. Smith. She had at least three custom ukuleles made for her by Martin, with the words "Ukulele Lady" inlaid on the fretboard (for more on these see Appendix C: Custom Ukuleles Made for Individuals). Breen struck deals promoting P'mico banjo-ukuleles and Bacon banjos, and surely would have been happy to have a similar arrangement with Martin ukuleles. Martin however did not make customer endorsement deals. Unlike Roy Smeck, who turned to the Harmony Co. for an endorsement deal when it became clear that Martin was not an option, Breen it seems did not look elsewhere. Smeck, later in his career, talked about a downside of his Harmony

Above: Breen with a Martin 5K, from an instructional booklet, 1925.

Top left: Breen's business card

Bottom left: Breen and DeRose in a photo from their 1931 Christmas card.

contract—the fact that he was required to perform with Harmony-made ukuleles instead of his preferred Martins. Perhaps Breen was so attached to her Martin ukuleles she just could not bear to play something else.

Breen was friendly with the Martin family, and corresponded with them often. She dropped by the factory in 1927 in what C. F. III described as "an unexpected visit, much to our surprise and delight." She kept the Martin's updated on the news from the professional field in New York City, and sent photo updates with some regularity. When she sent the Martin's a photo from a fishing trip she had made with her husband, C. F. III responded: "We wish we could think that the Ukulele had been instrumental in landing these fish. This would be tremendous sales argument for the Ukulele."

Breen visited the Martin factory again on June 14, 1932, and selected a 5K ukulele. On June 26, 1932, May Singhi Breen performed as soloist on a radio program with Paul Whiteman & his Chieftains. The piece, titled "Inspiration," was written by Breen's husband Peter De Rose and Charles Harold. Described as a symphonic poem for the ukulele, it was a part of the ongoing efforts by Breen to have the ukulele taken seriously as a musical instrument. Breen sent a postcard to Martin to let them know about the upcoming performance, and C. F. III wrote to her the day after the performance:

> Congratulations on the complete success of your performance with Paul Whiteman last evening! Several of us here in the office heard and enjoyed your playing. It was a revelation as well as an "inspiration" even to us who thought we knew something of the possibilities of the Ukulele. It is hard to believe that the instrument you were using was one we know so well. More power to you in your efforts to place the Ukulele on a high musical plane.
>
> Congratulations to Mr. De Rose, too, as composer. You are a great team.

Breen responded days later: "I certainly appreciated your letter and you may rest assured it was a Martin Uke which did the trick in my performance with Paul Whiteman last Sunday—and a raft of letters from fans asking the make, etc."

Breen would remain devoted to her Martin ukuleles throughout her career. Her three custom inlaid ukuleles remain among the fanciest ukuleles ever to come out of the Martin factory.

Above: Headstock detail from Breen's "Ukulele Special" made by Martin in 1927.

Above: Postcard sent by Breen to Martin announcing her upcoming radio performance, June, 1932.

particular areas where further production was possible. In May of 1925, at a time when new customer accounts were being turned away, C. F. III wrote to the A. H. Balliet Corporation. Balliet was a well-known manufacturer of cigar boxes located in nearby Allentown, and was branching out into the area of ukulele production. C. F. III offered Balliet gross lots of hardwood ukulele pegs. He let them know that "we are also in a position to make for you such small parts as bridges, string nuts, Rosewood fingerboards, Spruce braces or similar items for which we have special machinery and material."

C. F. III wrote again soon after, sending the name of a gut string manufacturer to Balliet. It may seem strange that Martin was giving advice to what appears to be a competitor, but C. F. III's letter makes it clear that he didn't feel the Balliet ukuleles would be selling in the same market as Martin products. He enclosed samples of "imitation Gut Ukulele Strings which we believe to be very good value… On testing them we find the tone to be inferior to the high priced Gut strings we are using but we believe it to be better than the very cheap Gut Strings which you probably intend to use."

With orders already coming faster than they could be filled, Martin had no need for any advertising. Still, the requests came in and had to be turned away. When the editor of The *Music Trade News* wrote to Martin in February of 1925 suggesting Martin run an ad, Herbert Keller replied that "we are not in the market for any advertising now and will probably not be for some months to come." When their business manager wrote again later in the year again soliciting advertising, Herbert Keller replied "We wish that we might have you here and show you our order file. We consider new advertising under these circumstances would be a useless expenditure."

When the Wm. J. Smith Co. began publishing Frets magazine in 1925, Smith sent a request to Frank Henry asking him to run an Ad in the first few issues. Despite having turned down many other advertising offers, Frank Henry agreed to run an ad in Frets—probably because of his long business relationship with Smith. His letter to Smith offers some interesting insight into Frank Henry's plans for his company…

I will have Herbert write copy for May and June "Frets" and send it tomorrow or Saturday. Make it a quarter page and send bill.

It is not at all likely I will want to continue, in fact the better the response the less I will want it. It is not our field of operation. Our whole selling plan aims at dealers' trade with encouragement for big dealers to stay with us, and for all dealers to buy big. Our

C. F. Martin & Co., Inc.
Established 1833
Nazareth, Penna.
Price List effective March 1, 1926
Subject to change without notice

GUITARS

Style		Style	
2-17	$27.50	00-28	$75.00
0-18	35.00	000-28	80.00
00-18	40.00	0-42	105.00
000-18	45.00	00-42	110.00
0-21	50.00	0-45	150.00
00-21	55.00	00-45	155.00
0-28	70.00	000-45	165.00

HAWAIIAN KOAWOOD GUITARS

Style 0-18 K	$40.00	Style 0-28 K	$70.00

FLAT MANDOLINS

Style A	$25.00	Style C	$55.00
A-K	30.00	E	110.00
B	40.00		

TENOR MANDOLAS
(Flat Model)

Style A	$30.00	Style B	$50.00

UKULELES

Mahogany		Koawood	
No. 0 (Discontinued temporarily)		No. 1 K	$16.00
1 (See note below)	$14.00	2 K	20.00
2	17.50	3 K	30.00
3	27.50	5 K	55.00

TIPLES

Style T-18	$35.00	Style T-28	$70.00

TARO-PATCHES

Mahogany		Koawood	
No. 1 (See note below)	$18.00	No. 1 K	$22.00
2	24.00	2 K	28.00
3	35.00	3 K	40.00

CONCERT UKULELE

No. 1 (See note below)	$18.00

Prices are net and do not include case or bag

Note: Design changed as follows. (1) A **rosewood binding is added to the back.** (2) The finish is **natural color mahogany** instead of stained mahogany.

Price List from March 1, 1926. Note the temporary discontinuation of the Style 0 ukulele model. Also noted on the Price List are changes made to the Style 1 instruments—the addition of rosewood binding on the back of the instrument and the lighter natural finish.

in the middle of 1925 Martin added a new ukulele to its line of instruments. The tenor banjo, though, was a very different instrument compared to Martin's regular wooden-bodied line. The new ukulele required only a few minor modifications to an instrument that Martin had manufactured for many years—the taropatch.

Martin had made four-string taropatches on special order as far back as 1916 but they were never big sellers, possibly because many retailers didn't realize this was an option. In mid 1925 Martin decided to make up a few four-string taropatches with a slightly narrower neck and a standard ukulele bridge. This was now an instrument intended for four strings, and customers greatly approved. It took some time before they arrived at a name, but eventually it became known as the "Concert Ukulele." The company had been trying to pare down the number of different models it made, so they added just one style of concert ukulele, the Style 1C. Other styles could be special ordered, but the 1C was the only style advertised and cataloged. Martin sold ninety-one concert ukuleles in 1925, despite not adding it to its price list until late in the year. That is greater than the number of four-string taropatches that had been made in the nearly ten years they had been available.

The large increase in production in 1925 led to shortages in some of the materials Martin needed to make its ukuleles. Ukulele pegs were one item that Martin had a hard time keeping in stock. Patent pegs were used on both the koa and mahogany version of the Style 2 and 3 ukuleles, as well as on the Style 5K. The metal parts for the pegs were manufactured by the A. D. Grover company, while the ivory-colored plastic buttons supplied by Grover were manufactured for them by the Celluloid Company. Due to restructuring at the Celluloid Company, Grover had trouble filling its peg orders. That left Martin without the pegs needed for its most expensive ukulele models. In a letter to Grover in August, C. F. III discusses the difficulty the delays were causing: "We have about one hundred seventy-five fine ukuleles held up for lack of ivory buttons." By the middle of September the pile of instruments awaiting pegs had grown and the buttons had still not arrived. A letter to Buegeleisen and Jacobson about the button shortage mentions that "several hundred ukuleles are waiting for them

best growth comes as we succeed in putting teachers and dealers on a mutual basis so that teachers come to us for assistance only in small matters while placing their orders with dealers. The Crescendo was taken up to reach small town teachers who have no good store. It has done that work well enough and I feel sure that 'Frets' will do the same, but there is petty annoyance connected with such sales, inducing a state of mind which I believe retards our growth. To you I can speak out as only old friends speak to each other, so I will add that my ambition is to make this the main factory in the trade, known as a reliable supply house for popular instruments of quality.

Martin's tenor banjo had been waiting on the sidelines for years now, never quite being put into full scale production because of the ever increasing call for Martin's ukuleles. It may seem strange then that

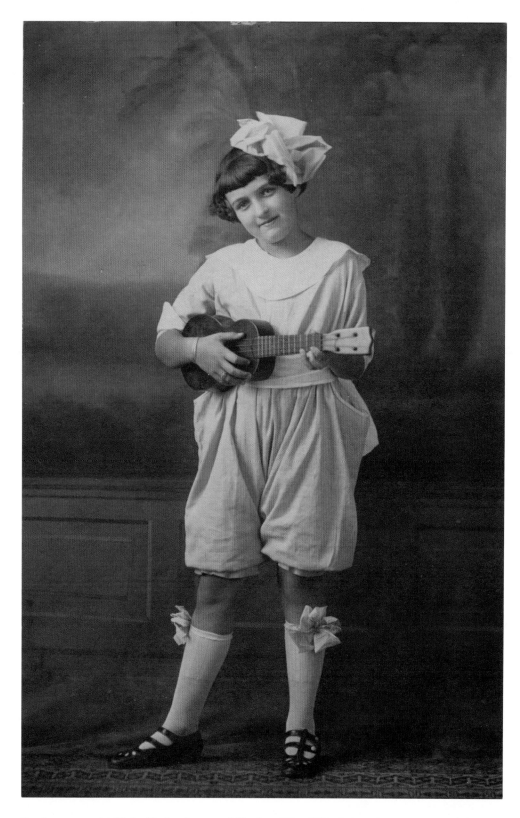

Twelve year old Viola Mott, who was billed as "The Little Entertainer", was a performer and teacher in Providence, Rhode Island. She sent this photo to Martin and let them know that she was "always in praise of the Martin."

1926 started off with the company coming off of its best year ever. In January the company had over 6,000 unfilled instrument orders, of which nearly 5,600 were for ukuleles. The great majority of these were Style 0 ukuleles, the company's least expensive, and least profitable, instrument. With production unable to keep up with orders, the decision was made to temporarily discontinue the Style 0 ukulele, effective March 1, 1926. Prior orders would be filled as instruments became available, but no new orders for Style 0s would be taken. C. F. III's Vice President's report in April of 1926 discusses the increasing workforce. Guitar orders were increasing, and for this reason C. F. III notes that "additional men have been placed on guitar construction rather than on ukuleles." After greatly expanding the factory in each of the previous two years, the company still could not produce instruments fast enough and therefore began to consider further expansion. The April meeting's minutes note that "on motion, the President was instructed to inquire into the price and advisability of buying the property adjoining the factory to the North."

In late April of 1926 a special second meeting of the Board of Directors was called to discuss prices. With demand outstripping supply, the need was felt to increase prices. The new prices went into effect on May 1st. The minutes of the meeting noted that "the reason for the increase is largely to provide money for enlargement and to provide a reserve for harder times." It was not yet clear that harder times were not all that far off. At the regular July meeting of the Board, the President's report noted that orders had declined during the second quarter. He added that "Judging by correspondence the decline is normal for the season, not caused by the raise of prices May first, and since it was desirable to reduce the unfilled orders the present condition is very satisfactory."

and as soon as they arrive we will finish these instruments and fill your orders."

In November of 1925 Landay Brothers, the retail branch of the jobbing firm Progressive Musical Instrument Co. (P'mico), placed a monumental ukulele order. Likely tired of delays in deliveries, Landay placed its order for the entire year of 1926, 1/12 of the order to be shipped on the first of each month starting in January of 1926. The order was for 600 Style 0, 360 Style 1, 300 Style 2, 120 Style 3, 240 Style 1K, 120 Style 2K, and 12 Style 3K. This order of over 1,700 ukuleles may be considered the zenith of the Martin ukulele boom of the 1920s, for within a few months ukulele orders would begin a long, steady decline.

Customer Endorsements

Throughout the 1920s Martin received dozens of requests for special deals on their ukuleles. Many performers asked to be supplied with instruments for free or at deep discounts in exchange for their promotion of the Martin brand either on stage or over the radio. Many other musical instrument manufacturers offered such endorsement deals. The instrument catalogs of many companies featured a large number of photos of popular performers and recording artists of the time. Alongside the photos these stars were quoted praising the company's instruments. Two of Martin's biggest competitors for the high-end ukulele market, Gibson and Lyon & Healy, both regularly featured these artist endorsements in their 1920s catalogs. Martin, however, stuck to its policy of not striking such deals and only offering a standard discount of twenty percent to professional players.

Wendell Hall and Johnny Marvin are two of the better-known ukulele players who sought endorsement deals, but there were many other lesser-known ukulele players also making requests. The Martins handled these requests respectfully, but always stuck to their established policy of supplying no more than the standard twenty percent professional discount.

When Mrs. Chas. Opunui wrote to C. F. III in 1922 inquiring about a Martin ukulele, she mentioned meeting Herbert Keller backstage at her production of "A Night in Honolulu" in Charleston, SC. Herbert wrote back, glad to hear that the Opunuis were "in this part of the country." He goes on to invite the Opunuis out to Nazareth, even offering to pick them up at the station in Easton. Mrs. Opunui wrote back later in the year, hoping to strike a deal. She relates that her manager said "if you will give me one of your best instruments, he will put an ad on all his programs in every town we play also a special ad in the local newspapers." She ends by saying "if you consider this kindly let me hear from you." It appears that Martin did not "consider" it—the letter appears to have gone unanswered.

In 1925, Martin appears to have at least considered changing their catalog style. The Southern California Music Company wrote to make a ukulele order and also went on to mention: "We are just wondering if you would be interested in receiving photographs of different movie stars who are using your instruments. We have sold them to Ethel Terry, Buster Keaton, Tom Murray and dozens of other stars and could get photographs of them playing your instruments and it might be you could use them for circulars or a catalog you might compile." Herbert Keller's reply was: "During the early summer we will be getting out a new catalogue and if we decide to change our regular form of catalogue and include pictures of the users of Martin instruments, we will take advantage of your very kind offer to get photographs of Movie stars for us." Perhaps he was just being polite, or perhaps the company was actually contemplating a change. Whatever the case was, the company decided against the artist endorsements and continued to issue a basic, understated catalog of its instruments for many years to come.

Vaudevillian Johnie Dunn wrote to Martin in 1925. "I, Johnie Dunn," he wrote, "now playing all big time vaudeville, have been using your uke and also recommending it for three years." Dunn relates that his $50.00 ukulele is in perfect condition, but he needs a back up because "if a string breaks I am lost because I only have the one uke." He continues: "I don't expect to get it free but I do expect a real, low price. I feel that you should make me a very attractive offer as I have advertised yours on the stage, and also in broadcasting." With Martin in its busiest period to date, Herbert Keller's reply is short and simple: "Many thanks for your kind words about our instrument. Your advertising is appreciated and we hope that we will be able to supply you to your complete satisfaction. Our regular Professional Discount is 20%." He also mentions that they are sending a catalog under separate cover.

Another 1925 request came from Richard Gilbert, who said he had "broadcast more than 150 times from 18 different stations in the past four months," always using a Martin taropatch. Gilbert fills an entire page with his varied accomplishments, claiming "before the close of this month I will be under contract with one or more phonograph recording companies to make records after the type of Cliff Edwards." He mentions that his taropatch is badly worn and has a crack in back, and ends by saying "As I use no other but Martin instruments, I feel that because of the advertising value of my constant and continued usage of the Martin Taropatch, you might be kind enough to present me with a new instrument." Herbert Keller's reply is, again, to the point: "We will be glad to take care of the work on your Taro Patch and judge from your description that this is covered by our guarantee; there will, therefore, be no charge for putting the instrument in first class condition."

In 1927 Charles E. Green, manager of the Parisian Red Heads, wrote to Martin. Calling the group "America's greatest girl band," Green wrote with regard to Miss Judy Fay, their ukulele player. Green was hoping to make an arrangement with Martin where Fay would mention the Martin name in performances and demonstrate Martin ukuleles with dealers in various cities, whereas Martin could reciprocate by mentioning the Red Heads in their national advertising. He added that "Miss Fay would also be pleased to try one of your very best instruments."

C. F. III responded, expressing the company philosophy: "So many of the best professional Ukulele players are using Martin instruments, because in them they find the tone and ease of action necessary for their work, that it would hardly be possible for us to make a suitable return for their advertising. We feel that we have done our share toward the success of the artist when we make it possible for him or her to have an instrument capable of expressing musical genius."

In April of 1925 a letter arrived from Volkein Brothers Music House in Pittsburgh, Pennsylvania. Although not ukulele-related, the exchange nicely illustrates Martin's thoughts on customer endorsements. The well-known guitar soloist Johnson Bane was in Pittsburgh, and was badly in need of a new guitar. Volkein details Bane's championing of the guitar, and makes a suggestion to Martin. "We believe it would be highly appreciated by Mr. Bane if you were to surprise him with an outright present of a Martin Guitar." Henry Keller's single paragraph reply makes the company's policy quite clear: "We

thank you kindly for your suggestion that we present an instrument to Mr. Bane, with a plate suitable engraved. His interest in the Guitar and his work for the Martin Guitar are valued fully, and your interest in the same things is similarly appreciated. You may say that we are not willing to pay for what we are getting, and that may be true; but the heavens will fall before C. F. Martin & Company give an instrument away."

Viola Mott, one of the many entertainers who wrote to Martin in praise of the company's instruments. She was also one of the few who never asked for any special deals or free instruments in exchange for her praise.

Gibson Scouts the Competition

One of the many interesting correspondence exchanges found in the Martin archives occurred late in 1924. Gibson, Inc. of Kalamazoo, Michigan was one of Martin's biggest competitors for the high-end guitar and mandolin market. Gibson was a much bigger company than Martin, having built its reputation during the era of mandolin popularity in the years around the turn of the century. But when the market for Hawaiian instruments surged in the late teens, Gibson did not actively pursue it. Gibson did not begin ukulele production and didn't offer guitars intended specifically for Hawaiian-style playing until long after the Hawaiian wave had crested. When the popularity of the ukulele again started to soar in the mid 1920s, Gibson decided to jump on the ukulele bandwagon before it was too late.

A change in management at Gibson in September of 1924 may have prompted the decision to go into ukulele production. Guy Hart was promoted to General Manager at Gibson in September of 1924. In October, barely one month after the promotion, Hart sent a letter to Martin asking for

**Gibson Uke-2
circa late 1920s**

information about Martin's ukuleles. He said that he had recently received a shipment of four Martin ukuleles, one each in Style 0, 1, 2, and 3, stating there was nothing on the package to "show from whom they came." The instruments apparently inspired Hart to consider a Martin-Gibson partnership of a sort. He continued: "In looking over these instruments, we became quite interested and wondered if you would consider making about two numbers for us with our name on them. We would, of course, want a few minor distinguishing marks added and perhaps an idea or two of our own incorporated." He asked about possible pricing and ended by saying "we would act in the capacity of a wholesaler with quite a large outlet."

A few penciled notes are made in the margin of the letter, likely by Frank Henry himself.

1. Building to order for jobbers is already established
2. All changes must meet with our approval
3. We must have the right to adopt any new ideas

These three notes establish the reason for agreeing to build for Gibson as well as the conditions under which such work would need to be done. Herbert Keller replied to Gibson:

Your letter of the 14th is at hand and has been read with interest. Your proposition is quite agreeable to us and we are willing to take up the matter in detail, as you may wish.

Price list is enclosed and the best discount, which we quote you, is 50%. Terms are net thirty days; there is no cash discount. This is our quotation; however, we should hasten to say that the present rush of orders makes it impossible for us to supply you, or any new customer, with instruments before 1925. Probably we will be able to do so early next year, but we would not care to promise definitely at this time.

If you would like to give us your ideas as to distinguishing marks or specialties that you would like to have incorporated in the instruments, perhaps, if we may offer a

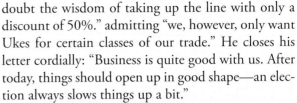

suggestion, the buying of instruments unfinished so that you can use your distinctive Gibson finish, we will be very glad to figure on it this fall.

Hart replied, asking about the discount for doing their own finishing, agreeing that "it would be to our advantage to carry out the established Gibson shades and finish." He also questioned whether Martin was offering up a deep enough discount on the instruments to make the plan feasible: "To be frank with you, we

**Gibson Uke-3
circa late 1920s**

doubt the wisdom of taking up the line with only a discount of 50%." admitting "we, however, only want Ukes for certain classes of our trade." He closes his letter cordially: "Business is quite good with us. After today, things should open up in good shape—an election always slows things up a bit."

Herbert Keller replied to Gibson, giving them quite a bit of information:

Your letter of the 4th has been laid aside for some time and we ask you kindly to pardon us for the delay in replying.

Enclosed you will find new price list, dated November 13th, on which there is a change in the price of the No. 0 and No. 1 ukuleles, making the net price of these instruments to you on the basis of our 50% quotation as follows:

No. 0	$6.00
No. 1	7.00
No. 2	8.75
No. 3	13.75

Using these figures as a guide, we quote you on Ukuleles unfinished, ready for wood filler and shellac, complete in all other ways but without pegs and strings, as follows:

No. 0	$4.74
No. 1	5.53
No. 2	6.91
No. 3	10.86

The reason for quoting without pegs and strings is the fact that these are put on after the varnish work is completed. If we were to put them on here for you it would be necessary for you to take them off. Furthermore, we suggest that in the item of pegs you will have an opportunity to vary our styles. There are several good wood pegs, also several good patent pegs on the market. We use Grover patent pegs which we consider the best.

...If there is any detail that you would like to have us go into more thoroughly, please call upon us for it.

It seems to us that what you said about business opening up after election has come true with a vengeance and we hope you will be able to take care of your share of it.

Unfortunately, that letter seems to have been the end of the discussion. It is possible Gibson felt the prices were too high and made the decision to manufacture their own ukuleles. Then again, Gibson may have been intending to go into manufacturing all along. They may simply have been looking for some inside information as to Martin's pricing and policies. Either way, there is no indication that Martin ever sent Gibson any ukuleles. In early March of 1925, less than four months after this exchange, Gibson announced its own line of ukuleles. Gibson ukuleles were initially made in three styles not completely dissimilar to Martin's Styles 0, 2, and 3.

This well-worn Gibson ukulele pamphlet is undated, but is likely from the later 1920s. The man on the cover, Doc Morris, was a Gibson endorser at the time. However, this pamphlet was discovered in Doc Morris' personalized hardshell case—along with his well-played Martin Style 2 ukulele.

Gibson may have patterned its standard ukulele styles after the Martin line-up, but they were willing to go above and beyond on special orders. On the left is a Gibson Florentine model ukulele, with hand painted Venetian scenes. On the right is the Gibson Poinsettia ukulele, which also featured hand painted designs and fancy inlays on the celluloid fingerboard.

The Decline

WE ARE STILL SUFFERING FROM THE DROP IN UKULELE PLAYING BUT HAVE MADE GOOD PROGRESS IN GUITAR SALES. THE GUITAR IS NOW POPULAR AND THE OPPORTUNITY FOR A LARGE BUSINESS IS HERE, BUT COMPETITION IS KEEN AND THE MANNER OF PLAYING IS CHANGED SO WE ARE STILL OBLIGED TO EXPERIMENT WITH NEW MODELS.

— F. H. Martin in his annual President and Treasurer's Report to the Board of Directors, January, 1931

By the October 1926 Board of Directors meeting the decline in demand for ukuleles had become clear. The President's report at the meeting began: "Demand has fallen off through the early fall so that it will be necessary to go over the whole situation in January. For the present no change is made except to re-instate the Style 0 ukulele effective January first, 1927." The Vice President's report speaks more specifically of the changing trends: "The notable feature of the third quarter was the change from ukuleles to guitars in production. With a smaller demand for ukuleles, a number of men have been transferred to guitar work." The number of men employed reached seventy-two, the most that would be employed for many years to come.

The change in public favor from ukuleles to guitars was noted across the country, not just at the Martin factory. A December 1926 editorial in Musical Merchandise magazine noted that guitar sales had increased fifty percent during 1926, while ukulele sales were noted as being about the same as in 1925. At Martin the growth of the guitar business was even greater, with guitar production in 1926 more than doubling from 1925 levels. 1926 would be Martin's largest production year, with very nearly 20,000 instruments produced—an annual total that the company did not surpass until 1971. The approximately 14,000 ukuleles sold that year is a number that never has been approached again. Although 1926 was Martin's best year for ukulele sales, some of that can be attributed to the large list of unfilled orders from 1925. Ukulele orders for the year dropped to just over 10,000. By the end of the year it was clear that ukulele orders were on the decline.

Still, as 1927 opened the outlook for the company was strong. They were coming off of their best sales year ever, during which they sold the most guitars by far in their history. However, with the new year came tragedy. Herbert Keller entered St. Luke's Hospital in Bethlehem on December 28th, and underwent surgery for an intestinal obstruction. On January 3rd, he died from peritonitis. His death was a sudden, shocking blow to the Martin family. Herbert Keller had served as the company's traveling salesman, visiting retail stores and taking orders for instruments. Based on correspondence, he was well-liked and highly respected by the dealers whom he visited. One of the many sympathy letters that the Martins received from customers was written by Wurlitzer employee J. C. Freeman. Freeman wrote that "on my return from California I learned for the first time of the death of your son and I wish to extend to you and to his brother my heartfelt sympathy. He was a fine, noble young man and we held him in the highest regard, and I can well imagine what such a great loss means to you both." Frank Henry replied: "I thank you for your letter of sympathy. Our loss is severe but we must carry on as best we can, hoping that we will honor the departed one by so doing as much as we can in any way."

Frank Henry's wife, Jenny Keller Martin, took Herbert's position on the Board of Directors, and C. F. III was elected Vice President and Secretary of the company. Herbert Keller had not been on the road for more than a year. With the large number of unfilled orders in 1926, attempting to increase production was more important than attempting to increase sales, and so Herbert had worked from Nazareth. But by 1927 production had caught up with orders and the company needed to look to build sales. A new traveling salesman was needed.

In May of 1927 Frank Henry asked New York City wholesaler Henry Stadlmair about a man who had formerly worked for Stadlmair and was being considered for the Martin job. Stadlmair lets Frank

Henry know that he can't recommend the man, saying "his sales did not meet with expectations." Stadlmair then goes on to suggest that his company's salesmen could represent Martin across the country, on a ten percent commission basis, "which is less than it would cost you to send out a traveler." Frank Henry replied:

> I think it will be best for us to keep looking for a suitable man. Your suggestion about having your branch travelers handle our line is plainly enough, even without long consideration, one that holds great promise, but I believe on the whole there are good reasons for keeping our former method. My son's work demonstrated the advantages of using this office as a base, and since he traveled according to our needs it was very economical.

The company eventually hired James Markley in 1928 to handle the traveling salesman position.

C. F. III's Vice-President's report at the January 1927 Board of Directors meeting made it clear that the ukulele craze was fading. "A sharp decline in orders for ukuleles affected production in several ways… In October production of the Style 0 ukulele was resumed and before the end of the year all ukulele production except this style was stopped, a large stock having been accumulated." His report at the July meeting was even gloomier. Seventeen men were laid off during March and April and the working hours were reduced. Ukulele sales were greatly reduced from the previous

Studio photo of Martin's newest ukulele offering, the Style 1T Tenor Ukulele, 1928

two years, yet still over 5,000 ukuleles were sold in 1927. The tenor guitar was added to the Martin line and helped guitar production remain near the record levels of 1926. C. F. III noted at the October Board of Directors meeting that "there have been no important changes in designs, and no new instruments, but several new ideas in guitars and ukuleles are now under consideration." Many changes to the guitar and mandolin lines would come in the next few years, along with one new model of ukulele, the tenor ukulele, introduced in 1928.

In 1927 the company did explore one way to increase sales—by increasing its discount to customers who purchased in quantity. For many years Martin had stuck with its standard maximum discount of fifty percent off the retail prices no matter how large an order. In April of 1927, after many years of jobbers requesting deeper discounts, Martin acquiesced. A discount of "50 and 10%" was instituted on orders from customers who did a large enough business. A discount of "50 and 10%" is equivalent to a fifty-five percent discount (the extra ten percent is taken off the already discounted price). The practice only lasted for a little more than a year. At the January 1929 Board of Directors meeting C. F. III noted: "The arrangement made with a number of jobbing houses in April of 1927 gave increasing trouble and was ended with most of them on the last day of December, 1928."

With the decline in business in 1927, the company took to soliciting new customers. Some of these were prospective customers who had been turned

Pole to Pole with "Ukulele Dick" Konter

Permanently on display at the Martin Museum, the "Konter Ukulele" is perhaps the most famous ukulele in the world. Formerly the property of Richard Konter, the early 1920s Martin Style 1K was actually on the plane that made the very first flight over the North Pole on May 9, 1926. It is covered with the signatures of many of the men on that arctic expedition, as well as many other notable names of the 1920s.

Richard Konter was a longtime member of the U.S. Navy, and was a veteran of both the Spanish-American War and the First World War. He was also an accomplished ukulele player. After retiring from the Navy he released his first ukulele method, titled *Dick's Ukulele Method* in 1923. He followed this with *Dick's Improved Ukulele Method* in 1924, shortly before volunteering for the arctic expedition that was being led by Commander Robert Byrd. The story of the ukulele and its famous flight was recounted by Konter in a 1952 letter to Martin. At the time, Konter was exchanging the ukulele for a Martin guitar. He explains how he got Floyd Bennett, Byrd's co-pilot, to hide the ukulele on the plane: "He hid the ukulele in the plane and thus it safely made this famous first flight over the North Pole, and upon their return, Bennett, several friends, and myself saw him take the ukulele from between the spare furs that were aboard."

Konter goes on to discuss the various signatures: "I immediately had every man I could reach on the expedition autograph the ukulele, with Byrd and Bennett's signatures being under the strings, and Ammundsen's and Nobile's, below the American's."

He then adds to the list of names: "Also, amongst these names are these:- President Cooledge; (?), Pershing; Kellogg; and Lindberg, just below the neck and above the sound hole, with Edison on the right side of the ukulele."

When Konter returned from the Arctic expedition he was quite a celebrity. He and his ukulele were mentioned in the *New York Times* on a number of occasions and celebrations were held in his honor in New York City. He brought the ukulele with him to many varied events and appearances. Eventually, he considered the idea of going into musical instrument sales, featuring, of course, the ukulele. He sent two letters addressed to "Mr. Fred Martin" late in 1927. In the first he explains his plan: "In the very near future I hope to go into the ukulele game, that is, selling all instruments, but specializing in ukuleles. I am very well known not only in Greater N.Y., but I have a small following in almost every city in the U.S., and I think I can make it a go."

Top Right: Konter published his first ukulele method in 1923, and this improved edition came out in 1924.

Left: The Konter Ukulele. 1920s Martin Style 1K ukulele that was flown over the North Pole during the Byrd Expedition. Byrd and his Co-pilot Floyd Bennett signatures can be seen between the soundhole and the bridge. Above the soundhole, among others, are the signatures of Calvin Coolidge and Charles Lindbergh.

He goes on to say he is only interested in selling the highest grade of instruments and relating that he is planning to pay cash for everything that he orders. In his second letter he makes it clear he is not afraid of the alleged declining ukulele market: "regardless of all the warning I am getting from all dealers, salesmen, etc., that it is a DYING GAME, or INSTRUMENT, I SAY IT IS NOT." He continues "I have that confidence in the UKE that I KNOW I CAN MAKE IT A GO." Martin responded by saying that the company will be "very glad to arrange to sell you whatever you may need whenever you are properly established. We cannot, of course, allow dealers' discount to anyone except he be regularly engaged in the retail music business and recognized as a dealer by the commercial agencies." Martin wrote again a few days later to try to arrange a meeting with Konter in New York, but it is not known if they ever did meet.

Konter would go on to participate in two Byrd expeditions to the South Pole, but it does not seem he brought along his famous Martin ukulele. By that time he had an association with the New York-based instrument makers the Favilla Brothers, who may have been more willing than Martin to exchange instruments for Konter's endorsement. He took Favilla instruments along with him to Antarctica, where a Favilla ukulele was flown over the South Pole, and its body was signed by members of the South Pole expedition.

Top right: Detail of the signatures on the front of the Konter ukulele.

Right: Konter with his ukulele at the White House.

Far right: Konter's second ukulele method. His *Ukulele System* was published after his return from his polar expedition.

The Players: Roy Smeck

oy Smeck was a remarkable multi-instrumentalist who was equally adept on guitar, steel guitar, ukulele, mandolin, banjo, and even the octa-chorda, an unusual eight-string guitar played in the Hawaiian style. Known as "The Wizard of the Strings," Smeck was friendly with the Martin family, and very fond of Martin guitars and ukuleles. Because Martin did not offer players endorsement deals, Smeck wound up endorsing Harmony and Gibson guitars, Bacon and Harmony banjos, as well as Harmony ukuleles.

Smeck's name comes up with some regularity in the Martin correspondence files. One example is a letter that came to Martin in 1927 requesting a price list for ukuleles. The writer wrote on behalf of his large group of ukulele players. He relates: "Most of the club are using the cheaper grade uke, but we have as our guest here this week Mr. Roy Smeck, commonly called the wizard of the string instrument. And he is using a Martin uke. And all the members are enthused over the quality." In 1933 another letter about Smeck arrived: "I had a very enjoyable weekend in New York City with Roy Smeck. He was playing at the Palace Theatre and won great admiration with his steel guitar playing. He tells me that his Martin steel guitar is the one instrument he could never replace."

Smeck himself wrote to Martin on a couple of occasions. In 1929 he wrote to acknowledge the receipt of a guitar and ukulele from Martin and let them know that he was "well pleased with both instruments." Addressing C. F. III, Smeck ends the letter by saying "I hope that Mrs. Martin and yourself will arrange to spend some time with us on your next trip to New York."

Top right: A poster from a Smeck performance in the 1970s, featuring a 1930s era photo of Roy with a Martin ukulele.

Right: Program from a Smeck performance in the late 1920s. The photo shows a Ditson model Style 5K ukulele at Roy's feet. It is unknown if this instrument was owned by Smeck.

away just a year or two earlier, when new accounts were being declined. In a letter to C. W. Sipe & Co. of Shelby, Ohio, in March of 1927, C. F. III wrote:

> In April, 1926, you favored us with an inquiry to which we were obliged to reply that our production was oversold and we could not accept any new accounts. This condition is now changed, so we write again to tell you that we shall be pleased to have your orders for immediate shipment.

In an attempt to re-establish ties to older customers, letters were sent out to many retailers who had not made recent orders. Here is an example of one such letter, sent by C. F. III to Stirling's Music House of Hazelton, Pennsylvania, in August of 1927.

> We are sorry to note that your name does not appear in our 1927 ledger,--in fact the last charge to your account was in July, 1924. This worries us, because we fear you were not pleased with our goods; or perhaps there have been other factors, beyond our control. Whatever the reason, we miss your orders.
>
> This year we have added several new numbers, shown on the cards enclosed; and we have improved our ukulele line by equipping all styles with fine patent pegs. We hope you will decide to select from the Price-list an assortment of styles for your fall stock. We promise prompt shipment and fine goods.

Martin introduced the tenor ukulele in 1928 and manufactured 181 of them during the year. This would be the last new ukulele model introduced until the baritone came out more than thirty years later. Like the concert ukulele three years earlier, the tenor was made in just one standard model, the Style 1T. It could however be special ordered in other styles right up to the top-of-the-line 5K Tenor. The tenor- and concert-sized ukuleles became the popular choices in the larger bodied ukuleles, and the interest in the eight-string taropatch virtually disappeared. The year 1927 was the last when taropatches were made in standard production. Over the next seven years only five more taropatches were made, the final one being built in the middle of 1935.

The ukulele would stay a consistent part of the Martin instrument lineup until the late 1960s, but never again would it rule the company as it had in the middle of the 1920s. From the late 1920s onward, the fortunes of the company rose and sank on the success of its guitars—ukulele and mandolin sales were rarely a major factor. At the Board of Directors meeting held in January of 1929, Frank Henry's combined President's and Treasurer's report made the situation clear:

> The bad conditions of the previous year continued. The ukulele came back a little but is now definitely out of fashion and cannot be reckoned on for a large part of the business. This loss has not yet been made up by an increase in guitars and mandolins, but there is a gain lately and prospects are better than a year ago.

The number of workers on the payroll had dropped from sixty-nine at the end of 1926 to forty-eight in 1927 and then to just thirty-seven by the end of 1928.

The company had a small loss for the year 1929, but Frank Henry's report in January of 1930 notes that "this loss is easily covered by the large sur-

As business slowed in the late 1920s Martin was more than happy to oblige when a customer requested a special order. They made nine style 5K tenors in 1929 and 1930.

The Players: Johnny Marvin

Johnny Marvin, who would later become one of the top crooners of the 1920s, worked the Vaudeville circuit early in his career partnered with Charles Sargent in an act billed simply as "Sargent and Marvin." In January of 1922 Marvin visited the Martin factory, purchasing a keratol-covered guitar case and trading in his old wooden case. The case cost $8.81, after the $1.00 allowance for Marvin's old case. It seems the purpose of Marvin's visit was to try to work out an endorsement deal. W. S. Williamson of the Southern California Music Company wrote Martin later in the year asking "do you know Johnny Marvin – ukulele player also uses a saw in his act?" Martin responded:

> In regard to Johnny Marvin, we can give you but little information. He called here last winter while playing the Keith theatre in Easton and had us do some little work on his Guitar and bought a new case for it. The real purpose of his visit was to try to make a business arrangement with us whereby he would advertise our instruments in return for receiving new instruments for his own use without charge. This being contrary to our established policy, we did not do any business with him. We enjoyed his visit but know nothing whatever about his character or habits.

In March of 1922 Martin received a telegram: "SEND IMMEDIATELY ONE TEN DOLLAR SPECIAL UKULELE KEITH'S THEATRE INDIANAPOLIS IND. SARGENT & MARVIN." Martin sent one "selected Style 0 Ukulele" by first mail that same day. Marvin wrote to Martin two more times that year, relating stories of how he was promoting Martin's instruments. Perhaps he was hoping Martin would reconsider their stance on player endorsements.

Even though Marvin wasn't getting paid by the company, he was indeed a supporter of Martin instruments. In September of 1922 a short article appeared in the *Music Trades* titled "Didn't Think Much About Ukuleles Until He Played." The article talks about the increased sales at Bush & Lane Piano Co.'s Portland, Oregon store caused by "John Marvin, ukulele player." The article mentions how Marvin "demonstrated to the Portland public what can be done with a Martin ukulele. The music played made the audience sit up and take notice."

Johnny Marvin became one of the most popular crooners of the 1920s, but he never did make any deal with Martin. He eventually landed an endorsement deal with the Harmony Co. of Chicago. In 1928 Harmony released the Johnny Marvin Professional Tenor Ukulele.

Johnny Marvin may not have worked out an endorsement deal with Martin, however, he did get a deal with Harmony, and apparently, Studebaker

plus accumulated in the good years before 1927, and since our dullness came on through a slump in the instrument trade it may be fair to average the poor years with the good and work for a return of profit without being discouraged."

Frank Henry's President and Treasurer's report presented at the January 1931 Board of Directors meeting showed that 1930 had been a good year in general, but not in terms of ukulele sales: "We are still suffering from the drop in ukulele playing but have made good progress in guitar sales. The guitar is now popular and the opportunity for a large business is here, but competition is keen and the manner of playing is changed so we are still obliged to experiment with new models."

The year 1930 had been the company's second best in total sales, trailing only 1926. At the beginning of 1931 the company was looking forward to bigger and better years to come. However, 1931 started a downward slide in ukulele sales that the company would not pull out of until the Second World War.

Frank Henry had long shown himself willing to experiment with new models to meet new musical tastes. In the period from the late 1920s through the Second World War no new ukulele models appeared, but a number of new mandolin and guitar models were added. Carved-top guitars and mandolins were introduced but these models never quite reached a popularity level that had any major long-term impact on profits. Another important addition was also made to the guitar line, a dreadnought model using the body shape from the largest of the guitars that Martin used to manufacture for the Chas. H. Ditson company. Ditson's store had gone out of business by early 1931 and within months Martin was marketing Dreadnought guitars under their own name.

The slowdown in ukulele production in the late 1920s was nothing compared to what the company would experience in the 1930s, when ukulele sales dropped to the lowest levels since their introduction.

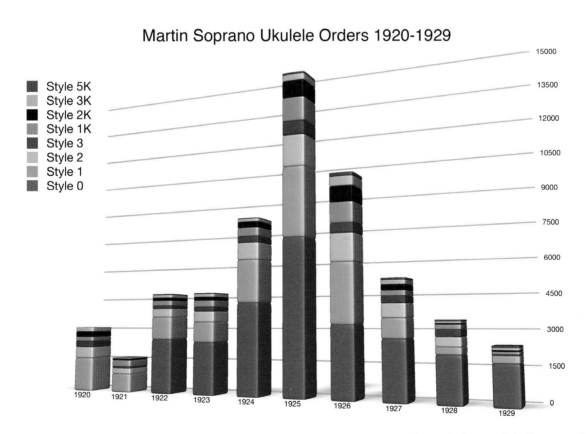

The decline in Martin ukulele orders in the years following 1925 was as rapid as their growth in the years leading up to 1925

Jimmie Rodgers: Father of Country Music & Ukulele Salesman

Jimmie Rodgers, known as "The Singing Brakeman" during his career, is now often credited as "The Father of Country Music." In 1928 Rodgers ordered from Martin what would become one of the best-recognized guitars of all time. The 000-45 model guitar was inlaid with his name in the fingerboard and "Blue Yodel" on the headstock. Rodgers' first recordings were released in October of 1927 and the recording of "Blue Yodel" later that year helped to make him a star.

In September of 1927, one month before the release of his first recordings, Jimmie Rodgers sent a guitar to Martin for repairs, and sent a letter along with instructions. Apparently not foreseeing his impending fame, he was looking for other ways to bring in money. He wrote asking Martin to repair the guitar and to send it back to him C. O. D. He then requests to also receive "prices on Ukes and Guitars. I want to buy some ukes for Fair Concessions, about 3 or 4 hundred. Please let me hear from you at once." He goes on to give a nice endorsement: "I want to say that I'm a Martin booster. I think you People Make the Best Uke & Guitar in the World. The reason I can say this is that I have owned String Instruments from every Country and the Martin is the Best."

In Frank Henry's reply he let Rodger's know when his repair would be completed. Because the company had made it a policy not to sell directly to individuals who lived in a city with a Martin agency, Frank Henry had to direct Rodgers elsewhere to obtain the ukuleles he desired:

> In answer to your request on prices on Ukes, we send our complete catalogue and ask that you kindly call on S. Ernest Philpitt & Son, 1300 G Street, who hold our agency for the city of Washington.

Jimmie Rodgers letter and business card from the Martin archives. When Jimmie Rodgers wrote to Martin in September of 1927 looking to buy "3 or 4 hundred" ukuleles to sell at fairs, he attached his business card. The card must have been new, for on it Rodgers describes himself as a "Victor Record Artist." Rodgers had recorded just two tracks for Victor in August of 1927, and at the time he wrote Martin in September those tracks had not yet been released.

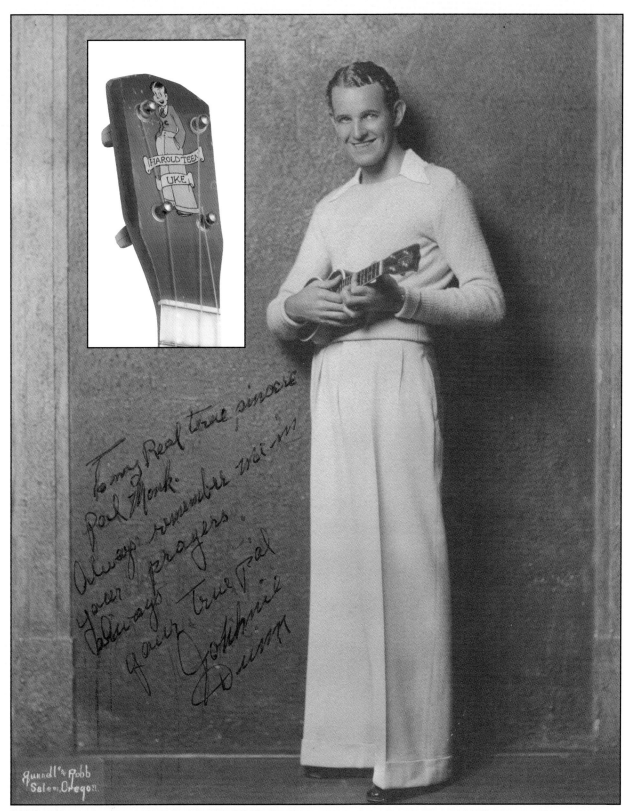

Vaudeville performer Johnie Dunn with his Martin Style 5K ukulele. Dunn also owned a second 5K custom ordered with his name inlaid on the headstock. Note Dunn's similarity to Harold Teen, the ukulele playing comic strip character featured on ukuleles manufactured by the Harmony Company (*inset*).

Depression, War, and the End of an Era

I JUST LEARNED ABOUT THE PASSING OF YOUR FATHER; HE MUST HAVE BEEN A GREAT MAN. ANY-
ONE WHO CAN KEEP HIS HEAD WHEN EVERYTHING ABOUT HIM IS TOPSY TURVY IS DESERV-
ING OF THE GREATEST RESPECT OF HIS FELLOW-MAN; TO ME, YOUR FATHER WAS SUCH A MAN AND
IN MY OPINION, C. F. MARTIN AND SON IS THE OUTSTANDING CONCERN OF ITS KIND, OF THE DAY.

—Guy Hart, President of Gibson, Inc., in a condolence letter to C. F. Martin III, 1948

The late 1920s had seen a big drop off in ukulele production at Martin. In the two year peak of 1925-26, Martin sold over 25,000 ukuleles. They sold fewer ukuleles in 1927, 1928, and 1929 combined than they had sold in 1926 alone. Still though, thousands of ukuleles were being sold every year. After dropping to a production of 2,675 in 1929, the company bounced back with over 4,000 ukuleles manufactured in 1930. The Stock Market Crash had occurred in October of 1929, but the effects of the Great Depression that followed were slow to develop. Ukulele production slipped to under 3,000 in 1931 but it was 1932 when it truly crashed. Fewer than 1,000 ukuleles were manufactured in 1932 and 1933 combined. That represents only four percent of the amount of ukuleles sold in the two-year peak just six years earlier. A combination of the poor economic climate and changing American musical tastes had dropped Martin ukulele production to its lowest annual totals ever.

The 1930s were not a good decade for Martin's ukulele sales. Fortunately, guitar sales remained reasonably strong. Through most of the decade Martin sold fewer than 1,000 ukuleles each year. Guitar sales, which were obviously more profitable, averaged over 3,000 annually. Due to the large factory space added during the ukulele boom, Martin had the room to expand its guitar and mandolin lines to attempt to meet popular demand. Carved-top guitars and mandolins along with new tenor guitar models helped Martin's bottom line for a few years. Many changes came to Martin's flat top guitars in the 1930s, including the change to fourteen fret necks on all the various guitar models. However, the biggest guitar introduction of the 1930s was the Martin dreadnought, shortly after the Chas. Ditson Co. went out of business. Today,

Martin dreadnoughts from the 1930s are among the most sought-after instruments ever made. In 1940, Martin made its first exploration into guitar electrification. As noted in the Board of Directors minutes: "In September the De Armond Guitar Microphone was added as a resale item. A patented product of Rowe Industries Inc., Toledo, O., this microphone works well on Martin Guitars and gives us an opening in the electric guitar field."

With ukulele sales lagging, Martin began to simplify its ukulele line. The last Style 2K ukuleles were made in 1931, although they continued to be listed in the Martin catalogs until 1934. By 1939 it appears that Martin's supply of figured koa had run out. The twenty-five Style 3K ukuleles and the twelve 5K ukuleles made in 1938 were the last of each of those models made in regular production until the re-introduction of these models nearly seventy years later. The supply of the plainer style koa wood used on the Style 1K ukuleles lasted a good bit longer. With the exception of two Style 2K ukuleles made in 1941, the only koa ukuleles made from 1939 to 1944 were Style 1Ks. Over 1,000 Style 1K ukuleles were made during that six-year stretch including a remarkable 375 in 1943 alone.

In 1941 business picked up considerably with both ukuleles and guitars selling in greater numbers. More ukuleles were sold in 1941 than in any of the previous ten years. Extra men were hired and working hours at the factory were increased. Income for the year was up nearly fifty percent over 1940 and even a price increase did not slow sales. However, the attack on Pearl Harbor in December of 1941 and the country's subsequent declaration of war against Japan and Germany left the company in an unsure position. At the January of 1942 Board of Director's meet-

Anita Page (*left*) and Joan Crawford (*right*), in a photo from MGM studios. A version of this photo appeared in *Musical Merchandise* magazine in May of 1930, in an article about the upcoming Music Convention. The caption there read: "Joan Crawford and Anita Page demonstrate a Martin Ukulele. Don't miss the convention displays."

In the 1920s through the 1930s, many ukulele manufacturers made special models intended to make their ukuleles stand out in the crowded market. Martin however, had a different philosophy, as made clear in a letter from C. F. III to the Chicago Musical Instrument Co. in 1927: "There will doubtless be efforts to stimulate business with novelties from time to time but we believe that our best policy is to make every effort to secure the standard, staple business with our regular line." *Top row, from left*: Harmony Harold Teen, Stewart Le Domino, Washburn by Lyon & Healy Shrine. *Middle row, from left*: Harmony Blue Crystal finish ukulele sold by B&J, Turturro Peanut Uke. *Bottom row, from left*: Betty Boop, Dayton Heart, and a hand-painted model by P'mico. The understated Martin ukulele line changed very little over the years. *Right*: A 1930s Style 2.

ing C. F. III discusses some of the changes to be expected during the war. "In 1942 rising costs, growing scarcity of supplies, and war-time restrictions are to be expected. It may even be necessary to turn part of our facilities over to government work." He ends on a positive note: "We hope, however, to do our part to win the war through Music to Maintain Morale."

One year later, at the January 1943 meeting, Frank Henry addressed some of his son's predictions:

> Nineteen forty two was a year of war, the first full year of participation by this country in the Second World War. It had its effect on this business, enough to tell yet not as severe as in some lines of business. We were not able to secure any contracts for war work, which confined us to our own line of manufacture the amount of which was controlled by

government restrictions in the use of scarce materials. Also the loss of men to the armed services and to munition plants crippled operations to some extent.

Restrictions limited the amount of metal that could be used in musical instruments. C. F. III specified these restrictions in his 1943 report to the Board of Directors. "Beginning March 1 Limitation Orders L-37 and L-37A of the War Production Board limited the use of critical materials to 75% the quantity, by weight, used in 1940 and to 10% of the total weight of each instrument." These restrictions, coupled with the difficulty in acquiring all materials including wood led to changes in production at the factory. The 1943 report also mentions that "fewer guitars and more ukuleles were made." The metal-heavy mandolin and the tiple became Martin's first casualties of the

C. F. III, right, is telling Michael J. Ross, of Ross Music Store, Akron, Ohio, when he might expect the next shipment on his earlier orders at the 1947 National Association of Music Merchants (NAMM) convention.

war, with the archtop guitar line also being discontinued in 1942.

Martin fared much better during the wars years than many of the other musical instrument makers of the time. Because they are made almost completely of wood, guitars and ukuleles were some of the very few musical instruments that could continue to be made with the wartime restrictions in place. Outside of the frets, ukuleles could actually be made without any metal at all. Although Martin had been using only metal patent ukulele pegs on its ukuleles since 1927, the war years brought a switch back to wooden pegs. An undated company memo noted some of the changes that needed to be made because of the wartime restrictions: "Substitutes for metal parts are being used wherever possible and practical. A rigid ebony bar now gives guitar necks the same guaranteed strength as the steel bar it replaces. Wood pegs take the place of metal patent pegs on ukuleles, which can be made in fair quantities." The ukulele's small size and lack of metal helped to bring it back to a place of prominence in the Martin line.

No new accounts were opened, and current customers were limited to at most the same amount of instruments they had ordered in 1941. Mandolin production ceased when stock of metal parts ran out in 1942. Tiples were not produced from 1941 through 1945. During the war, guitar production held pretty steady at between 3,000 and 4,000 guitars per year. Ukulele production actually increased during the war years. In the nine years from 1932 to 1940 Martin had manufactured over 1,000 ukuleles in single a year just twice. In 1943 alone Martin manufactured over 2,500 ukuleles.

Had it not been for their loss of labor, Martin could have sold even greater numbers of instruments during the war years. Some workers were drafted and others left to work in munitions plants. New workers were brought in to help make up for the losses. The 1944 Vice President's report notes the hiring of "two older men, two boys and two girls" and mentions that "the girls, working in the glue room under foreman Deichman have done well." By January of 1944 orders were booked ahead for about eight months, with many orders outright refused because the company was unable to make enough goods.

In 1944 an aging Frank Henry Martin transferred some of his duties and took on more of a part-time role in the company. C. F. III became General Manager and took on some of his father's duties. Frank Henry retired in 1945 but stayed involved with the company. After the end of the war in 1945, ukulele production continued along at a few thousand instruments per year. In 1948, with Martin on the verge of its second major era of ukulele production, they lost the man who had started it all. Frank Henry Martin died on April 9, 1948 marking the end of an era for the guitar company. 🎻

Frank Henry Martin and his son C. F. Martin III pose for a photo just outside of the front entrance of the North Street factory. When Frank Henry died in 1948, the Martin Company was left in the good hands of C. F. III, Frank Henry's only remaining son, much as Frank Henry had taken charge with the passing of his father sixty years earlier.

Frank Henry Martin, head of the C. F. Martin & Co. from 1888 to 1945, a period many consider the company's time of greatest growth and innovation.

The Players: The Hawaiians

The 1925 Martin catalog describes their ukuleles as follows: "These instruments are built on guitar principles, and are made as light in weight as durability will permit. Natural air-drying, careful gauging, scientific bracing, make the tone that is responsible for their widespread use, which reaches to the home of the ukulele, Hawaii." There is no question that Martin ukuleles and guitars were very popular among Hawaiian musicians from the time they were introduced.

On March 25, 1916, Martin sold a Style 1 ukulele, serial no. 20, to Major Kealakai. The sale ledger notes that it was to be sent "C.O.D. on approval." Because there is no sign of it being returned, one can only assume that Kealakai was pleased with the instrument. Kealakai was likely the first native Hawaiian to try out a Martin ukulele. Many important Hawaiian musicians would follow in Kealakai's footsteps, adopting Martin ukuleles and guitars as their instruments of choice. Martin was really the only mainland company to produce instruments that grew popular enough in Hawaii to rival the popularity of the Hawaiian-made instruments.

Major Kealakai, was given the name Sergeant Major by his father, a Sergeant Major under the Hawaiian King Kamehameha V. He dropped the Sergeant and was known simply as Major, or sometimes by the Hawaiianized version of the name, Mekia. Kealakai was a member of the Royal Hawaiian band in the 1890s and toured the North America and Europe from around that time until 1920, when he went back to Hawaii to become the Conductor of the Royal Hawaiian Band. It is probable he took his Martin instruments back to Hawaii at the time, possibly giving Martin some high-profile exposure in the islands.

Ernest Kaai, Honolulu, 1917.

Although Kealakai was likely the first Hawaiian musician to play a Martin ukulele, others had been familiar with Martin guitars for many years. Hawaiian musicians had been touring the country for years, some with the Bird of Paradise show and others on the Vaudeville stage. There is no question that some had picked up Martin guitars in their travels. Ernest Kaai was one such performer, having appeared on the West Coast in 1907, 1909, and 1914. Kaai was a noted instrumentalist who was an accomplished ukulele, guitar, and mandolin player. His 1906 work *The Ukulele (A Hawaiian Guitar*

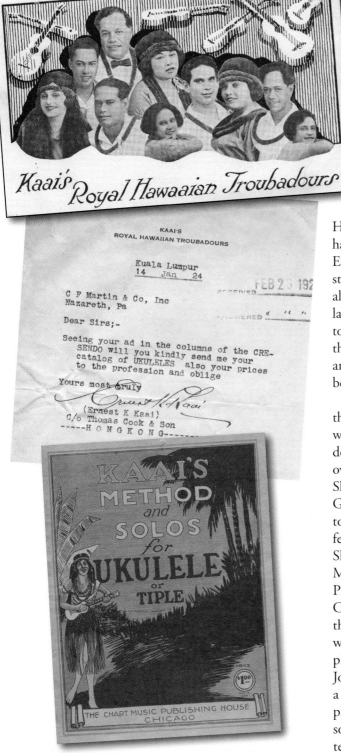

Top: Postcard of Ernest Kaai's Royal Hawaiian Troubadours, who toured the Far East with Kaai in the 1920s. *Middle:* Letter Kaai sent to Martin in 1924 from Kuala Lumpur. *Bottom:* 1916 Ukulele Method written by Kaai.

and How to Play It), published by Wall Nichols Co., is the earliest known ukulele method book. In the midst of a long tour of the Far East, Kaai wrote to Martin in January of 1924 from Kuala Lumpur, Malaysia. He requested a catalog of ukuleles and also the prices charged to the profession. Martin sent along the catalogs and quoted their standard twenty percent professional discount. Kaai wrote back in October of 1924, this time from Brisbane, Australia. He put in an order that included a Style 28 model guitar in Grand Concert size, a Style 2 taropatch, and a tiple, as well as cases and strings. He requested a special bridge for his guitar that could handle the tension of steel strings as well as the Far East climate, which he described as "rather trying on stringed instruments." He mentions that his band already features three Martin guitars. Just three days later Kaai sent a second note to Martin, asking them to hold the order for further instructions. He states that his band's "movements are uncertain at present and it may be that we should be starting for Hawaii before very long."

Joseph Kekuku is often credited as the inventor of the Hawaiian steel guitar style of playing. Kekuku too was a Martin player. Less than a month after Kekuku's death in Dover, New Jersey, in January 1932, his widow wrote to Martin looking to sell Kekuku's guitar. She asked "if for a consideration you could use the Guitar for adv. purpose. The Guitar has a wonderful tone even tho it was patched up after Joseph Kekuku fell down two long flights of concrete stairs with it." She goes on to relate how her husband advertised for Martin: "I can show you a full page in an Orpheum Program stating Joseph Kekuku "always plays on the Celebrated Martin Guitar." She offers to come out to the factory to talk matters over. C. F. III's response was respectful of course: "Although we never had the pleasure of meeting your distinguished husband, Mr. Joseph Kekuku, we had great respect for his ability as a Guitarist and as a pioneer in the Hawaiian style of playing." He extends his condolences: "We are very sorry to hear of his untimely death and we wish to extend our sincere sympathy in your bereavement." But he goes on to deliver the bad news: "For advertising purposes his Guitar would be of little value to us because Guitars are now built somewhat differently and it would hardly due to advertise the new style with an

old instrument, as you will understand."

He goes on to recommend a number of Martin dealers in New York who may be interested in purchasing the guitar if she is looking to sell it.

The Martins were familiar with the Joseph Kekuku story, as is evidenced by a series of correspondence back in 1927 with Bergstrom Music in Hawaii. In January of 1927 C. F. III wrote to Bergstrom Music to inquire about an article that had recently appeared in the *New York Times*. The article was titled "Steel Guitar Playing Invented by Hawaiian." The article discussed the new manuscript by Helen Roberts that had been published in Hawaii by the Bishop Museum. Roberts had related the story of Joseph Kekuku, who as a boy came upon this new way of playing the guitar. Martin wanted Bergstrom to send a half dozen copies of the manuscript, mentioning that they had a number of customers who are interested in the subject. Bergstrom responded that the cost would be four dollars a copy, so before ordering they wanted to let Martin know the price. They went on to give a little bit of the history:

We have with us a Hawaiian by the name of

Major Kealakai who was a boy and grew up with Joseph Kekuku mentioned in your letter. The straight guitar was then in use having been brought over by the Portuguese and these boys first got the idea of playing a guitar in steel fashion by trying to imitate the actions of some German sailors off a German ship here at the time, about 1882. These men made up a bass violin out of a cracker box and a bass drum from an empty salmon barrel, and a narrow long box strung with two steel wires and a metal belaying pin run up and down and the strings strummed with the thumb. This latter instrument is what the boys tried to imitate on the guitar, first with a pen knife and another tried a file and Mr. Kekuku was the first to try a file. Mr. Kekuku is now in New York and has been for many years and possibly could give you a verification of this or his version of it if you could get in touch with him. You might be able to locate him through the National Vaudeville Artists' Association of New York.

C. F. III wrote back thanking the Bergstrom people for the information and noting that he didn't think "the report prepared by the Bishop Museum would give us sufficient additional information to warrant the charge of four dollars." He lets Bergstrom know

Hawaiian Musicians were clearly fond of their Martin ukuleles. *Clockwise from top left:* Johnny Ukulele (Johnny Kaaihue), Bill Ali'iloa Lincoln, Eddie Kamae, and Ray Kinney

that he is making an effort to get in touch with Kekuku "to verify the very interesting version you give of the beginning of Steel Guitar Playing." He goes on to relate: "We are interested to learn that Major Kealakai is with you. The writer has a very pleasant recollection of meeting the Major ten or eleven years ago in the M. Doyle Marks Company's store in Elmira, N. Y." C. F. III had been on a business trip at the time, and Kealakai was performing. He continues: "we had a very pleasant conversation together. We trust he is enjoying his work with you and would appreciate your conveying to him our kind regards."

Another of the many Hawaiians who corresponded with Martin was the Hawaiian composer and musician Johnny Almeida. Almeida is often referred to as "the Dean of Hawaiian Music" and was a prolific composer and a master of the guitar, ukulele, and mandolin. Many of his songs are considered Hawaiian language standards to this day. Blind since he was young, Almeida still was very involved in all aspects of Hawaiian music throughout his life. He was the musical director for the Matson Navigation Company in the 1920s, whose ships sailed between Hawaii and the West Coast. Almeida wrote in to Martin in 1925: "I have just recently opened a Hawaiian Studio and am

teaching Orchestral Instruments in Honolulu." He goes on to praise Martin instruments: "I have been using your instruments for years and am very well satisfied with them, both for Island use and Tourist Trade, on board of ships." He goes on to say that he is interested in using Martin instruments exclusively and wants to be able to purchase instruments direct from Martin. He requests full information and price list.

Martin graciously thanked Almeida for the good words about their instruments, but let Almeida know that Bergstrom Music had their sole agency in Hawaii and so they would not be able to supply him directly. They also note that they are so overbooked that they are not taking on any new accounts anyway. Still they sent along their catalog and offered their services for "any special orders that you may place with our agents."

In 1934 Frank J. Vierra became the Conductor of the Royal Hawaiian Band. Although the full Royal Hawaiian Band featured band instruments of a typical brass band rather than guitars and ukuleles, in the 1930s the band also had a string ensemble. The string ensemble featured ukulele and guitar players, and in September of 1934 Vierra wrote to Martin, offering

The Royal Hawaiian Band String Ensemble, 1934. Featuring Lena Machado, Soprano, (*seated left of center*), Elizabeth Alohikea (*seated right of center*), and led by Peter Opunui (*seated center*).

high praise for the instruments the string ensemble had received through Thayer Piano Co. Ltd. of Honolulu. "The use of these wonderful instruments in our string ensemble has more than doubled the efficiency of our organization and added very materially to the attractiveness of our programs through their beautiful tone qualities. This band played a very prominent role during the recent visit of President Franklin D. Roosevelt to Hawaii and the string ensemble came in for its share of honors due in a large measure to the splendid new instruments furnished by you."

Included with Vierra's letter is a black and white photo of the string ensemble. The ensemble featured soprano Lena Machado and mezzo soprano Elizabeth Alohikea. These two women, both legendary singers and composers of Hawaiian music, played ukulele also. The band also has three other ukulele players, four guitarists, two Bass players, a violinist, and a flutist.

Anyone looking for evidence of the popularity of Martin ukuleles with Hawaiian musicians need look no further than the covers of Hawaiian music albums from the 1950s–1970s. Above is just a sampling of the many albums featuring a Hawaiian musician with a Martin ukulele. *Top row, from left:* **John Lukela, Nelson Waikiki, Alfred Apaka, Poncie Ponce.** *Middle row:* **John Almeida, Johnny Ukulele (Kaaihue), Mungo (Harry Kalahiki), Don Baduria.** *Bottom row:* **Al Kealoha Perry, Eddie Kamae, George Kainapau, and Andy Cummings.**

Television, Folk Music, and Rock 'n' Roll

A PANEL OF MUSICAL INSTRUMENT INDUSTRY LEADERS AGREED THAT ARTHUR GODFREY, A RED-HAIRED ENTERTAINER WHO CAN BE HEARD ALMOST ANYTIME ANY DAY ON RADIO OR TELEVISION, WAS THE GREATEST THING THAT EVER HAPPENED TO THE UKULELE.

The *New York Times,* "Music Merchants See Rise in Sales," July, 1950

After a great drop in ukulele production in the depression era of the 1930s, Martin ukulele sales climbed again in the 1940s. Martin produced about 3,000 ukuleles per year from 1943 to 1948, at a time when they were producing roughly 5,000 guitars annually. However, the ukulele was about to move back into the production lead. A number of factors contributed to the resurgence of interest in the ukulele in the late 1940s and early 1950s, but most people agree that one important element was a red-haired entertainer who was taking the new medium of television by storm. After many years as a star on the radio, Arthur Godfrey became one of the biggest stars of the early years of television. By the beginning of 1949, Godfrey was hosting two major television shows, often playing ukulele on the air. He is given much of the credit for the incredible success of the inexpensive new plastic ukuleles brought to the market by Mario Maccaferri, but the exposure that Godfrey gave to the ukulele led to increased demand in the high-end of the market as well. In 1949, Godfrey's first full year of television broadcasting, Martin's ukulele produc-

tion more than doubled. Almost 20,000 ukuleles were produced in 1949 and 1950, nearly matching the peak production rates they had reached during the ukulele craze twenty-five years earlier. The years 1949–1951 would be the final three that Martin would produce more ukuleles than guitars. Ukulele production then dropped back to about 4,000 to 5,000 a year, a rate at which it would continue until the middle of the 1960s.

Godfrey commonly used a Martin tenor ukulele to accompany his voice, but around 1950 he struck up a deal with the Vega Co. to use his name on a new larger baritone ukulele. Vega and Favilla each sold good numbers of baritone ukuleles in the 1950s, but Martin was a little slow getting into the act. Finally, in 1960, Martin added a baritone ukulele to its line—its first new ukulele model in over thirty years.

Annual guitar production surpassed 6,000 for the first time in 1953, and would stay at about this level for the next ten years, despite growing demand for guitars. While the guitar had long held the position of prominence in the Martin line,

Arthur Godfrey and Janette Davis sing as Godfrey plays a Martin tenor ukulele.

For fun filled hours, anytime, anywhere. Martin Ukuleles

In the Summer, in the Spring, Anytime, Anywhere

Nothing beats the enjoyment you can create
For your friends or yourself when you
Play a Martin Uke. Anytime, Anywhere,
Musical Pleasure available with the
Happiest of all Musical instruments—
A ukulele by Martin
Accepted as the world's standard in ukuleles.

C. F. MARTIN & CO., INC.
ESTABLISHED 1833
NAZARETH, PA., U.S.A.

1-C—CONCERT Mahogany body and neck with rosewood fingerboard. Ornamented and finished same as Style 1 standard size ukulele. The body is larger and the strings longer, increasing the volume of tone.

1-T—TENOR Mahogany body and neck; 14 frets clear to body, rosewood fingerboard, bridge. Ebony nut, ivory saddle. Body bound with dark plastic, bordered and inlaid with black and white. Dark mahogany color. Nickel-plated pegs black buttons. Body is 8⅜ inches wide at the bridge, with a string length of 17 inches. Slightly larger Concert

This ukulele pamphlet from the early 1960s may well have been Martin's last effort to bolster ukulele sales. With guitar sales booming, there would soon be little reason for Martin to continue to advertise its small instruments.

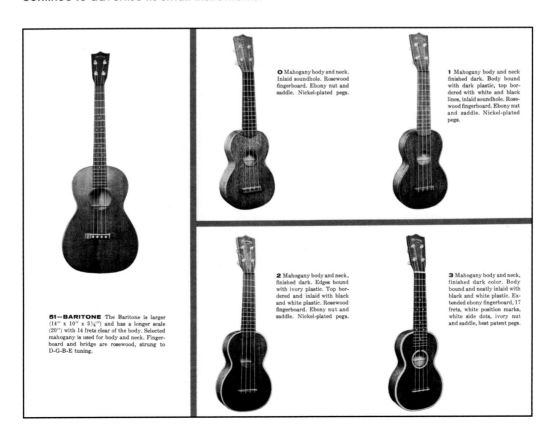

51—BARITONE The Baritone is larger (14″ x 10″ x 3¼″) and has a longer scale (20″) with 14 frets clear of the body. Selected mahogany is used for body and neck. Fingerboard and bridge are rosewood, strung to D-G-B-E tuning.

O Mahogany body and neck. Inlaid soundhole. Rosewood fingerboard. Ebony nut and saddle. Nickel-plated pegs.

1 Mahogany body and neck finished dark. Body bound with dark plastic, top bordered with white and black lines, inlaid soundhole. Rosewood fingerboard. Ebony nut and saddle. Nickel-plated pegs.

2 Mahogany body and neck, finished dark. Edges bound with ivory plastic. Top bordered and inlaid with black and white plastic. Rosewood fingerboard. Ebony nut and saddle. Nickel-plated pegs.

3 Mahogany body and neck, finished dark color. Body bound and neatly inlaid with black and white plastic. Extended ebony fingerboard, 17 frets, white position marks, white side dots, ivory nut and saddle, best patent pegs.

Early 1950s Dole Pineapple advertisement featuring a Martin Style 3 soprano.

Not a shadow of a doubt
with Kotex

Protection without fail — you can trust the *absorbency* of Kotex* completely, for this is the napkin made to stay safe . . . and to stay *soft*, chafe-free, while you wear it.

Comfort that lasts — because Kotex holds its shape; retains its comfortable fit. There is no roping, twisting or pulling.

Freedom from outlines — for of all leading brands, Kotex alone has flat, pressed ends. Another important reason why Kotex is America's first choice in napkins. Discover which size is best for you . . . Regular, Junior, or Super.

More women choose Kotex
than all other sanitary napkins

Made for each other — Kotex and Kotex sanitary belts. Why not buy two belts . . . *for a change!*

Pure silk fashions a shirtwaist costume of gentle grace. The blouse with poet collar, push-up sleeves. The skirt, six yards of pleats. In heather rose, frosty blue. By Sloat, at leading stores. Skirt about $40, blouse about $25.

*T. M. REG. U. S. PAT. OFF.

MAY, 1954   63

This 1954 Kotex advertisement featured a modern, confident woman of the 1950s playing a ukulele. Martin may have inadvertently received a little free advertising here, as the ukulele the woman is holding features an easily read C. F. Martin & Co. decal. The ukulele is a Style 0 soprano, Martin's biggest selling instrument.

in the early 1950s it still lagged behind the ukulele as far as the total number the company had ever made. This changed sometime in 1955 when total guitar production finally caught up with ukulele production.

A few changes occurred in the Martin ukulele line between the end of the Second World War and 1960. Koa wood and pearl inlay were no longer options. All ukulele models were now made from mahogany and featured circular celluloid position markers on the fretboard. The Style 3 ukulele first lost its celluloid ornament on the front of the body and then lost the stripes down the center of the fretboard, both during the first half of the 1950s. The Martin ukuleles produced in the 1950s were less fancy than some of their earlier models, but they were still unsurpassed in tone.

At about the same time the baritone

Top: **In 1960 the stamp used inside the bodies of Martin instruments was changed, with the addition of the line "MADE IN U. S. A."** *Bottom:* **Workers in the new factory working on ukuleles, 1964.**

ukulele was added to the Martin line in 1960, the design of the tenor ukulele was changed. The new tenor had a longer neck that met the body at the fourteenth fret rather than the twelfth, a feature that was already incorporated into the new baritone model. Another change to Martin instruments that came in 1960 was the addition of the words "Made in U.S.A." under the standard Martin stamp inside the body. Previously Martin had stamped "Made in U.S.A." separately on the back of the headstock of instruments that were being sent abroad. With no serial numbers in their ukuleles, this change is one important aspect in helping to date vintage Martin ukuleles.

In the 1950s, Elvis Presley helped to popularize rock 'n' roll, and demand for guitars grew across the country. Unable to produce more than about 6,000 guitars a year, Martin was beginning to feel the limits of its aging North Street facility. In the early 1960s demand for Martin guitars continued to grow. Folk music was popular around the country, but the company just couldn't make instruments fast enough. Also, the company was starting to experiment with electric guitar models, hoping to stay on top of the changing musical styles of the time. It is noteworthy that the company found the time to make thousands of ukuleles every year at a time when they were falling further and further behind on their guitar orders. The company built a large new factory in Upper Nazareth and completed the move in July of 1964. The new factory would help Martin greatly increase its guitar production, but the Martin ukulele was about to hit some hard times. 🎻

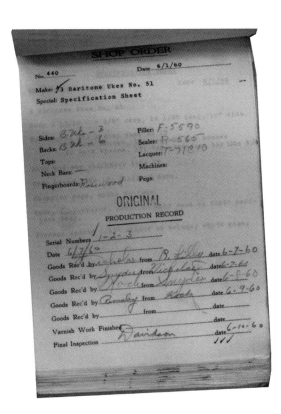

Above: Shop order for the original three baritone ukuleles, dated June 7, 1960.

Right: Early catalog photo of the new baritone ukulele model, 1960.

The Long Lull

AMERICANS ARE BECOMING MORE MUSICAL. WE NOW HAVE MORE THAN 44 MILLION AMATEUR MUSI-CIANS, COMPARED TO 20 MILLION IN 1950. ONE IN EVERY 4.6 PERSONS PLAYS AN INSTRUMENT. MORE THAN TWICE AS MANY PLAY THE PIANO AS THE GUITAR—23.5 MILLION TO 11 MILLION. BUT, ALAS, THE NUM-BER WHO CAN STILL STRUM A UKULELE HAS FALLEN IN TEN YEARS FROM 1.5 MILLION TO A HALF A MILLION.

Hal Boyle, *Spokane Daily Chronicle*, July, 1968

The decline in Martin ukulele sales in the late 1960s has long been attributed to the rise in rock and roll and the electric guitar, and there is no denying that these two factors played a large role. The folk movement of the 1960s and the folk-rock era that followed caused an unprecedented demand for Martin guitars. As guitar production at Martin went from a little over 5,000 guitars a year in the early 1960s to a peak of over 20,000 guitars produced in 1971, the ukulele became little more than an after-

thought at the company. However, there were other factors that contributed to the decline and eventual disappearance of the Martin ukulele line. The smaller demand for ukuleles in the 1960s led to smaller, less frequent production runs, which in turn made the ukuleles costlier to produce. Prices went up rapidly in the later 1960s and 1970s, greatly outpacing the increase in Martin guitar prices, and outdoing inflation as well. The higher prices, in turn, caused demand to drop even further. The Style 0 ukulele, introduced in

Beginning in 1966, the Martin ukulele line had been narrowed down to just four models. *Above from left to right*: Style 0 and Style 3 sopranos, Style B51 baritone, and the Style 1T tenor.

Above: Postcard view of the new Martin factory on Sycamore St. opened in 1964. *Below:* Ukulele production was still going strong in the early years of the new factory. Racks of ukuleles are shown in this photograph taken just months after the new factory had opened.

Here is a mysterious photo of a Style 3K from the Martin archives. The black & white photo suggests that this ukulele was likely made sometime before the 1970s, while the fretboard markings date it to after 1950. The only problem is that production records don't show any Style 3K ukuleles made between 1938 and 1981.

UKULELES

0

Genuine mahogany body and neck, with an ebony nut and bridge saddle and a fingerboard of rosewood. White pegs hold the strings, and black and white rings are inlaid around the soundhole. Flat lacquer finish is in natural color.

3

With a body of quarter-sawn mahogany, bound and inlaid with black and white trimmings, and a shaped neck, also of genuine mahogany, this ukulele provides very fine tone. It features an extended fingerboard of ebony containing 17 frets and marked with white position dots. The nut and bridge saddle are of genuine ivory. Strings held by high-quality patent pegs. Finished in dark color.

1·T

Featuring 20 frets (14 clear of the body) aligned and spaced on a rosewood fingerboard, hand-shaped neck of genuine mahogany providing easy extended action, and a selected rosewood pin-style bridge. Positions indicated by white side markings and dots on the face of the fingerboard. Dark, satin-finished body bound in appropriate trimming, with black and white lines inlaid around the soundhole. Fine, soft tone.

51

This Baritone model is a larger ukulele with a longer scale (14 frets clear) utilizing quarter-sawn mahogany for the body and a hand-shaped neck. Select rosewood is used in the bridge and fingerboard. The Baritone is strung to D-G-B-E tuning, guitar pitch. Its clear resonance and beauty result from the fine workmanship, choice materials, and careful satin finishing it receives.

26

The Final Four. The year 1965 was the final regular production year for the Style 1 and Style 2 soprano ukuleles as well as the Style 1C Concert ukulele. The once extensive Martin ukulele line had been narrowed to just four models, Style 0 and Style 3 sopranos, the Style 1T tenor, and the Style B51 baritone. These same four ukulele models represented the Martin line from 1966 through 1994 when ukulele production in Nazareth ceased.

1922 with a price of $10, sold for $35 in 1965. By 1977 the retail price of a Style 0 had skyrocketed to $500!

Martin narrowed its ukulele line after 1965 by ending production of Style 1 and Style 2 sopranos just as they approached the fiftieth anniversary of their addition to the Martin line. The concert ukulele was also discontinued, forty years after its introduction. Only four ukulele models remained, Style 0 and Style 3 sopranos, the Style 1T tenor, and the Style B-51 baritone. For a little over ten years these four models were the standard Martin ukulele line.

In 1977 the ukulele was taken out of standard production, and became available on special order only. By that time, Martin had produced a total of over 190,000 ukuleles in the first sixty years of production. As the public's interest in the ukulele faded many used Martin ukuleles became available at flea markets, antique stores, pawnshops, and music stores. The Martin company was unable to produce new ukuleles at a price that could compete with it's own previously-owned instruments. Also, vintage Martin ukuleles had few of the problems that are often associated with vintage guitars. While a vintage guitar might need a neck reset, adjustment of the action, or a re-fret, vintage Martin ukuleles were relatively problem-free. The shorter necks and lower-tension nylon strings meant vintage Martin ukuleles could be made nearly good-as-new by simply putting on a fresh set of strings. It would be many years before the demand for its higher-end vintage ukuleles would drive their prices up to a level at which Martin could compete by producing new instruments.

With prices higher than even the cleanest vintage examples, very few new Martin ukuleles were ordered from the late 1970s to the early 1990s. In

The Martin S0 Ukulele, introduced in 2000, was the first of Martin's new ukulele models.

1993 ukuleles were dropped from the Martin catalog, although a few were still made occasionally on special order. From 1995 to 2005 virtually no new ukuleles were made in Nazareth. However, the once-again growing popularity of the ukulele in the 1990s had the company looking at how to best get back into the ukulele business. In 1992 Martin had introduced a new small-bodied travel guitar called the Backpacker. These inexpensive guitars were built at Martin's facility in Navahoa, Mexico and sold surprisingly well. This led to the introduction of Backpacker ukuleles in 1997. Although the idea of a travel-ukulele is rather redundant, for a few years these were the only ukulele models marketed by Martin. A few hundred were produced each year from 1997 to 2002.

In 2000 Martin again started to build standard shape soprano ukuleles, again at its Mexican facility. The new S0 uke was similar in some ways to the classic Style 0, with its unbound body of solid mahogany, but there were many differences in the construction and finish of the S0 compared to vintage Martin ukuleles. With a suggested retail price of $299, the S0 was quite a success in the entry-level ukulelc field. Nearly 1,000 were sold each year between 2001 and 2005. In 2003 Martin announced an upgraded version of the S0 ukulele, named the HS0. The HS0, like the S0, was assembled in Mexico, but it had construction details that made it more like their vintage models, including a standard kerfed lining inside the body. Perhaps more importantly, it was finished in satin laquer in Nazareth, to more closely approximate the finish of vintage Style 0 ukuleles. This was the first regular production work on ukuleles in Nazareth in quite some time, but it wouldn't be long before ukuleles were again being built from start to finish in the Martin factory.

Martin HS0 ukulele, introduced in 2003.

Above: Mike Longworth, an inlay artist from Tennessee, was brought to Nazareth by Martin in 1968 to bring back the Style D-45 Dreadnought guitar. Longworth soon took on the role of company historian, and in 1975 he authored the first book detailing the company's history and instruments: *Martin Guitars: A History*. Although he was known as a banjo player and was brought to Martin to work on guitars, Mike Longworth had a great fondness for the ukulele. After he retired from Martin, Longworth built ukuleles in his free time, including some extensively inlaid models.

Top right: Longworth attended a number of Ukulele Expos organized by the Ukulele Hall of Fame Museum, including one held in West Orange, New Jersey, in April of 2000. In this photo he is being photographed by professional photographer Greg Heisler.

Right: In the 1970s, Longworth did the inlay work on this custom-ordered Martin ukulele.

Resurgence

WE'VE GONE FROM MAKING NONE OF THESE TO THOUSANDS OF THEM. IT'S HEART WARMING TO ME—MY GRAND-FATHER AND GREAT-GRANDFATHER WOULD GET A BIG KICK OUT OF THE FACT THAT THE UKULELE IS BACK.

—C. F. Martin IV, from his YouTube series "A Word from Chris"

Nearly ten years after the last Martin ukuleles had been produced in Nazareth, Martin announced a new era in its ukulele production in 2006. However, Martin decided not to produce the same styles it had been making on special order in the 1990s, they instead chose a model that had not been produced in over sixty years, their top-of-the-line Style 5K. Vintage 5K ukuleles had increased in value in the collector's market and could sell for $10,000 or more. The new instruments were hotly anticipated by the ukulele world, but with a retail price of $5,199 it was obvious that the new 5K would have a somewhat limited market. Martin ukulele fans hoped for the best, knowing that sales of the 5K could be the deciding factor in whether Martin would delve deeper into ukulele production with other models. The new 5K was very true to the original, with only minor changes in the specifications. The new model was greeted with very good reviews in the ukulele community and even with its steep price tag sold well enough to encourage Martin to look for more opportunities in the ukulele market. The 139 instruments produced in 2006, the first full year of production, represented an annual total only surpassed once in the original run of 5K production, in the peak production year of 1926.

The next ukulele model that Martin introduced was also a recreation of one of their fanciest models. In the 1930s, C. F. III had a special ukulele built for his wife Daisy Allen Martin. The "Daisy" ukulele has the inlays of a Style 5K, but is made of beautifully figured Cuban Mahogany. The original "Daisy" ukulele has long been on display in the Martin Museum. Martin made Style 5 ukuleles in mahogany only for a few special orders in the 1920s and 1930s

Style 5K

Style 5 Daisy

The new Martin 5K ukulele, introduced in 2006, was the first ukulele built in regular production by Martin in Nazareth since the 1970s. This batch of 5Ks was photographed while in production in 2007.

The original Daisy ukulele. Built in the 1930s for C. F. Martin III's wife Daisy Allen Martin. Now a permanent fixture in the Martin Museum, this instrument was the inspiration for Martin's new limited edition Style 5 Daisy ukulele, introduced in 2007.

and again in very small numbers around the Second World War, when koa was unavailable. Introduced in 2007, the new "Daisy" ukuleles were also made from beautifully figured mahogany. They also had another distinction—they were the first limited-edition Martin ukuleles, with a production run limited to one hundred instruments.

Because Martin had started at the high-end of its ukulele model range when getting back into ukulele construction in Nazareth, it was only logical that they follow up the success of the Style 5s with their next fanciest model, the Style 3. In 2008 Martin created a new line of Style 3 ukuleles that blended the old with the new. Along with the Style 3 soprano in mahogany and the Style 3K in koa, Martin added a new Style 3C in cherry. The 3C was the first Martin ukulele in their Sustainable Woods series. It is constructed completely of woods from certified sustainable wood forests, including cherry, basswood, and katalox. With retail prices ranging from $2,000 to $2,600, the new Style 3 models were a much more affordable alternative to the ultra high-end Style 5 models.

In 2010, Martin introduced an innovative new ukulele model, the 0XK. Taking inspiration from their popular X Series guitars, The 0XK has top, back, and sides made from High Pressure Laminate (HPL), with the koa wood grain photographically reproduced. The neck on the 0XK is also a laminate, a material called Stratabond. The HPL ukulele carries a retail price of $399, making it the most affordable ukulele Martin has produced at Nazareth in over 35 years.

In 2008, Martin re-introduced Style 3 ukuleles. The new models brought back some Style 3 features that hadn't been seen since the World War II era, including the celluloid ornament at the bottom of the body, square and diamond pearl fingerboard inlays, and the black and white stripes down the center of the fingerboard. Shown are the Style 3 in mahogany (*left*), Style 3K in koa wood (*center*), and the Style 3C in cherry (*right*).

Long-time Martin employee Willard "Buddy" Silvius working on one of the new Style 3K ukuleles introduced in 2008.

In January, 2011, Martin introduced the model S1 ukulele. Like the earlier S0 ukulele, the S1 is made in Martin's Mexican plant. Unlike the S0, the S1 is built much in the style of Martin's classic ukuleles. With a dovetailed neck joint, cedar linings, and an inlaid rosette, the S1 is a traditional style ukulele that is also affordable. Retailing at $499, the S1 is Martin's least expensive solid wood ukulele.

In July of 2011 Martin announced an exciting new line of Style 2 ukuleles. The big news of the announcement was the first new concert and tenor sized ukuleles in Martin's new ukulele line. Style 2 mahogany and Style 2K koa instruments were announced in soprano, concert, and tenor sizes. Priced between $1,449 and 1,649 the new Style 2 instruments are surprisingly affordable.

In January of 2012, Martin, in a sense, combined two of its newer creations by offering more affordable concert and tenor models made in its Mexican facility. The C1K concert ukulele and the T1K tenor are both made from solid koa wood. At $629 and $649 respectively, they are

Style 0XK

Style S1

The New Martin Style 2 Line, Introduced in 2011

Style 2 Tenor

Style 2 Concert

Style 2 Soprano

Style 2K Soprano

Style 2K Concert

Style 2K Tenor

Warner Bros. recording artist LP's instrument of choice is a new Martin Style 2 Concert Ukulele. Decades after many would-be Martin ukulele endorsers were turned away in the 1920s, in 2012 LP became the first ukulele player to be featured in an advertisement for Martin ukuleles.

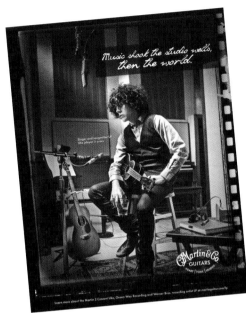

the most affordable option for any player interested in Martin's larger ukulele models.

In January of 2013 Martin announced their first Commemorative Custom Artist Ukulele, the 1T IZ. The 1T IZ commemorates Hawaiian ukulele player and singer Israel Kamakawiwoʻole. Known around the world simply as Iz, Kamakawiwoʻole is best known for his stirring rendition of "Somewhere Over the Rainbow/Wonderful World," but in Hawaii he was anything but a one-hit wonder. Before his death in 1997, Iz was the most popular musician in the islands.

Iz began his recording career in the 1970s with the Makaha Sons of Niʻihau. By the time Iz started his solo recording career in the early 1990s, the Makaha Sons were the most popular traditional group in Hawaii. Iz released four solo albums between 1990 and 1996, but it was his 1993 release, "Facing Future," that contained the song that would posthumously propel him to international fame. Kamakawiwoʻole died from weight-related health issues in 1997 at the age of 38.

Iz's ukulele of choice was a 1960s Martin Style 1T

C1K Concert   T1K Tenor

Israel Kamakawiwoʻole with his Martin tenor ukulele.

tenor. The new 1T IZ is made from quilted mahogany, and features a beautiful inlay on the headstock featuring a hibiscus flower in pink pearl and "IZ" in Hawaiian koa wood. The 1T IZ is the first Martin instrument to use PegHed tuners. PegHeds look like wooden friction pegs, but have internal gearing that allows for quick, accurate tuning. They give the instrument a more traditional look, compared to the geared side tuners used on the new Style 2 Tenor ukuleles. Each 1T IZ has a paper label inside signed by Marlene Kamakawiwoʻole, Iz's wife.

The ukulele is clearly experiencing a world-wide resurgence, and it is once again an important part of Martin's production. By early 2013 Martin was offering a ukulele lineup with 15 different model choices. This is the largest number of four-string ukulele models the company has ever offered. Ukulele fans around the world are hoping that this new era of popularity is not a passing fad, and that Martin will continue to develop and build high quality ukuleles for many years to come.

1T IZ Tenor

General Information on Martin Ukuleles

Introduction

The serial numbers on Martin guitars provide a simple way to determine the year a guitar was built. With a large enough database of guitars, it is easy to determine when even minor changes were made to the Martin guitar line. Martin ukuleles, however, are notoriously difficult to date accurately, because of their lack of serial numbers. It is impossible to determine when specifications to the ukulele line changed by simply examining existing instruments.

Although the dates of specification changes weren't all kept in a single spot at Martin, there is enough material available in their archives to pin down the dates of many changes. Between their order books, sales books, correspondence files, inventory logs, and more, there is a wealth of useful information that can be used to sleuth out when specification changes occurred.

Martin's inventory books are especially helpful in identifying the materials that they were using at any given point in time. Martin did a careful inventory of the factory at the end of each year. Everything was listed with its estimated value: machinery, cut and uncut wood, ivory, bone, celluloid, pearl, glue, strings, tuning machines and pegs, finished and unfinished instruments and instrument parts, cases and bags, stationary, office furniture, and sundries. Some of the main appointments people use to date Martin ukuleles are headstock decals, types of frets, types of tuning pegs, and fretboard inlays. All of these items were inventoried every year, and these inventories help to provide a clearer time frame of the various changes to Martin's ukulele models.

Stamps and Headstock Decals

Until the 1930s, all standard Martin ukuleles were stamped "C. F. Martin & Co. Nazareth PA" on the back of the headstock and inside the sound hole. The earliest examples have the stamp inside the soundhole running perpendicular to the back braces. Shortly after serial numbers were discontinued in mid-1916, Martin began stamping the ukuleles parallel to the back braces.

In the 1930s Martin began to use decals on their instrument's headstocks. The first record of a decal order took place in June of 1932 when Martin sent $46.92 to F. Palm & Co. These early decals had no black border around the gold letters. By 1933 F. Palm & Co. had become The Palm Brothers Decalomania Co. In January of 1934 Palm Brothers sent Martin the first guitar decals with black-bordered letters, noting in their letter that "we believe that you will find that the black outline 'sets off' the gold lettering, besides giving you the added protection around the edge where it is needed." C. F. III replied that they were pleased with the new decals and soon placed an order for 5,000 pieces, enough to last "at least a year." It seems that Martin started using these relatively large decals on their ukuleles at around the same time they began using them on their guitars. There are examples of ukuleles with the original large non-bordered decal, as well as others with the large bordered decal. These ukuleles were stamped on the back of the headstock as well as having the decal on the front. The reason not too many of these ukuleles with the large decals show up is that Martin was not making many ukuleles in the couple of years the large decals were in use. Martin's ukulele production in 1933, the only full year where large decals would have been used, was only 320 instruments, the least it produced any year between 1916 and 1973.

In June of 1934, C. F. III again wrote to Palm Brothers, this time with a new request: "Now we need a

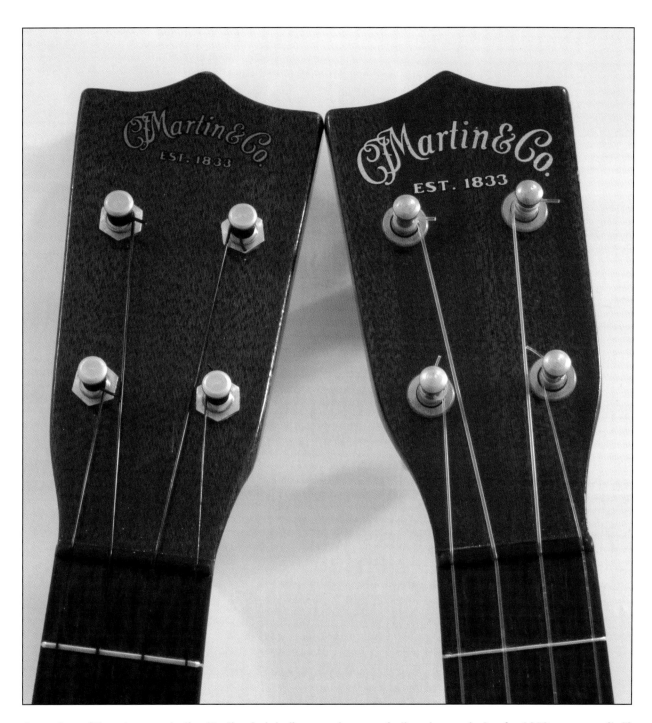

A number of the changes to the Martin ukulele line can be seen in the above photo of a 1950s soprano (*left*) and one from 1932-34 (*right*). The 1930s instrument has the larger guitar decal that was used for at most a couple of years, only until smaller ukulele decals were ordered in 1934. The 1950s ukulele features Waverly no. 2014 hexnut tuners, while the 1930s ukulele has Grover Simplex tuners. You can also see in the photo that the frets are different on the two ukuleles. The 1930s ukulele has bar frets while the ukulele from the 1950s has T-frets.

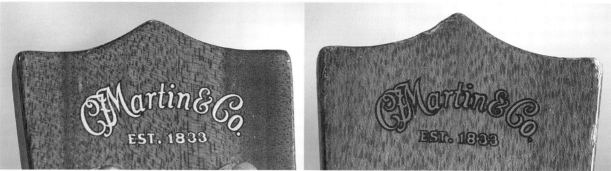

At least two different versions of the small ukulele decal were used by Martin. A*bove* *left*: Headstock decal from a 1930s Style 1, showing very shiny gold lettering. A*bove* *right*: Headstock decal from a 1960s Style 0, showing a duller, darker gold coloring in the lettering. There is no clear timeline as to which decal was used when.

similar design but smaller for use on our Ukuleles. It should not be more than 1-3/8" long. Would it be possible to use the same lettering in this small design?" The first 5,000 ukulele specific decals were ordered in July, at a price of $13.75 per 1,000. For a very short time Martin continued to stamp the back of the headstock even with the new ukulele decals, but this practice likely had ended by the end of 1934. The original Palm Brothers decals had bright shiny gold lettering. At various times Martin used a different decal with a duller gold color, but it is unclear exactly when each type of decal was in use.

Fretboard Position Markers

The earliest Martin ukuleles and taropatches had no position markers on the fretboard. The first time position markers are specifically mentioned is on a revised price list dated February 1, 1918. A small note at the bottom of the price list reads: "UKULELES and TARO-PATCHES: All styles inlaid with position marks." This change could have occurred as early as 1917, or it may have happened in the first month of 1918. Initially, all three ukulele styles had markers at the fifth, seventh, and ninth frets. Styles 1 and 2 had small celluloid dots, while the Style 3 had pairs of inlaid pearl squares on the fifth and ninth frets and a bow-tie pearl inlay on the seventh fret. In 1920 the position markers were changed to the fifth, seventh, and tenth frets. This change may have been inspired by a large ukulele order from the Chas. H. Ditson Co. In February of 1919, Ditson ordered 500 Ditson Model Style 1 ukuleles, fifty a month for ten months. On these ukuleles Ditson specifically requested "Position Dots at 3-5-7-10th frets both on side and on fingerboard." These Ditson Model ukuleles may have been the only Style 1 Martin-made ukuleles with position markers on the side of the fretboard, this is a feature usually only seen on Style 3 and Style 5K models.

Once the change was made to a standard of markers at frets 5-7-10, there were few changes to the specifics on the fretboard inlays, except on the Style 3 models. On Style 1 and Style 2 ukuleles the only change that occurred after 1920 was a slight change to the size of the dots used. The general trend is that the earliest ukuleles had the smallest position marker dots, and a change was made to larger dots sometime in the 1940s. There were many changes to the markers on the Style 3 model ukulele over the years. The earliest Style 3 ukuleles used a rosewood fingerboard with black and white lines inlaid down the center. When position markers were added in late 1917 or early 1918, two solid pearl squares were used on frets five and nine, while a pearl bow-tie inlay was used at fret seven. In 1920 when Martin switched the position markers to frets five, seven, and ten, they also changed the inlay at fret seven to two solid pearl diamonds. It was also at about this time that they started to use ebony for the Style 3 fingerboard instead of rosewood. In the 1930s the solid diamonds and squares were changed to slotted diamonds and squares. Based on their inventories, this occurred in 1936, the last year that they inventoried solid diamonds and squares. The slotted diamonds and squares were the same as those used on

Style 0

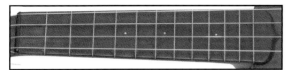

1922–ca.1945

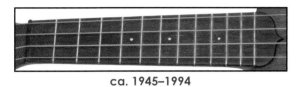

ca. 1945–1994

Styles 1 & 2

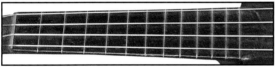

1915–1917

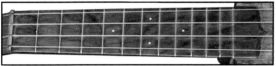

1918–1920

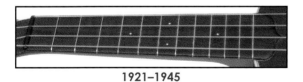

1921–1945

~1945–1994

Style 3

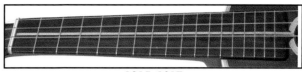

1915–1917

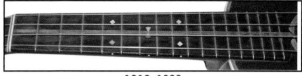

1918–1920

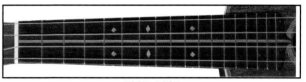

1921–1936

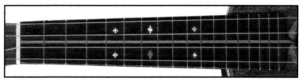

1936–1947

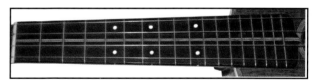

1947–ca. 1955

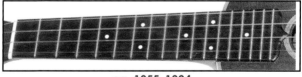

ca. 1955–1994

Style 5

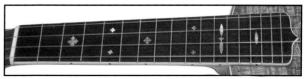

1922–1944

some of Martin's guitars of the time.

The Style 3 fretboard continued to change over the years. The slotted pearl squares and diamonds were first replaced by celluloid dots around 1947. A more major change occurred around the mid 1950s, when the stripes down the center of the fretboard were eliminated and a new pattern of dots was used—one dot at frets five, ten, and fifteen, two dots at frets seven and twelve.

The inlays on the Style 5K were not only Martin's most elaborate, they were their most consistent. The standard pattern, which featured intricate inlay at frets three, five, seven, ten, twelve, and fifteen, remained unchanged for the duration of the model's lifetime, 1922–1941.

Frets

Before the 1930s, all of Martin's fretted instruments were equipped with bar frets. Bar frets are just what they sound like, a simple metal bar inlaid into the fretboard. The cross-section of a bar fret is rectangular, but with a somewhat rounded top edge. Martin began using T-frets on its guitars in the 1930s. This has led many to speculate that they would have started using T-frets on ukuleles at about the same time. This does seem to hold true for Martin's tenor ukuleles, but the change to T-frets on Martin's concert and soprano size ukuleles came much later.

Martin first inventoried T-fret wire long before they began to use it regularly on their instruments. The T-fret wire was first used regularly on guitars in 1934, but the only fret wire for ukuleles that was being inventoried at the time was the standard bar stock. Supply shortages due to World War II prevented Martin from getting the standard nickel-silver bar fret wire for ukuleles. The 1944–1946 Martin inventories list iron wire for ukulele frets. The first mention of T-fret wire specifically for ukuleles is seen in the January, 1948, inventory, which suggests the switch was made sometime in 1947.

Bindings

Binding is the decorative material on the edges of an instrument where the top and back meet the sides. All three of Martin's original ukulele models, the Styles 1, 2, and 3, had bindings on their top edge. The Style 1 had rosewood binding on its top edge but no binding on the back. Binding was added to the back of the Style 1 in 1926. In 1936 a switch was made from rosewood to a tortoise shell plastic binding. The change from rosewood to tortoise binding likely occurred at the same time on Style 1C concert ukuleles and Style 1T tenors.

Styles 2 ukuleles featured an ivory-colored celluloid binding with a single thin black line on the front, and a plain ivory-colored celluloid binding on the back. Style 3 ukuleles featured a wider seven ply celluloid binding on the front edge with alternating ivory-colored and black layers. On the back they had a simpler ivory-colored celluloid binding with a single black stripe.

The Style 0 ukulele, introduced in 1922, was Martin's first instrument with no bindings at all. Also in 1922 Martin added the Style 5K ukulele to their line. The Style 5K was Martin's only ukulele model with inlaid pearl. The binding was an ivory-colored celluloid with black stripes on the side and top as well as the inlaid pearl. The same style of binding was used on both the top and back of the instrument. In the 1925-26 Martin catalog the description of the 5K model indicates "pearl inlay in top, back and sides," a statement that has puzzled Martin ukulele fans for many years. No known examples exist of an original Martin 5K with pearl on the sides. Because 1925 and 1926 were the two biggest years of production for the Style 5K, it seems certain that if Martin was actually inlaying the sides of the instrument in those years, examples would be known. Therefore, it seems that the catalog description must have been in error.

Styles 1 and 1K: 1915–1936 (front)

Styles 1 and 1K: 1936–1966 (front)

Styles 2 and 2K:1916–1966 (front)

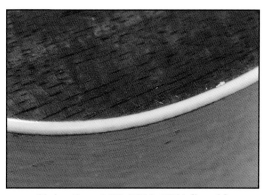

Styles 2 and 2K: 1916–1966 (back)

Styles 3 and 3K: 1916–1994 (front)

Styles 3 and 3K: 1916–1994 (back)

Styles 5 & 5K 1922–1945 (front)

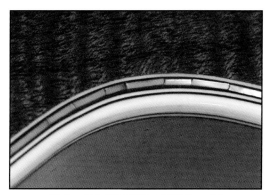

Styles 5 & 5K 1922–1945 (back)

Tuning Pegs

In 1907 Martin made its first six ukuleles for Bergstrom Music in Honolulu. While there is no indication in the archives as to of what type of tuning peg was used, since these first ukuleles were likely patterned after a Hawaiian-made ukulele sent by Bergstrom, it is reasonable to assume that wooden friction pegs were used. These pegs may have been supplied by Bergstrom as there is no mention of ukulele pegs in any of the expense or inventory books of the period.

The first record of Martin purchasing ukulele pegs is in August of 1915, when they purchased one gross of wood ukulele pegs for $2.00. These are likely the pegs they used on their first production ukuleles, which they began selling in October of 1915. While there is no record of where Martin purchased these pegs, it wasn't too long before Martin began to get its wood pegs from the Southern California Music Company. Wooden pegs were standard equipment on all Martin ukulele models in the teens and early 1920s. According to the early inventories and expense books, the earliest of the wooden pegs were made from a type of wood called "almiqui" also known as bulletwood or South American mahogany. Later Martin experimented with ebony pegs, although it isn't clear if they actually shipped ukuleles equipped with ebony pegs. Later the wood pegs they used were made of "ebonized" maple—maple stained black to take on the appearance of ebony. For a time in 1924 Martin sought out someone who could make them a quality peg made from rosewood, but

Hardwood Pegs
Style 0: 1922–1927
Style 1: 1915–1927
Styles 2, 3: 1915–1921
Most Styles: 1943–1945

eventually gave up and continued with the maple pegs they were using.

Martin sold a good number of ukuleles without pegs to the Chas. H. Ditson Co. in New York. These Ditson model ukuleles with the special Ditson dreadnought shape were equipped by Ditson with Champion Key tuners. Martin records show that they purchased 100 Champion Key tuners themselves in November of 1920, probably for ukuleles that were special ordered. The Champion Key tuners were intended for banjo or guitar headstocks, and are a little bit bulky for use on a ukulele. It is possible that this is why Martin did not adopt them for regular use. Ditson's use of Champion Keys did have a small effect on Martin's ukulele specifications. Because they were generally used on bigger instruments, there was some trouble using them on the thinner headstocks of the Martin ukuleles. Ditson wrote to Martin in 1922 suggesting that they "make the peg end of your Ukuleles a trifle thicker as we have a great amount of trouble making the Champion pegs hold." Martin replied that "a sixteenth of an inch at this point will answer your purpose and this can be added without much trouble."

Champion Key Pegs (white)
Some Ditson Models
Some special orders
1920–1925

In April of 1921 Martin purchased sixty ukulele pegs from A. D. Grover & Son. A version of these Grover pegs would become the first "patent pegs" regularly adopted for the Martin ukulele line. By late 1921 Martin was supplying patent pegs on their higher grade ukuleles. The specific pegs used varied some early on, as can be seen in Martin correspondence with R. S. Williams & Sons Co., a Canadian manufacturer and importer. C. F. III wrote in a February, 1922 letter that "on our Style 3, Style 3-K and Style 5-K we are now regularly using patent pegs, wither Grover, Champion or Universal of the standard type." Soon however Martin would settle on the Grover tuners as the tuners of choice for its high-grade models. Waverly Novelty Co., Grover's big competitor in the musical instrument hardware market, fought hard to get Martin to adopt its tuning pegs. Martin was not interested in Waverly's cheap "ten-cents-a-set article," considering the wooden pegs they were using to be their equal in ease-of-use and superior in appearance. When Waverly came out with a better peg, Martin purchased a quantity to use on instruments when they were specifically requested by a customer. One such customer was the Rudolph Wurlitzer Co., who requested Waverly pegs on some of their Customer Model ukuleles in 1922.

Grover spring-loaded
Some Style 3 ukuleles: 1921

Various models of Grover pegs were used as standard equipment on Martin ukuleles continuously from late 1921 up until the Second World War. Originally they were used only on Style 3, Style 3K, and Style 5K ukuleles, but the Style 2 was also upgraded from wooden pegs in September of 1922. The new Style 0, and the Style 1 and Style 1K would continue to be equipped with wooden pegs until early 1927. By February of 1927, all Martin ukuleles were being shipped with patent pegs.

A change to the model of Grover pegs used occurred in late 1923. In December of 1923 Grover announced a new nickel plated, grooved-barrel peg. In an article in the *Music Trade Review*, Mr. A. W. Grover is quoted as saying: "While very few things in this world are ever perfect, I feel that we are now offering the trade an article that approaches more nearly perfection than anything on the market to-day." The article also

Grover spring-loaded
w/ ivoroid buttons
Styles 2, 3, 5K:
1922–1923

Grover no. 76 Pegs
Styles 2, 3, 5K: 1923–1927

Grover Simplex no. 88 Pegs
Styles 2, 3, 5K: 1927–1929

states that "C. F. Martin & Co., Nazareth, Pa., makers of one of the finest ukuleles in the trade, have adopted the new Grover peg on ukuleles of their manufacture." Martin referred to these as no. 3 pegs, but the Grover designation was no. 76. Martin ordered all of these new pegs with ivory-colored celluloid buttons. The ivory-colored buttons cost more than black buttons did, but Martin preferred their appearance and was willing to pay extra to set their instruments apart from those of other manufacturers. Although Martin used these grooved-barrel tuners for only about three years, this stretch was the biggest period of ukulele production in the company's history, explaining why they are seen on so many vintage Martins.

When Martin introduced the Style 1C Concert ukulele in 1925, like other Style 1 models, it was given wooden friction pegs. In January of 1927 Grover announced a new "Simplex" peg with a smooth, rounded barrel. Martin quickly adopted the no. 88 model, with ivory-colored buttons, and used it on Style 2 and higher ukulele models. By early 1927, Martin began to use Simplex pegs on all their ukulele models. Simplex pegs no. 92 with black buttons and knurled knobs were used on the Style 0, Style 1, and their new Style 1C Concert ukuleles, while Simplex pegs with the more expensive ivory-colored celluloid buttons were used on all of the high-end Style 2, 3, and 5K models. Based on their inventories, by 1929 Martin was using Grover Simplex pegs with knurled barrels on all models, no. 92 with black buttons and no. 94 with ivory-colored buttons. Nearly all Martin soprano ukuleles made between late 1927 and the Second World War were equipped with the Grover Simplex pegs of one style or another.

Grover no. 94 Simplex Pegs
Styles 2, 3, 5K: 1927–1937

When the Style 1T Tenor ukulele was introduced in 1928, it too used the no. 92 Simplex pegs with black buttons.

After the US entered the Second World War at the end of 1941, Martin could no longer obtain the Grover pegs it had been using for years. According to their inventories, they had no Grover tuners remaining by the beginning of 1943.

Grover no. 92 Simplex Pegs
w/ black buttons
Styles 0, 1: 1926–1942
Style 1C Concert: 1927–1942
Style 1T Tenor: 1927–1942

Waverly Pearl Pegs
Some special orders 1920s

They had a small supply of new tuners from Waverly, which it seems they reserved for their high-end ukuleles. Martin went back to using wooden pegs on most of their ukuleles once the Grover tuners ran out. This is noted in a memo found in the archives, that reads: "Substitutes for metal parts are being used wherever possible and practical. A rigid ebony bar now gives guitar necks the same guaranteed strength as the steel bar it replaces. Wood pegs take the place of metal patent pegs on ukuleles, which can be made in fair quantities."

There are many existing examples of Martin ukuleles with wooden tuning pegs and standard decals on the headstock. Because these decals were not used until 1934, it has led some Martin experts to speculate that Martin continued using wooden pegs on some models well into the 1930s. Most evidence from the Martin archives seems to contradict this notion. In March of 1927, in a letter to H. A. Stiles & Co., a wooden ukulele peg manufacturer, C. F. III wrote: "We advise that we have discontinued the use of Wood Ukulele Pegs in favor of the Patented Metal Peg." However, in May C. F. III wrote to Peate's Music House, Inc., of Utica, New York: "We are introducing the patent pegs gradually and are still shipping quite a number of instruments with wooden pegs." Look-

Kluson no. 566 Pegs
Style 0: 1946–1956
Styles 1, 2: 1946–1948

ing through the order books of the period, there don't appear to be any dealers who continued to order ukuleles with wood pegs after Martin had upgraded to patent pegs. However, Martin continued to inventory changing numbers of wood ukulele pegs through 1935. It is likely these pegs were being used

Waverly no. 2014 w/white buttons
Style 0: 1956–1994
Styles 1, 2, 3: 1949–1994
Style 5: 1941–1942

for repairs or replacements rather than as standard equipment on new ukuleles. No wooden pegs are found in the Martin inventories between 1936 and 1943. From 1943 to 1945 Martin manufactured over 5000 ukuleles, and it is likely nearly all were supplied with wooden pegs. Over 500 of these were Style 1K ukuleles, the last koa ukuleles Martin would make in standard production for sixty years.

In 1944 Martin acquired some Champion pegs which it began using on its concert and tenor ukuleles. In 1946, after the war was over, Martin

Waverly Baritone Pegs (white)
Style B51 Baritone: 1960–1994

purchased a supply of pegs from the Kluson Co. Kluson no. 566 keystone tuners became standard

equipment on Style 0, 1, and 2 ukuleles for a short time. In 1948 they began using Waverly no. 2014 pegs on Style 1, 2, and 3 ukuleles, but they continued to use the Kluson tuners on the Style 0 model. The Waverly pegs are easy to identify as they have a hexagonal grommet on the front side of the headstock, and they are sometimes referred to as "hexnut" tuners. For a short time Style 1 ukuleles received Waverly hexnut tuners with black buttons, but soon only white buttons were used. At some point in 1956 Martin stopped using the Kluson tuners and all soprano models from that point on were equipped with Waverly hexnut pegs with white buttons. Concert and tenor ukuleles used a version of the Champion peg with black buttons. Baritones used a larger, banjo style Waverly peg.

Champion Pegs (black)
Style 1C Concert: 1944–1965
Style 1T Tenor: 1944–1994

Martin Ukuleles by Style

Style 0

In the 1920s, after physicists had established the first, second, and third laws of thermodynamics, they realized another more fundamental law of thermodynamics should also be recognized. This law eventually came to be known as the zeroth law of thermodynamics. Similarly, in the 1920s Martin already had three well-established ukulele models, numbered 1, 2, and 3, when they decided to introduce a new lower-priced ukulele model. Their Styles 1, 2, and 3 were in increasing order of ornamentation and price, thus the new simpler model was designated the Style 0.

On December 29, 1921, Martin took its first orders for the new ukulele model. On that date their two biggest customers of the time, New York City retailers Chas. H. Ditson and Wm. J. Smith, each ordered twelve Style 0 ukuleles. Martin sent out new product postcards in February announcing the model:

A new number at a popular price. Neatly designed and finely built of mahogany, with rosewood fingerboard, ebony nut, and hardwood pegs. Natural color finish hand rubbed, clean and velvety in appearance. Martin Quality Throughout.

The Style 0 was an instant success. In January of 1922, the very first month of sales, the Style 0 became Martin's biggest selling model. Over 1,600 Style 0 ukuleles were sold during that first year, roughly the same number of ukuleles Martin had sold in all styles in 1921. Writing to Hawkes & Son, a retailer in London, C. F. III had this to say about the new style:

We have lately added to our line of Ukuleles a new style known as No. 0, listed at ten dollars, and the response of the domestic trade to the announcement of this style has been most gratifying. In this country there is a wide market for a strictly high grade instrument at this price. Does not the same condi-

tion exist in London? We should be very glad to have an opportunity to make a sampler shipment.

The profit margin on the Style 0 ukulele was quite small, and production needed to be checked regularly. In late 1921 when the style was first made up, an analysis was done and it was estimated that the amount it cost to make a Style 0, including labor, material, and overhead costs, was $4.71. With most dealers receiving a fifty percent discount off of the retail $10 price, Martin was generally receiving $5.00 for each Style 0, making a profit of just 29 cents for each one sold. But the Style 0 paid in other ways. The company knew that increasing sales in one model could help with sales of others. In a letter to the Lyon & Healy company in October of 1922 Frank Henry discusses the strategy:

There is a better time coming; we have had a steady ukulele trade all this year and at present are ordered far ahead. We believe the immediate future is so good that Lyon & Healy, Martin, and all other good factories will have plenty of business. Our great success is the ten dollar style, but it is surprising how many fine ones are added in making up orders. If we may suggest, the surest way to sell what you have on hand is to put in a large number of the No. 0, the ten dollar one, which will draw trade and make openings for the others.

The other way to make the Style 0 more profitable was to find ways to reduce the cost of production. Careful cost analyses were done each year, and in 1922 after the company was in full production for some time, the estimated production cost had dropped to $4.22. As labor and material costs increased in the following years, the price needed to be raised to keep the style profitable. In July of 1923 the price was raised to $11.00 and in November of 1924 to $12.00. The price raises weren't due solely to rising costs, but rather simple supply and demand was at work. When Martin couldn't produce ukuleles fast enough to fill orders, a price increase could sometimes help the company get caught up. But the increase in price of the Style 0 did not seem to slow demand.

Even with the factory expanding in 1924 and again in 1925, by early 1926 Martin had fallen so far behind in the production of the Style 0 that they were forced to discontinue the model temporarily. C. F. III explained the reasoning in his report at the July 1926 Board of Directors meeting: "In the ukulele line the No. 0 ukulele was discontinued temporarily on March first because of the continual increase of back orders, and greater emphasis will be placed on the production of the finer styles, for which there is good demand." Orders dropped off in the second half of 1926, allowing Martin to get caught up. The Style 0 was reinstated on January 1, 1927. It again quickly became Martin's most popular instrument. Nearly half of the 5,500 ukuleles Martin made in 1927 were Style 0s.

The Style 0 would remain an important instrument for Martin for many years to come. Even as the popularity of the ukulele ebbed and flowed over the coming decades, in nearly every year from 1922 to the mid 1960s Martin sold more Style 0 ukuleles than any other single model of instrument they made. With the exception of the depression year of 1933, Martin made at least 400 Style 0 ukuleles every year from 1922 to 1968.

Studio photo of a late 1920s Style 0.

Retouched photo for use in Martin catalog.

Style 0 Specifications:

1921:	First orders received
1922:	First sales. First cataloged. Solid mahogany top, back, and sides. No body bindings. Single small fingerboard position dots on frets five, seven, and ten. Wood friction pegs. Mahogany bridge w/ebony saddle, ebony nut. Bar frets. Stamped inside soundhole and on back of headstock: "C. F. Martin & Co., Nazareth, PA."
1927:	Grover Simplex pegs with black buttons replace hardwood pegs.
1932:	Large guitar style decal added to front of headstock. Still stamped on back of headstock.
1934:	Standard ukulele size decal on front of headstock. No stamp on back of headstock. A small number of ukuleles have both the small decal and the stamp on the back of the headstock.
1942-1945:	During some of the war years wooden pegs were used.
1946:	Kluson no. 566 keystone tuning pegs first used.
1947:	Bar frets replaced by T-frets.
1956:	Waverly hexnut tuners replace Kluson tuners.
1960:	Made in USA stamped inside soundhole under Martin stamp.
1977:	Available by special order only.
1994:	Discontinued.

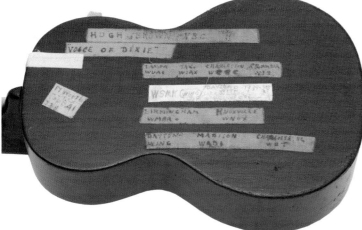

Above and right: 1920s era Style 0 originally owned by Hugh Brown. Brown was an entertainer who called himself "The Voice of Dixie" and performed with his Style 0 on radio stations throughout the Southern United States. He used white cloth tape to temporarily repair cracks in his ukulele. This white tape made a good place for him to document his various appearances.

Style 0 | Style 0

ca. 1930

1960s

Style 1

The original Martin ukulele line introduced at the end of 1915 consisted of soprano ukuleles in three styles designated simply as Styles 1, 2, and 3. The Style 1 was the plainest model, and it retailed for ten dollars. The earliest models had serial numbers, but a separate series of serial numbers was used for the otherwise identical ukuleles Martin was making for the Chas. H. Ditson Co. of New York City. Until the introduction of the Style 0 in 1922, the Style 1 was Martin's biggest selling instrument every year starting with its first full year of production, 1916.

Style 1 specifications:

1915: First made and sold. Solid mahogany top, back, sides, and neck. Twelve fret rosewood fingerboard. Bar frets. Rosewood bound top. Wood friction pegs. One-piece mahogany bridge/saddle. Maple nut. No fingerboard inlays. Serial number on neck block. Stamped inside soundhole and on back of headstock: "C. F. Martin & Co., Nazareth, PA." Stamp inside soundhole originally perpendicular to the back braces. Many small construction details different from model even a year later.

1916: Serial numbers dropped. Bridge made with separate maple saddle. Stamp inside body parallel to back braces.

1917 -1918: Small circular position markers added to fingerboard. One each at the fifth and ninth frets, two at the seventh fret.

1920-1921 Fret marker positions changed from frets five, seven, and nine to five, seven, and ten. Ebony nut and bridge saddle.

1926 Rosewood bindings added to back of instrument.

1927: Grover Simplex tuners w/black buttons replace friction tuners.

1932-1934: Large logo decals used on headstock, stamp on back of headstock.

1934: Small logo decals on headstock. No stamp on back of headstock.

1936: Celluloid tortoise shell binding replaces rosewood binding.

1942-1945: During some of the war years wooden pegs were used again instead of patent tuners.

1946: Kluson keystone tuners (no. 566) were used for a short time after the end of the Second World War.

1947 T-frets replace bar frets.

1948: Waverly hexnut tuners (no. 2014) with white buttons.

1960: "Made in U.S.A." added to stamp inside soundhole.

1966: Discontinued.

THE

HAWAIIAN UKULELE

MANUFACTURED BY

C. F. MARTIN & CO.

STYLE No. I

PRICE
$10.00

A neat and durable instrument, original Hawaiian model. Body and neck of mahogany in an artistic dull finish. Rosewood fingerboard, accurately fretted, scientific scale.

Unexcelled tone of rich quality and full volume.

Style 1K specifications:

1917: First made on special order for Southern California Music Company. Solid koa top, back, sides, and neck. Twelve fret rosewood fingerboard. Bar frets. Rosewood bound top. Wood friction pegs. Koa bridge w/ maple saddle. Maple nut. Small circular position markers on fingerboard, one each at the fifth and ninth frets, two at the seventh fret. Stamped on back of headstock: "Southern California Music Company, Los Angeles."

1919 First made as part of standard Martin line. Stamped inside soundhole and on back of headstock: "C. F. Martin & Co., Nazareth, PA."

ca. 1920 Rosewood binding added to back of instrument.

1920-1921 Fret marker positions changed from frets five, seven, and nine to five, seven, and ten. Ebony nut and bridge saddle.

1927: Grover Simplex tuners w/black buttons replace friction tuners.

1935: Small logo decals on headstock. No stamp on back of headstock. (No Style 1K ukuleles were made between 1932 and 1934).

1936: Celluloid tortoise shell binding replaces rosewood binding.

1942-1944: During the Second World War wooden pegs were used again instead of patent tuners.

1944: Discontinued.

Style 1: Serial no. 105

1916

Style 1

Style 1

ca. 1927

ca. 1956

ca. 1920

ca. 1927

Style 2

Style 2 specifications:

1916:	First sale. Solid mahogany top, back, sides, and neck. Twelve fret rosewood fingerboard. Bar frets. Celluloid bound top and back. Wood friction pegs. One-piece mahogany bridge/ saddle. No fingerboard inlays. Serial number on neck block. Stamped inside soundhole and on back of headstock: "C. F. Martin & Co., Nazareth, PA." Stamp inside soundhole originally perpendicular to the back braces. Many small construction details different from model even a year later.
1916:	Serial numbers dropped. Bridge made with separate saddle. Stamp inside body parallel to back braces.
1917 -1918:	Small circular position markers added to fingerboard. One each at the fifth and ninth frets, two at the seventh fret.
1920-1921	Fret marker positions changed from frets five, seven, and nine to five, seven, and ten. Ebony nut and bridge saddle.
1922:	Grover patent tuners w/white buttons replace friction tuners.
1923	Grover grooved barrel tuners first used.
1927:	Grover Simplex tuners w/white buttons first used.
1932-1934:	Large logo decals used on headstock, stamp on back of headstock.
1934:	Small logo decals on headstock. No stamp on back of headstock.
1942-1945:	During some of the Second World War wooden pegs were used again instead of patent tuners.
1946:	Kluson keystone tuners (no. 566) were used for a short time after the end of the Second World War.
1947	T-frets replace bar frets.
1948:	Waverly hexnut tuners (no. 2014) with white buttons.
1960:	"Made in U.S.A." added to stamp inside soundhole.
1966:	Discontinued.

Style 2K specifications:

1917:	First made on special order for Southern California Music Company. Solid koa top, back, sides, and neck. Twelve fret rosewood fingerboard. Bar frets. Celluloid bound top and back. Wood friction pegs. Koa bridge w/ maple saddle. Maple nut. Small circular position markers on fingerboard, one each at the fifth and ninth frets, two at the seventh fret. Stamped on back of headstock: "Southern California Music Company, Los Angeles."
1919	First made as part of standard Martin line. Stamped inside soundhole and on back of headstock: "C. F. Martin & Co., Nazareth, PA."
1920-1921	Fret marker positions changed from frets five, seven, and nine to five, seven, and ten. Ebony nut and bridge saddle.
1922:	Grover patent tuners w/white buttons replace friction tuners.
1923	Grover grooved barrel tuners first used.
1927:	Grover Simplex tuners w/white buttons first used.
1931:	Last produced in regular production.
1934:	Discontinued.

Style 2

ca. 1930

Style 2K

ca. 1927

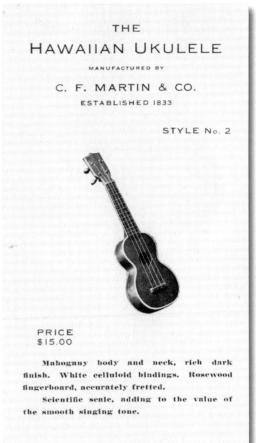

THE
HAWAIIAN UKULELE
MANUFACTURED BY
C. F. MARTIN & CO.
ESTABLISHED 1833

STYLE No. 2

PRICE
$15.00

Mahogany body and neck, rich dark finish. White celluloid bindings. Rosewood fingerboard, accurately fretted.

Scientific scale, adding to the value of the smooth singing tone.

Style 3 specifications:

1916:	First sale. Solid mahogany top, back, sides, and neck. Seventeen fret rosewood fingerboard (at least one surviving example has an eighteen fret fingerboard). Bar frets. Seven-ply black and white celluloid bound top; three-ply celluloid bound back. Wood friction pegs. One-piece mahogany bridge/saddle. No position markers. Five-ply black and white stripe down center of fingerboard. Kite-shaped celluloid inlay on headstock, celluloid ornament inlaid at bottom of body beneath the bridge. Serial number on neck block. Stamped inside soundhole and on back of headstock: "C. F. Martin & Co., Nazareth, PA." Stamp inside soundhole originally perpendicular to the back braces. Many small construction details different from model even a year later.
1916:	Serial numbers dropped. Bridge made with separate bone saddle. Ivory nut with black stripe. Stamp inside body parallel to back braces.
1917 -1918:	Pearl position markers added to fingerboard. Two squares each at the fifth and ninth frets, bow-tie inlay at seventh fret.
1920:	Kite ornament on headstock eliminated.
1920–1921	Fret marker positions changed from frets five, seven, and nine to five, seven, and ten. Bow-tie inlay at seventh fret changed to two elongated diamonds.
1921:	Grover patent tuners w/ivoroid buttons replace friction tuners.
ca. 1923	Plain ivory-colored nut replaces white-black-white nut.
1923	Grover grooved barrel tuners with ivoroid buttons first used.
1927:	Grover Simplex tuners w/ivoroid buttons first used.
1932-1934:	Large logo decals used on headstock, stamp on back of headstock.
1934:	Small logo decals on headstock. No stamp on back of headstock.
1936	Slotted diamonds and squares replace solid diamonds and squares on fingerboard.
1942-1945:	During the Second World War wooden pegs were used again instead of patent tuners.
1946:	Kluson keystone tuners (no. 566) may have been used for a short time after the end of World War II, otherwise wooden tuners were continued.
1947	T-frets replace bar frets. Circular celluloid dots replace slotted pearl squares and diamonds on fingerboard.
1948:	Waverly hexnut tuners (no. 2014) with white buttons.
1950	Ornament at the bottom of the body eliminated.
ca. 1955	Fingerboard stripes eliminated. New dot pattern on fingerboard with single dots at frets five, ten, and fifteen, double dots at frets seven and twelve.
1960:	"Made in U.S.A." added to stamp in soundhole.
1977:	Available by special order only.
1994:	Discontinued.

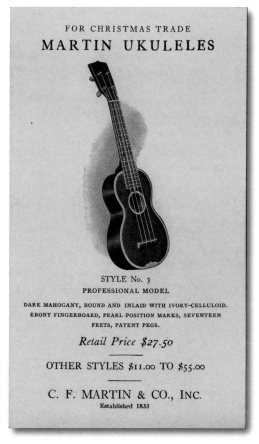

FOR CHRISTMAS TRADE

MARTIN UKULELES

STYLE No. 3
PROFESSIONAL MODEL
DARK MAHOGANY, BOUND AND INLAID WITH IVORY-CELLULOID.
EBONY FINGERBOARD, PEARL POSITION MARKS, SEVENTEEN
FRETS, PATENT PEGS.
Retail Price $27.50

OTHER STYLES $11.00 TO $55.00

C. F. MARTIN & CO., INC.
Established 1833

Style 3K specifications:

1917:   First made on special order for Southern California Music Company. Solid koa top, back, sides, and neck. Seventeen fret rosewood fingerboard. Bar frets. Seven-ply black and white celluloid bound top; three-ply celluloid bound back. Wood friction pegs. Koa bridge w/ ivory saddle. Ivory nut with black stripe. Pearl position markers on fingerboard, two squares each at the fifth and ninth frets, bow-tie inlay at seventh fret. Five-ply black and white stripe down center of fingerboard. Kite-shaped celluloid inlay on headstock, celluloid ornament inlaid at bottom of body beneath the bridge. Stamped on back of headstock: "Southern California Music Company, Los Angeles."

1919   First made as part of standard Martin line. Stamped inside soundhole and on back of headstock: "C. F. Martin & Co., Nazareth, PA."

1920:   Kite ornament on headstock eliminated.

1920–1921   Fret marker positions changed from frets five, seven, and nine to five, seven, and ten. Bow-tie inlay at seventh fret changed to two elongated diamonds.

1921:   Grover patent tuners w/ivoroid buttons replace friction tuners

1923   Grover grooved barrel tuners with ivoroid buttons first used.

ca. 1923   Plain ivory-colored nut replaces white-black-white nut.

1927:   Grover Simplex tuners w/ivoroid buttons first used.

1932-1934:   Large logo decals used on headstock, stamp on back of headstock.

1934:   Small logo decals on headstock. No stamp on back of headstock.

1938:   Last made in regular production.

1939:   Discontinued.

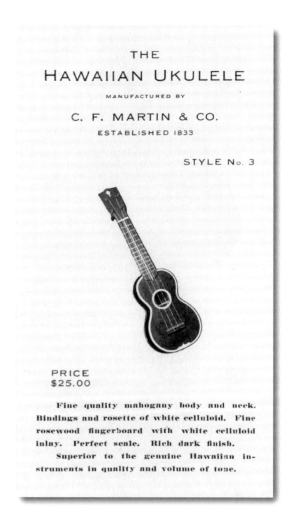

THE
HAWAIIAN UKULELE
MANUFACTURED BY
C. F. MARTIN & CO.
ESTABLISHED 1833

STYLE No. 3

PRICE
$25.00

Fine quality mahogany body and neck. Bindings and rosette of white celluloid. Fine rosewood fingerboard with white celluloid inlay. Perfect scale. Rich dark finish.

Superior to the genuine Hawaiian instruments in quality and volume of tone.

ca. 1917

ca. 1920

Style 3

ca. 1962

Style 3K

ca. 1920

Style 3K

Style 3K

ca. 1927

ca. 1936

Toward the end of 1921 Martin experimented with two new ukulele styles. The Style 0 was added to create a new lower-priced ukulele of uncompromised quality. At the other end of the spectrum, they introduced the fanciest ukulele on the market.

On December 29, 1921 Martin sent a new model of ukulele to Wm. J Smith in New York City. The instrument was a Style 5K, but lacked the pearl inlaid headstock veneer. Martin spent the month of January having two different New York City companies make up samples of headstock inlays to determine the price. The Louis Handel Co. was chosen after they offered to inlay the headstock veneers for sixty cents a piece. When Smith ordered a second 5K in February, Martin wrote to Smith to see if he wanted to return the original ukulele to have the headstock veneer applied. Smith replied that he "took the liberty of selling it for $42, owing to it not having the extra inlay." He added "I am satisfied however to have you bill it to us at the regular price." In another example of the Martin Company putting fairness in front of profit, C. F. III wrote back: "We enclose herewith a bill for fifty per cent of the price you got for the No. 5K ukulele left with you on consignment. We appreciate your willingness to accept a bill for the regular price, but we prefer to be allowed to share the reduction with you."

The release of the 5K allowed the Martin Company to proclaim itself the maker of the finest ukulele in the world. Their confidence shows in correspondence with dealers and associates alike. For example, in April of 1922 the company wrote to A. D. Grover, the maker of the pegs Martin was using on its high-end ukuleles. Martin had heard that Grover was going to be displaying its prod-

ucts during the Guild convention. Frank Henry wrote: "It occurs to us that possibly you would like to add to your display one of our Style 5-K ukuleles, listed at fifty dollars, which is regularly equipped with Grover Pegs." He continued: "..The 5-K is a very handsome instrument, easily the best now on the market, and perhaps it would be of value to you to have it associated with your line." Grover accepted the offer agreeing that it "will undoubtedly be to our mutual advantage." Before the 5K, Martin may have claimed to have the best sounding ukuleles or the best ukuleles for the price, but now they could simply claim "best on the market."

The original Martin Style 5K ukulele was made for less than twenty years, but in reality nearly all were made in the first ten years of production. Except for a total of twenty-four 5K ukuleles (one dozen were made in both 1936 and 1938), no 5K ukuleles were made after 1931. Fewer than 750 Style 5K ukuleles were manufactured in total in their original production run, all between 1921 and 1938.

There were no substantial changes made to the 5K model specifications during its short production run, although the 1925-26 Martin catalog suggests otherwise. The 1923 catalog's description includes the description "Pearl inlay around the sound hole and along front and back edges of the body." The 1925-26 catalog changed the wording of the description line to read "pearl inlay in top, back, and sides, and around sound-hole." This wording in the catalog has left collectors looking for the elusive 5K with pearl inlay on the sides of the body as well as the top and back. The wording is most likely a simple mistake, unless perhaps Martin planned to change the model but then never did. The years 1925 and 1926 were Martin's two biggest production years for the Style 5K, with well over 250 5Ks ordered. These two years account for roughly one third of total 5K production, so you would expect a pretty good number of 5K ukuleles to show pearl on the sides if the catalog description was correct. In fact, when former Martin inlay artist and historian Mike Longworth first heard about the recently discovered custom Style 5 ukulele made for May Singhi Breen, his first questions was: "Is there pearl inlay on the sides?"

By 1938 when the last twelve 5K ukuleles were built, Martin was either finding it difficult to find koa wood, especially the fancier grade used on the high-end koa instruments, or it had stopped trying. By 1941, the company had apparently run out of the fancy koa wood, and for the first time offered a Style 5 ukulele made from mahogany. Soon after the U. S. entered the Second World War at the end of 1941, pearl-bordered instruments were dropped from the Martin catalog. A total of only twenty mahogany Style 5 ukuleles were made in 1941 and 1942. Add in the other four that had been made earlier by special order, and you have one of the rarest Martin ukulele models.

Style 5K specifications:

1921:	First sale. Solid figured Hawaiian koa wood top, back, and sides, mahogany neck. Seventeen fret ebony fingerboard bound with ivory-colored celluloid. Bar frets. Celluloid and pearl bound top and back. Pearl soundhole rosette. Grover patent pegs with ivoroid buttons. Koa bridge with ivory saddle. Ivory nut. Pearl position markers at frets three, five, seven, ten, twelve, and fifteen. Stamped inside soundhole and on back of headstock: "C. F. Martin & Co., Nazareth, PA."
1922:	First cataloged. Figured koa wood headstock veneer inlaid with pearl scroll.
1923	Grover grooved barrel tuners with ivoroid buttons first used.
1927:	Grover Simplex tuners w/ivoroid buttons first used.
1934:	Small logo decal on back of headstock. No stamp on back of headstock.
1938	Last manufactured.
1940	Last cataloged.
1941	Discontinued.

Style 5 specifications:

1941:	First manufactured (except for earlier special orders) and first and last cataloged. Solid figured mahogany top, back, and sides, mahogany neck. Seventeen fret ebony fingerboard bound with ivory-colored celluloid. Bar frets. Celluloid and pearl bound top and back. Pearl soundhole rosette. Figured mahogany headstock veneer inlaid with pearl scroll. Waverly pegs with white buttons. Mahogany bridge with ivory saddle. Ivory nut. Pearl position markers at frets three, five, seven, ten, twelve, and fifteen. Stamped inside soundhole: "C. F. Martin & Co., Nazareth, PA." Small decal on back of headstock.
1942:	Discontinued.

Style 5K

ca. 1930

Style 5

ca. 1941

Taropatches

All taropatch models were made with the same appointments as the corresponding soprano model.

Style 1 Taropatch specifications:

1916:   First sale.
1918:   First included on price list.
1919:   First included in catalog.
1927:   Last regular production.
1931:   Discontinued.

Style 2 Taropatch specifications:

1917:   First sale.
1918:   First included on price list.
1919:   First included in catalog.
1927:   Last regular production.
1931:   Discontinued.

Style 3 Taropatch specifications:

1917:   First sale.
1918:   First included on price list.
1919:   First included in catalog.
1927:   Last regular production.
1929:   Discontinued.

Style 1K Taropatch specifications:

1919:   First sale.
1921:   First included on price list.
1921:   First included in catalog.
1927:   Last regular production.
1929:   Discontinued.

Style 2K Taropatch specifications:

1919:   First sale.
1921:   First included on price list.
1921:   First included in catalog.
1927:   Last regular production.
1930:   Discontinued.

Style 3K Taropatch specifications:

1919:   First sale.
1921:   First included on price list.
1921:   First included in catalog.
1927:   Last regular production.
1930:   Discontinued.

TAROPATCH NO. 1

TAROPATCHES
These are shaped like the ukuleles, only larger, same material and styles. Made regularly with eight strings, or with four strings to order.

No. 1. $17.60
No. 2.   22.00
No. 3.   33.00

ca. 1917

MARTIN

HAWAIIAN

TARO-PATCH FIDDLES

—

SUPERIOR IN TONE

—

Made By

C. F. Martin & Co.

Nazareth, Pa.

Established 1833

Style 1
$20.00

Style 1
Body and neck of mahogany in a fine dull finish. Rosewood fingerboard, accurately fretted; four white position marks.
Price : : $20.00

Style 2
Bound front and back with white celluloid. A very effective design.
Price : : $24.00

Style 3
Finely bound and trimmed with white celluloid. Extended fingerboard, seventeen frets. Pearl position marks. *Professional Model.*
Price : : $36.00

Above top: Taropatch paper pattern from 1917.
Above: Taropatch product postcard, ca. 1920.
Preceding page, bottom left: Style 2 taropatch.
Preceding page, bottom middle: Retouched version of photo for catalog.
Preceding page, bottom right: First catalog taropatch listing, 1919.

Style 1 Taropatch

ca. 1919

Style 2 Taropatch

ca. 1924

Style 3 Taropatch

ca. 1924

Style 1K Taropatch

ca. 1923

Style 2K Taropatch

ca. 1924

Style 3K Taropatch

ca. 1920

Style 3K Taropatch

ca. 1924

Ditson Style 3 Taropatch

ca. 1917

Concert Ukuleles

In 1920 many companies making Hawaiian instruments made both ukuleles and taropatches. The standard ukulele was about 21 inches long and had four strings. Although there were a few companies producing smaller versions of the ukulele, often referred to as "midget" ukuleles at the time, there were none regularly producing a larger version with four strings.

For a larger instrument, the taropatch was really the only choice. The taropatch is an eight-string instrument with a body that is larger than the body of a soprano ukulele. The eight strings are in four unison pairs, tuned and played like a standard ukulele. The taropatch had been a regular part of the Martin ukulele line from nearly the beginning—they were first made in 1916. From the beginning taropatches were available on special order in a four-string version and priced the same as the eight-string version. This option was first mentioned in Martin's price list that went into effect on July 1, 1918, but Martin sold very few of the four-string model. From 1916 to 1923, Martin sold a total of only sixty taropatches of the four-string variety, and twenty-seven of these were in the special mini-dreadnought body shape made for Chas. H. Ditson.

It is difficult to say for certain what company first produced a larger-bodied four-string ukulele as part of its standard offerings, but Lyon & Healy, the large Chicago-based firm, was certainly one of the first. Lyon & Healy introduced what they called a tenor ukulele in their 1922-23 catalog, which was sold under Lyon & Healy's "Washburn" brand, and was 24 ½ inches long. The catalog suggested it be tuned "D, G, B and E—one fifth lower than the ukulele."

In 1925 Martin started to experiment with a new larger-bodied uke, possibly spurred on by correspondence with two different customers. In late April 1925 the Tom Brown Music Co., a Chicago retailer, wrote to Martin asking about a Style 1 four-string taropatch that they had special ordered but not yet received. In the letter they state: "This instrument was ordered as a sample instrument with the intention on our part of carrying these as regular stock if in our opinion they would be popular." The next section of the letter might have whetted Martin's appetite: " The fact that

we have at least six or eight customers dropping in from time to time, all waiting to see this instrument, proves to us that this instrument will be popular."

Martin wrote back apologizing for the delay and offering to send immediately a four-string taropatch in Style 3K that could be used temporarily as a sample, subject to return for full credit when their original order was received. The company apparently liked the sample, as they soon ordered six Style 1 and one Style 2 taropatches, all with four strings.

Before completing the Tom Brown taropatch order Martin received a letter from the New York City Wurlitzer branch also requesting a larger model four-string ukulele. Wurlitzer had a customer by the name of Harry S. Robinson, a performer who they described as having "no equal, I think, not barring Cliff Edwards, better known as 'Ukulele Ike'." Robinson had been trying the Lyon & Healy tenor model, and was looking for something similar but with a little deeper body. He sent detailed diagrams with measurements of the Lyon & Healy tenor, and made suggestions as to how much deeper it should be. The Martin company was in a hugely busy production period at this time in 1925 and was in no position to try to construct a completely new size instrument. They wrote back to Wurlitzer: "Since the making up of a new model requires considerable time, we will first submit for Mr. Robinson's examination a special Ukulele constructed with a Taro Patch body and neck of the same width as a Ukulele." As they made up this special instrument, they must have realized that others might be interested in something similar. C. F. III brought the new instrument and met with Robinson at Wurlitzer's New York City store in the middle of June.

The meeting was likely a success, for just days later they wrote back to the Tom Brown Co.: "In regard to your order for six No. 1 and one No. 2 Taro Patch, Four-String Model, we wish to offer the suggestion that it might improve these instruments for your purpose to have the neck worked to the same dimension as a Ukulele neck, and the strings spaced like the strings on a Ukulele, using a Ukulele bridge. The sample instrument sent you last month had a Taro Patch neck and the strings spaced far apart as on a Taro Patch."

The Tom Brown Co. replied that they thought it would be a "great thing if you would change the neck of the four-string Taro Patch, as per your letter." Martin wrote back, intrigued by the interest: "We find that there is some demand for an instrument of this type on account of the greater volume of tone as compared with the ukulele." C. F. III continues, surveying the interest: "We have in mind to add this number to our ukulele line, calling it a Tenor, or Barytone, Ukulele. What do you think of the sales possibilities of such an instrument?"

The reply from the Tom Brown Co. may have been the final incentive that Martin needed to adjust their line-up:

We believe that the name 'Tenor Ukelele' is better fitted to this instrument than baritone. Lyon & Healy here has had such an instrument on the market for some time, and we have had so many inquiries for one such that we placed the orders for these with you, and just between ourselves, wish to say that we have had the Washburn Tenor Ukelele alongside of this instrument, and it sells at $30.00, and our customers have all, without exception, stated a preference to even your $18.00 instrument. We shall be anxious to receive the instruments into our stock at the earliest possible convenience.

The new instrument was seen as one that could be used by professionals in stage, radio, and recording work. C. F. III wrote in September to Gene Klingman, a performer who was looking to do some recording: "The writer had the pleasure of hearing Mr. Harry Robinson make several records with one of these instruments in the Okeh studio. Comparing it to a No. 5K which Mr. Robinson had been using and to which he was very partial. The large instrument was distinctly superior in the opinion of all of us who heard the test, showing much more volume and 'cutting through', as the studio men say, with much better effect."

Martin eventually chose to call their new instrument a "Concert Ukulele" apparently to highlight the fact that the instrument was intended to have a greater volume than a soprano, making it perfect for performers. That name had first been mentioned to them in a correspondence with Buegeleisen & Ja-

cobson in May of 1925, when they wrote to Martin asking if they manufactured "Concert size Ukuleles." Herbert Keller responded with interest: "We do not make Concert Size Ukuleles. What are they? We are very much interested to learn of this new instrument." The name caused some confusion, and it took some time before everybody started using that name. In September of 1925 both the *Music Trade News* and the *Music Trade Review* carried short articles mentioning Martin's "New Baritone Ukulele." Buegeleisen & Jacobson wrote in to Martin having seen the notice in the trade papers and asked about the "Baritone Ukulele." Martin replied that "we have on file your order for two Tenor, or baritone or Concert Ukuleles No. 1" all of which meant the same thing at the time. The concert ukulele was added to the Martin price list in September of 1925, taking the place of the discontinued tenor banjo.

Concert Ukulele Specifications: Style 1C

1925:	Solid mahogany top and back (both one-piece), sides, and neck. Twelve fret rosewood fingerboard. Bar frets. Rosewood bound top and back. Wood friction pegs. Mahogany bridge. Maple nut. Small circular position markers on fingerboard, one each at the fifth and ninth frets, two at the seventh fret. Stamp on back of headstock and inside body.
1927:	Grover Simplex tuners with black buttons replace wooden friction pegs.
1932:	Large logo decals used on headstock.
1934:	Small logo decals on headstock. No stamp on back of headstock.
1936:	Celluloid tortoise shell binding replaces the rosewood binding.
1942-1945:	At times during the Second World War wooden pegs were used again instead of patent tuners
1946	Champion tuners with black buttons. These tuners were first inventoried in 1946, but may have been used in the later 1930s also.
1947:	T-frets become standard equipment.
1965:	Discontinued.

Style 0C | # Style 1C

ca. 1931

ca. 1928

Style 2C

ca. 1925

Style 3C

ca. 1928

Style 1KC

Style 2KC

ca. 1924

ca. 1936

Style 3KC

ca. 1928

Style 5KC

ca. 1925

Tenor Ukuleles

Lyon & Healy introduced their tenor ukulele in their 1922-23 catalog. The Washburn tenor was 24 ½ inches long overall. Martin introduced its concert ukulele in 1925, breaking into the four-string larger-bodied ukulele market. The Martin concert ukulele was 23 inches long overall. Soon many other companies also introduced larger models. Most companies referred to these as tenor ukuleles. Gibson put out its tenor ukulele by 1928. At 25 inches long, the Gibson tenor was bigger and deeper-bodied than many of the other oversized ukuleles already on the market.

In July of 1927, Martin answered a customer who had asked if they make a tenor ukulele. C. F. III's responded: "We do not list a Tenor Ukulele but we make a Concert Ukulele which we consider better than the Tenor Ukulele because the scale is not quite as long. We have found that the Tenor and Concert Ukulele are so near alike that we do not care to make both."

However, less than one year later Martin introduced its own Tenor Ukulele. Because no 1928 correspondence survives, the origins of the tenor ukulele are far less detailed than the origins of the concert ukulele. Based on the comments above, Martin was not interested in offering another ukulele that was only slightly bigger than its concert ukulele. They also likely didn't want to have to go to the trouble of coming up with a completely new body size for the new instrument. However, at the time, Martin was experiencing a big drop off in ukulele sales and was willing to experiment to satisfy customers.

Martin had been making tiples for many years using its obsolete terz guitar body molds. By 1928 interest in the tiple was declining. Martin made the decision to make a larger four-string ukulele using the same molds they used to make tiples and the Martin tenor ukulele was designed. It was 25 ½ inches overall and very nearly three inches deep. It was a far different instrument than the concert ukulele. Giving the new instrument a style designation of 1T, the Martin tenor ukulele had a more guitar-like pin bridge and an extended fretboard with a total of 17 frets.

In 1960 the design of the Martin tenor ukulele was changed. Before 1960 the neck met the body at the twelfth fret, but the post 1960 tenors have a neck that connects at the fourteenth fret. Fans of Martin guitars already know that a similar change was made to the Martin guitar line in the early 1930s. By 1934 Martin was offering nearly its entire guitar line in fourteen fret versions. What most people don't know is that Martin also tried out the fourteen fret tenor ukulele in the 1930s. According to production records, Martin made four fourteen fret tenors in 1934, and three more in both 1935 and 1936. There is a pattern in the Martin archives dated April 2, 1936 for a fourteen-fret tenor ukulele, where some experimentation was being done.

Martin ceased ukulele production in Nazareth in 1994, then started making sopranos again in 2005. Tenor-sized ukuleles are possibly the most popular size among serious modern ukulele players, and many hoped that Martin would again re-introduce their tenor sized instruments. These players got their wish in 2011 when Martin announced new Style 2 tenor ukuleles in both mahogany and koa.

MARTIN *TENOR* UKULELE

Style No. 1-T

MAHOGANY BODY, BOUND WITH ROSEWOOD; MAHOGANY NECK;
ROSEWOOD FINGER BOARD AND BRIDGE; EBONY NUT,
IVORY SADDLE, BLACK PINS.
RUBBED LACQUER FINISH, DARK COLOR.

Tone of Guitar Quality, with Great Carrying Power

Price, $25.00

Tenor Ukulele Specifications: Style 1T

1928:	Solid mahogany top and back (both two-piece), sides, and neck. Seventeen fret rosewood fingerboard, twelve frets to the body. Bar frets. Rosewood bound top. Grover Simplex tuners with black buttons. Rosewood pin bridge with black pins. Ebony nut. Circular position markers on fingerboard, one each at the fifth and tenth frets, two at the seventh fret. Stamp on back of headstock and inside body.
1932:	Large logo decals used on headstock.
1934:	Small logo decals on headstock. No stamp on back of headstock.
ca. 1934	T-frets replace bar frets.
1936:	Tortoise shell celluloid binding replaces rosewood.
1942-1945:	At times during the Second World War wooden pegs were used again instead of patent tuners
1946	Champion tuners with black buttons. These tuners were first inventoried in 1946, but may have been used in the later 1930s also.
1960	Neck with fourteen frets to the body. Position marks at frets five, seven, ten, twelve, and fifteen. "Made in U.S.A." added to stamp inside soundhole.
1994	Discontinued.

Left: One of the final studio photos of the 12 fret tenor taken in the late 1950s.

Right: One of the first studio photos of the new 14 fret tenor taken in the early 1960s.

Style 1T

Style 2KT

ca. 1950

ca. 1929

Style 3T

ca. 1929

Style 5KT

ca. 1929

Baritone Ukulele: Style B51

The largest member of the ukulele family, the baritone ukulele, was first developed in the late 1940s. In a 1951 baritone ukulele self-teaching method book written by Herk Favilla, it is stated that "Favilla was the first to manufacture the Baritone Ukulele." This may be true, but at around the same time the Vega Company of Boston, Massachusetts was working on their version of the instrument. The Vega baritone ukulele was designed by banjoist Eddie Connors. Story has it that Arthur Godfrey asked Connors to design the instrument for him when Connors was employed by Vega.

Under the leadership of C. F. III, the Martin company was rather conservative, and did not generally dive into new markets as soon as they appeared. This was certainly the case for the baritone ukulele, for it was a full ten years after its introduction before Martin decided to move forward with its own version.

Although they likely did not know it at the time, Martin did play a role in the development of the Arthur Godfrey baritone ukulele designed by Eddie Connors for Vega. This fact only came to light because Martin eventually purchased the Vega Co. in 1970, and took hold of historical documents from the company. Among these documents are quite a number of pieces pertaining to the original construction of the Vega Arthur Godfrey baritone ukulele.

It appears from these documents that Vega was contemplating a new design as far back as 1948. One typed sheet refers to the new instrument as the "Vega Tenor

Paper pattern made from a 1948 Martin tenor ukulele. This pattern appears to have been used by the Vega Company as a basis for its new baritone ukulele model. It was signed at the bottom by Eddie Connors, in 1949.

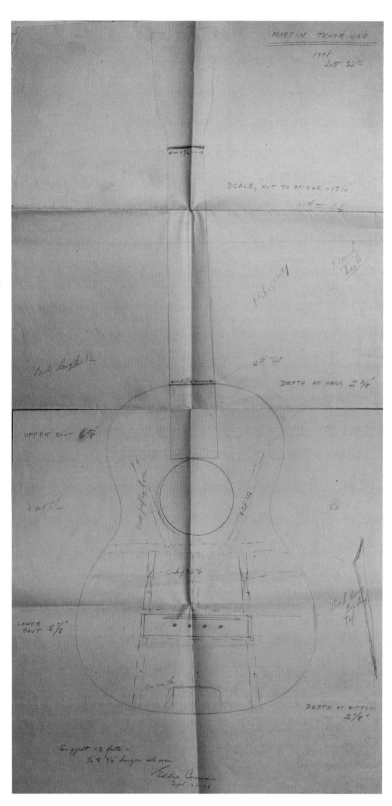

Ukulele," but the word tenor is crossed out by hand and replaced with the word "baritone." Another has a heading: "Production June 1950 Baritone Ukulele" and "First 25 sample lot" and provides information about the labor and setup costs of putting out this lot.

From a Martin perspective, the most interesting piece from the Vega archives is a paper pattern. It is a carefully drawn pattern labeled on top "MARTIN TENOR UKE, 1948, List 32.00." The pattern shows the dimensions and bracing pattern of a Martin tenor ukulele. On the bottom it reads: "Suggest 13 frets, 1/2" to 3/4" larger all over" and is signed "Eddie Connors, Sept 23, 49." So, as it turns out, the Vega Arthur Godfrey model baritone ukulele was designed to basically be a larger version of the Martin tenor ukulele.

Martin made its first batch of three baritone ukuleles in June of 1960. Some of the early baritones, perhaps just the first batch, were made with tie bridges but soon they were making them with the standard pin bridges. The baritone did not change much at all from that point on. Like other models of Martin ukuleles, the baritone was only available by special order after 1977. It remained a part of the Martin line until ukulele production in Nazareth ceased in 1994. To date, it is the only size Martin ukulele that has not been reissued.

Style B51

ca. 1960

Right: This ukulele may be one of the first baritone ukuleles made by Martin in 1960. The unusual features, the tie bridge and the large fretboard position dots, suggest it may have been a very early model if not a prototype.

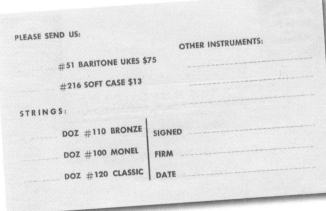

PLEASE SEND US:

OTHER INSTRUMENTS:

#51 BARITONE UKES $75

#216 SOFT CASE $13

STRINGS:

DOZ #110 BRONZE   SIGNED

DOZ #100 MONEL   FIRM

DOZ #120 CLASSIC   DATE

Above: Postcard sent to dealers with ordering information about Martin's new baritone ukulele model, including accessories like the soft shell case and strings.

Style B51   Custom Koa Baritone

ca. 1960s

ca. 1980s

Custom Spruce Top Baritone

Custom 5K Baritone

ca. 1980s

ca. 1980s

Custom Ukuleles Made for Individuals

Under the supervision of Frank Henry Martin, the Martin Co. was always ready to try new things to meet the public's needs. When there was a demand from a large number of people, new models were created. Even when the demand was from a single person, Martin was often willing to meet the needs of the individual. There are many letters in the Martin correspondence files requesting special models, unusual inlays, and other custom features. Except during their busiest periods, Martin was agreeable to most requests.

Don Becker

A small wooden box in the Martin archives holds various metal stamps that were used by the company to mark instruments. There are Martin stamps and stamps of a number of companies for whom Martin made instruments. Among the stamps is one odd one, however. The stamp reading "Made Especially for Don Becker" stands out as the only one that was made for use on one specific instrument. One might assume that it was used on a very fancy guitar at some point, but it turns out it was instead made for use on a ukulele—a one of a kind ukulele.

The story of the custom ukulele made for Donald Becker is a veritable saga in the Martin correspondence files. Donald Becker was a ukulele-playing radio performer in Cincinnati in the late 1920s before going on to co-write the long-running radio soap opera "Life Can Be Beautiful." The Wurlitzer company wrote to Martin in January of 1929, saying the Mr. Becker was "very anxious to procure the very finest ukulele that can be made." They sent along special designs for the headstock and the fret markers, and asked that Martin stamp the ukulele inside "Made Expressly for Don Becker." Martin wrote back the day after receiving the letter. They were excited about the idea, opening their reply: "The opportunity you give us to make up a special Ukulele for Mr. Don Becker is too good to miss and we assure you we will do everything we can to provide Mr. Becker with a very fine ukulele." They did not know what they were getting themselves into.

Martin suggested a Style 5K type of instrument,

MADE ESPECIALLY FOR DON BECKER

but made of figured mahogany. They mention their fondness for this wood, relating that if they could get enough figured mahogany that they would use it on all their fine ukuleles "because we think it is finer for tone than Curly Koa." For ornamentation, they said that they would incorporate the designs sent by Mr. Becker as well as conventional ornaments at other frets. They suggested that Mr. Becker might prefer to have his name inlaid on the fingerboard instead of the headstock, mentioning that they had inlaid "Ukulele Lady" on the fingerboard of the custom May Singhi Breen ukulele they had made a few years earlier.

Martin wrote again in February, giving details of the ornamentation they planned for the ukulele. They had made arrangements with a New York City engraver to engrave Mr. Becker's name and coat of arms in gold and black on a veneer of pearl Pyralin for the peg head. The body was to be made of "Curly Mahogany, finished dark with Duco lacquer." The pegs were to "be of internal gear type, as small as possible." The instrument was to be supplied with a $20 "plush lined case, with zipper coverite to protect the instrument." A proud C. F. III wrote: "This makes a hundred dollar outfit and we believe it will be the handsomest Ukulele outfit we have ever offered." The instrument was entered into the order book on February 20th: "1 Special Uke in case for Don Becker" It was the most expensive ukulele Martin had ever booked.

Pyralin was a type of pearly plastic veneer made by the DuPont Corporation that is today affectionately referred to by vintage instrument collectors as "mother-of-toilet-seat." Although it had been in use on various toiletries for a number of years, in 1929 Pyralin was a relatively new material in the world of musical instruments. At that time it was primarily being used on banjos, including some high-end instruments. It was not a material with which Martin had experience, so they wrote to Epi Stathopoulo of the Epiphone Banjo Corporation requesting information. Stathopoulo eventually sent Martin a piece of Pyralin three inches wide by twelve inches long, which Martin had engraved as per Mr. Becker's instructions.

The ukulele was completed and sent off to Cincinnati, but Martin did not hear back right away. C. F. III wrote a short note to Wurlitzer in April: "We are wondering whether Mr. Becker was pleased with the special Ukulele we made for him. We will appreciate a report from you." The reply they received must have been quite unexpected.

Wurlitzer wrote that Mr. Becker was "sadly disappointed" in the ukulele. He was unhappy with the engraving that had been done on the Pyralin fingerboard, and was not impressed with the instrument's

tone. Ralph Rigio, the Wurlitzer representative, said he too was disappointed in the appearance of the ukulele calling the engraving "exceptionally bad." Mr. Becker refused to accept the instrument, and Rigio worried about losing the sale, noting "we fear he is liable to go over to Gibson's for his special job."

C. F. III replied, suggesting he meet with Rigio and Becker at the Wurlitzer store when he visits Cincinnati in the coming weeks. The next letter from Wurlitzer states that they are returning the instrument for the work that had been discussed in this meeting. This work included removing all the Pyralin, having "Don Becker" inlaid on the headstock in pearl, and sanding down the entire body to "increase the volume of tone." Martin estimated the work would take two to three weeks. Presumably Mr. Becker was ultimately satisfied with the instrument, as the only further correspondence regarding the ukulele came nearly three years later when it was sent back to Martin to have the bridge replaced.

It is interesting to note that what was likely Martin's first, and last, instrument to feature a Pyralin fretboard and headstock veneer was stripped of its Pyralin just months after it was built.

In the 1930s Pyralin became a popular material for use on the fretboard and headstock of inexpensive ukuleles. *From left:* Bruno Maxitone, P'mico by Harmony, Art Nouveau by Harmony, Unknown maker crystal finish, Vagabond by Harmony.

May Singhi Breen

May Singhi Breen was a popular radio star of the 1920s known as the Ukulele Lady. She partnered with songwriter Peter DeRose, who she eventually married. Breen was a vocal advocate for the ukulele as a serious musical instrument, and wrote method books, did ukulele arrangements for sheet music, and even recorded a 78 RPM ukulele lesson for Victor Records. She is also the single person who ordered more custom ukuleles from Martin than any other.

Breen was an early adopter of the top-of-the-line Martin 5K ukulele. She posed with her 5K in many of her early photos used in method books and sheet music from the mid 1920s onward. In 1924 Wm. J. Smith published Breen's ukulele method. It featured photos of the various chord positions, and the Martin 5K is displayed prominently. In 1925 Smith wrote to Martin about having a special ukulele made up for Breen: "You have no doubt heard of May Singhi Breen the popular radio artist and teacher of the *N.Y. Graphic* Ukulele club," wrote Smith (The *New York Graphic* was a tabloid newspaper of the time). Smith ordered a special ukulele, a "#5 mahogany." He told Martin they wanted to put a plate on the headstock reading: "Presented to etc. etc." In the busy year of 1925 a special order like this would generally take quite some time, but coincidentally Martin had already begun working on a Style 5 mahogany model. Frank Henry wrote to Smith "It has been so difficult to secure the fine koa required for this number that we have been considering the use of figured mahogany, which costs about as much as Koa but it is much easier to get, and we are inclined to believe has a better tone." He went on to say that they had made three of these mahogany Style 5 ukuleles, and they were already in the finishing room. He suggested the headstock veneer could easily be changed later to allow for a plaque. He sent all three mahogany Style 5s to Smith to let him select one.

Smith was interested in the new model, and not just the one for Breen. Before receiving the three ukuleles he wrote to Martin and said "I suppose you will not object if we keep a couple of them instead on one." Martin shipped the three Style 5 mahogany ukuleles along with two Style 5K ukuleles that Smith had previously ordered. As it turned out, Breen chose one of the 5Ks over the new mahogany models. Still Smith kept and apparently sold two of the three mahogany Style 5s, and returned the third a few weeks later. At the time of the return he wrote about having another instrument made up for Breen.

Smith ordered a "special ukulele, made with mahogany body, but not figured." He requested a very dark finish and suggested that the ukulele should "retail for about $75." In Smith's words that meant it would have "about $50 worth of inlay." He suggested mother-of-pearl inlay around the headstock "similar to the way you inlay your Style 45 Guitars." He also suggested gold-plated tuning pegs.

This ukulele was entered into the order book as a "Special Style 3," although its specifications in many ways were more similar to those of a Style 5 instrument. C. F. III wrote back and suggested that

Custom Style 5 ukulele made for May Singhi Breen circa 1930.

they "inlay Miss Breen's full name or initials on the headpiece of the instrument instead of the usual pearl design." At first Smith thought this was a good idea, but he soon reconsidered. He wrote to Martin: "We have decided not to put Mrs. Breen's name or initials on the ukulele that you are making for her. You can make it up the way you think would look best without the initials." He went on to explain his decision: "Mrs. Breen owes me quite a bit of money, and it is possible that we will have a break with her before long, and I figured that if we had her name put on the instrument we would be unable to sell it to anyone else, but it will be easily enough sold if it is just made up in a general way." This ukulele was completed and sent to Smith at the beginning of December. At the time it was the fanciest (and most expensive) ukulele that the Martin company had ever made.

In February C. F. III wrote the following letter to Smith:

A few days ago our mutual friend, The Ukulele Lady, May Singhi Breen, paid us an unexpected visit, much to our surprise and delight. We enjoyed the music which she gave us and news she had from the professional field in New York.

She instructed us to make another special Ukulele for her, using selected Curly Mahogany, inlaid like the one we sent you about two years ago, with the addition of having her name inlaid in the head plate, and the words 'Ukulele Lady' inlaid in the fingerboard. She directed us to forward the instrument to you for her, saying that she always bought her Ukuleles through you if possible.

We have booked the order in your name, according to the acknowledgement enclosed. Is this satisfactory to you?

Smith wrote back to say "it will be alright to book the order and when it's ready ship it to us." Martin, however, shipped the ukulele directly to Breen when it was completed. Smith wrote again in June:"In regard to the special ukulele that you shipped to May Singhi Breen, I am sorry that you shipped this directly to her. She owes us two or three hundred dollars, which has been on our books for more than two years, and she's a pretty hard customer to get any money from." He was hoping to send it to her C. O. D., and explained that he was "afraid I'll have a deuce of a time trying to collect for this instrument."

The May Singhi Breen ukulele was one of, if not the, fanciest ukulele that the Martin Co. ever manufactured. The inlaying on the fingerboard may have been a Martin first, although the inlay work was actually done by a specialist in New York and not at the Martin factory. Having "UKULELE LADY" inlaid on the fingerboard may well have been the idea that led Martin to suggest to Jimmie Rodgers that he have his name inlaid on the fingerboard of the 000-45 he special ordered in 1928. Soon afterwards, large numbers of cowboy and country singers were sporting guitars with their own names on the fingerboard.

Breen wrote to Martin in July of 1927 to say how pleased she

"Ukulele Special" made for May Singhi Breen in 1927 and built to her own specifications. It is almost certainly the fanciest ukulele Martin had ever made at the time. In the early 1930s Breen had the ukulele electrified, and unfortunately it was permanently altered.

was with the ukulele. "I should have written you long ago to tell you how thrilled I was with the Ukulele Special. I have received a lot of publicity over it...The Ukulele is wonderful...It sure was worth waiting for and without a doubt the best Ukulele in existence."

She included a newspaper clip about how she had been presented the ukulele by her husband as part of a celebration of her fourth anniversary on the radio. The article mentions "the instrument is strikingly handsome with a beautiful pearl inlay which reads 'May Singhi Breen – The Ukulele Lady.'"

Breen had at least two other custom ukuleles made for her by Martin in the following years. One is another curly mahogany Style 5, and one is a Style 5K. Both have "Ukulele Lady" inlaid on the fingerboard and her name inlaid on the headstock.

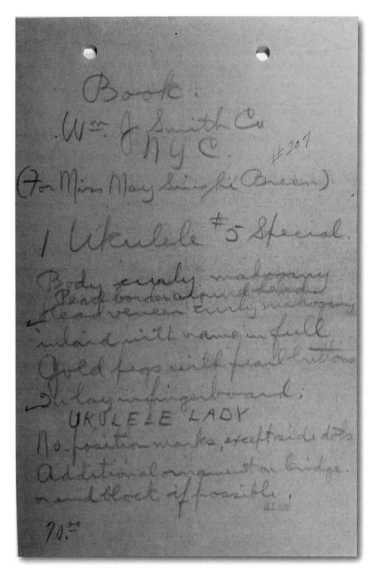

Right: The original order for the #5 Special ukulele made for May Singhi Breen in 1927.

Below: A special two ukulele carrying case, with two of May Singhi Breen's ukuleles still inside. The ukulele on the bottom is a standard 1930s era Style 3, while the ukulele on top is a 5K with custom inlays on the fingerboard and headstock.

Custom Ukuleles for Other Individuals

Buster Keaton

In March of 1924 Tom Murray wrote to Martin from the Charlie Chaplin Studios of Los Angeles, CA. Murray was an actor who had worked in a number of movies, some with Chaplin himself. Murray had purchased a Martin ukulele from the Southern California Music Company, and was now interested in ordering one to be presented to Buster Keaton: "I want to make Buster Keaton a present of a taropatch uke one good one with screw keys and his name BUSTER KEATON in mother of pearl below the bridge or around the sounding hole." Murray hoped to have the ukulele shipped directly to him rather than through a music store, noting that he had many picture friends and that he might sell quite a few of these custom inlaid ukuleles. Martin responded, but sent Murray to their sole agent in the region, the Southern California Music Co. to make the order. Martin suggested the name be inlaid on the headstock, noting "we do not consider it advisable to inlay on the body."

A few weeks later, Martin received the order from SoCal, for one Style 3 taropatch with "the name 'Buster Keaton' inlaid as per letter." The sale was recorded in April of 1924. This taropatch is likely the same one Keaton is seen with in his 1930 movie *Doughboys*. At one point in the movie, Keaton's co-star Cliff Edwards uses two drumsticks to play a tune on the taropatch as Keaton holds the instrument and frets the chords.

H. & A. Selmer

Although the Company was producing far more instruments than it ever previously had, in 1922 they still were willing to build unusual instruments to the specifications of the customer. A series of letters between Martin and H. & A. Selmer shows that Martin very nearly made an odd variation of its taropatch. C. F. III's reply to Selmer's request for the special instrument explains that it will take about six weeks and confirms the instrument's specifications: "We understand what you want is a regular four-string Taro-Patch with Patent Pegs, but with a body of the same shape as our Flat Mandolin. The top, of course, would be flat like a Taro-Patch and not beveled back of the bridge like a Mandolin. The bridge would be the same as on a regular Taro-Patch. We will await confirmation of the order."

Unfortunately, the order was never completed. Selmer wrote back to let Martin know that the customer "has decided to use one of the Martin taro-patches we have in stock, having it rebuilt to suit his ideas. We are taking care of this matter in our shop."

Al Peterman

In August of 1925, A. M. Peterman wrote to Martin requesting a 5K soprano with his name inlaid. The reply from Martin let him know the charge would be fifty cents per letter—a total of five dollars. After hearing the price, Peterman requested that Martin just inlay his nickname, "AL." The ukulele was never completed though. Peterman wrote again in October and cancelled the order, saying he was "in no position to handle this at present." He instructed Martin to keep the dollar he had sent for the inlaying, to "help you to pay for the trouble I have put you to." C. F. III wrote back, saying that the order had been cancelled. As always, the company treated the customer fairly. They also returned the dollar, noting "since that work had not yet been started, there is (no) reason why we should retain the money."

Johnie Dunn

Johnie Dunn wrote to Martin in 1925 hoping to get a discount on a 5K ukulele he wanted to use as a back-up to his main instrument. He ordered a 5K in December of 1926 with his name inlaid on the headstock. It is one of a very rare group of surviving examples of custom model Martin ukuleles from the prime era of ukulele popularity.

Katsuyuki Yoshida

In 2001 Eric Clapton had Martin build him a custom OM-45 guitar. Katsuyuki Yoshida, a good friend of Clapton from Japan, ordered a very special ukulele from Martin around the same time, with some of the same features found on Clapton's guitar. Martin made a custom Style 45 Concert ukulele for Yoshida, with a spruce top, Brazilian rosewood back and sides, and pearl inlay around the body, soundhole, and on the headstock.

Left: Long time Martin employee Fred Castner poses with the Clapton/Yoshida ukulele while it was being built. *Right:* Martin's Dick Boak with the completed ukulele.

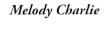
Melody Charlie

In regular production, Martin only manufactured concert-sized ukuleles in one style, Style 1C. Occasionally they would make custom concert ukuleles, like this rare Style 5K Concert. No record could be found for this particular ukulele in the Martin archives, but it was likely made in the late 1920s or early 1930s. Style 5K Concert ukuleles are extremely rare, this is almost certainly the only one with custom inlay. Another custom feature on this ukulele is the set of geared tuners.

Custom Sunburst Tenor

This unique instrument is another of Martin's mysteries. Featuring a sunburst-stained spruce top and Brazilian rosewood back and sides, as well as Style 5K style pearl inlay, this ukulele is truly one of a kind. Likely dating to the 1930s, no specific mention of this instrument could be found in the Martin archives.

Mystery Style 3

Nothing is known about the origins of this very unusual Style 3 soprano. It features solid ivory friction pegs and a mandolin-style bridge, as well as a two-piece back with an inlaid center strip. The fact that it has no fingerboard inlays suggests it may have been made before 1918. It has the Martin stamp inside the soundhole (twice) but not on the back of the headstock.

Grandma's Ukulele

This ukulele was special-ordered by a music store owner when Mike Longworth was working at Martin. Longworth did the inlay work, including inlay on the sides of the body, and the custom fingerboard and headstock inlays.

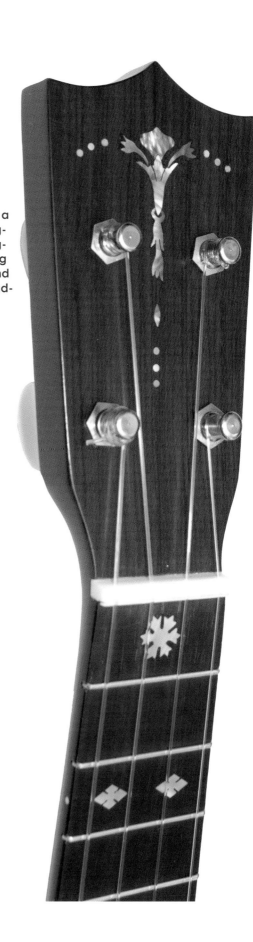

Martin Employee Instruments

Employee "5K" Style Taropatch

Martin made taropatches in Styles 1, 2, and 3, in both mahogany and koa. They never made a Style 5K taropatch, even on special order. That makes this employee instrument the next best thing. Made of solid koa wood and bound top and back with pearl, the body is very much what a Style 5K would look like. The bound extended fretboard is another 5K feature. The fingerboard inlays are like those from a Style 3. There is no pearl inlay on the headstock, as would be found on a typical Style 5K. The headstock features a large guitar-style decal, similar to those used on some ukuleles around 1933.

Employee Soprano #1

Employee Soprano #2

The soprano ukuleles on this page and on the previous page are both Martin employee instruments. Each of these instruments was most likely built in the late teens. Both feature spruce tops and Brazilian rosewood back and sides. Each also has a unique guitar-like bridge.

Employee Taropatch

This unique taropatch was made by Martin employee Charles N. Anglemire. Anglemire worked for Martin from 1906 to 1917. It features a solid ivory bridge, ornate headstock inlays, and top-of-the-line mandolin tuners with inlaid buttons.

Martin Ukuleles Made for Other Companies

Determining the exact number of ukuleles made by Martin but marked with the names of other companies is not possible. There are simply too many missing or contradictory pieces of information in the Martin archives for anyone to be able to state exact totals.

Most of the information for these numbers comes from the original sales and order ledger books still held in the archive. Prior to 1922, when ukuleles were sold any special marks were generally noted in the sales ledger. A record reading "8 Uke No. 1 Smith Stamp" would denote eight Style 1 ukuleles marked with a special stamp bearing the name of the Wm. J. Smith Co. rather then the standard Martin stamp. The only companies that had their own special stamps used prior to 1922 were Ditson, Smith, and the Southern California Music Company. In 1922 Martin started to push the idea of Customer Model instruments and a number of other companies got their own stamps on the ukuleles they ordered. Many of these ukuleles had slight differences in their specifications, to make them look a little different than the standard Martin line. In 1922 Martin marked these Customer Models in their sales books by appending a "C" after the style. A sales ledger entry of "10 uke No. 2-C" was used to denote ten Style 2 Customer Model ukuleles. Most of the minor differences made to these customer models lasted only about a year, and by the beginning of 1923 Martin was simply supplying their regular models with the stamp of the particular distributor. Between 1923 and 1925 many of the Customer Model ukuleles had the standard Martin stamp inside the soundhole and the special customer stamp on the headstock only. In some cases, both the Martin stamp and the customer stamp were used on the headstock. The Customer Model designation had been discontinued well before 1925 when the new concert-sized ukulele took over the "C" notation.

Bergstrom Music Company

In December of 1907, Martin made six ukuleles for the Bergstrom Music Company of Honolulu, Hawaii. The specifications for these ukuleles are unknown. It is also not known whether these instruments were marked with the Martin name. Assuming that Bergstrom sold these instruments, they may have added a paper label inside the soundhole, as they did with ukuleles made for them by various Hawaiian manufacturers.

Buegeleisen & Jacobson (S. S. Stewart)

Buegeleisen & Jacobson, also known as B&J, was a New York City based jobbing firm. Jobbers were musical instrument distributors who bought instruments from various manufacturers and sold the goods to musical retailers through their catalogs. B&J had a number of trade names under which they sold instruments, including Mele and S. S. Stewart. B&J added their Mele label to some of the Martin ukuleles they sold, but when Martin offered them a Customer Line, they chose to sell their Martins under the S. S. Stewart name.

Buegeleisen & Jacobson

Martin Style	1922	1923	1924	1925	1926	Total
0	0	0	150	150	25	325

Chas. H. Ditson & Co.

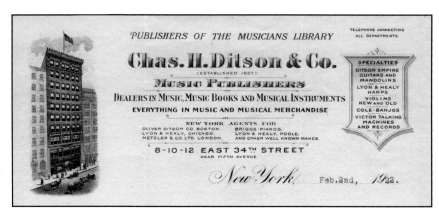

In correspondence with The Southern California Music Company in the summer of 1915, Martin mentions that they are starting to build ukuleles for "the New York Trade." Although no particular dealer is mentioned, there is no doubt that Martin was referring primarily to Chas. H. Ditson & Co., the New York retail branch of the Boston-based Oliver Ditson Company. In July of 1915 the Martin expense book shows that $3.25 was used to purchase "1 Steel stamp 'Oliver Ditson Co,'" a stamp that would eventually be used to denote ukuleles and guitars made for both the Chas. H. Ditson store in New York City and the Oliver Ditson Co. store in Boston. The earliest production ukuleles made for Chas. Ditson received separate serial numbers from the ukuleles Martin was selling to all other retailers. In the beginning, Ditson ordered more ukuleles from Martin than all other customers combined. A total of 170 Ditson-stamped ukuleles received serial numbers before Martin decided to stop numbering ukuleles, while only 140 Martin ukuleles received numbers during that same period. These Ditson ukuleles were identical to the early Martin ukuleles, with the exception of the stamps used.

In 1916 Martin began to make ukuleles for Ditson with a special body shape. Ditson's small goods department manager Harry Hunt worked with John Deichman at Martin designing a unique line of instruments. Guitars in three sizes were developed, along with ukuleles and taropatches, all with the unusually wide waists that set these instruments apart from the standard Martin line. The largest of these guitars was given the dreadnought designation, named for the Royal Navy's Dreadnought, a battleship launched in 1906. Collectors today often refer to the Ditson ukuleles as mini or baby dreadnoughts, but at the time Martin denoted them simply as "Ditson Models."

When reading through Martin sales ledgers, it is not always easy to tell whether a ukulele being sold to Ditson is a special Ditson model or a standard Martin model with a Ditson stamp. When taropatches were added to the Martin line-up in 1916, the very first models were sold to Ditson. On the first few taropatch orders, some were denoted as "Spanish Models" while others were "Regular Models." The "Spanish Model" was most likely used to denote the new body shape being made for Ditson. When the first ukuleles with the new shape were sold to Ditson in November of 1916, they were denoted in the sales ledger as "Ditson Ukes" "Own Model." Two each were sold in Styles 1, 2, and 3. Later Martin ledger shorthand would use the letters D. M. (Ditson Model) or D. H. M. (presumably Ditson-Hunt Model) to denote ukuleles with the special Ditson body shape.

Soon however, the sales book starts listing Ditson taropatches by Ditson model number. The various model numbers were 14, 18, 24, 28, 34, and 38. Based on the pricing, it seems obvious that the Ditson numbers were based on the style number (first digit) and the number of strings (second digit). Thus, a Style 18 Ditson was an eight-stringed taropatch with Style 1 specifications and the special Ditson body shape, and a Style 34 was a four-stringed taropatch with Style 3 specifications. Oddly, one Ditson Style 35 was sold late in 1916, which, if it followed the same numbering scheme, would suggest a five-string model of some sort.

Ditson made many special requests on the various early ukulele and taropatch models, and Martin seemed happy to oblige. Some of the early Style 3 Ditson ukuleles and taropatches were specially "varnished and polished," an option for which Martin charged $1.50 per instrument. Beginning in 1917 Ditson sometimes ordered ukuleles without pegs, an option for which they were credited twenty cents per instrument. On many of these models Ditson fitted Champion Key "patent" pegs in place of the wooden pegs that Martin was using at the time. Ditson also ordered their ukuleles with non-standard fingerboard inlays. In 1919, when Martin was still placing fret markers on the fifth, seventh, and ninth frets, Ditson put in a large order for Style 1 Ditson Models with position marks at the third, fifth, seventh, and tenth frets, with side position markers as well. Ditson Model Style 3 ukuleles also show a number of different fretboard inlay patterns. Some are marked at frets five, seven, and ten, while others have inlays at the third and or fifteenth frets as well.

In addition to their "Own Model," Ditson sometimes would order "Regular Model" ukuleles with the Ditson stamp. Eventually Martin started to consistently denote Ditson model ukuleles with a D.M. designation in their sales ledgers. After Martin phased out their Customer Model lines around the beginning of 1923, they began to put their name back on all of the instruments they were making. Ukuleles made for Ditson after this time generally had the Ditson stamp on the back of the headstock and the Martin stamp inside the soundhole.

Chas. H. Ditson Models

	1915	1916	1917	1918	1919	1920	1921	1922	1923	1924	1925	1926	Totals
Martin Models with Oliver Ditson Stamp													
Style 1	3	250											
Style 2	0	143											
Style 3	0	99											
Style 1 Taropatch	0	13											
Style 2 Taropatch	0	6											
Style 3 Taropatch	0	6											
Style 1 Taropatch (4 string)	0	1											
Style 2 Taropatch (4 string)	0	0											
Style 3 Taropatch (4 string)	0	0											
Totals	3	518											521
Ditson Models with Oliver Ditson Stamp													
Style 0	0	0	0	0	0	0	0	168	73	75	120	100	**536**
Style 1	0	15	222	104	453	100	51	111	24	72	108	100	**1360**
Style 2	0	2	40	0	40	50	52	37	24	18	12	50	**325**
Style 3	0	2	105	0	0	50	3	15	21	18	24	50	**288**
Style 1K	0	0	0	0	0	0	12	0	0	0	0	0	**12**
Style 2K	0	0	0	0	0	0	0	0	0	0	0	0	**0**
Style 3K	0	0	0	0	0	0	0	0	0	0	0	0	**0**
Style 5K	0	0	0	0	0	0	0	3	9	0	10	0	**22**
Style 1 Taropatch	0	40	30	0	0	0	0	0	0	0	0	0	**70**
Style 2 Taropatch	0	20	22	0	0	0	0	0	0	0	0	0	**42**
Style 3 Taropatch	0	26	30	0	0	0	0	0	0	0	0	0	**56**
Style 1 Taropatch (4 string)	0	11	0	0	0	0	0	0	0	0	0	0	**11**
Style 2 Taropatch (4 string)	0	7	0	0	0	0	0	0	0	0	0	0	**7**
Style 3 Taropatch (4 string)	0	9	0	0	0	0	0	0	0	0	0	0	**9**
Totals	0	132	449	104	493	200	118	334	151	183	274	300	**2738**
											Grand Total		**3259**

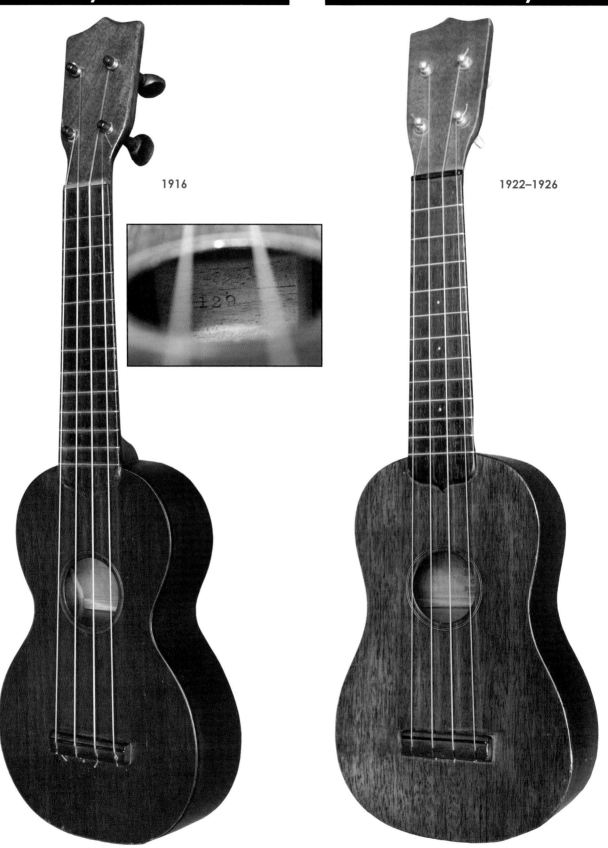

Ditson Style 1: Serial no. 129

1916

Ditson Model: Style 0

1922–1926

Ditson Model: Style 1

Ditson Model: Style 2

1919

1921–1926

1916–1917

1922–1924

Ditson Model: Style 5K   **Ditson Taropatch: Style 3**

1922–1926

1916–1917

Oliver Ditson & Co.

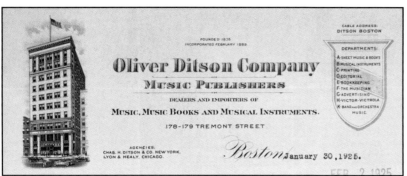
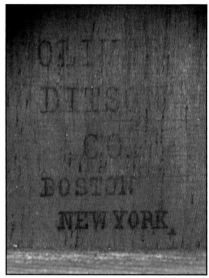

Unlike Wurlitzer or Sherman Clay, whose retail chains received their goods from their headquarters, the Oliver Ditson Co. of Boston and the Chas H. Ditson Co. of New York were run as separate businesses. Each store ordered and paid for their own goods, and they even had different tastes in the instruments they ordered. The Boston store only sold ukuleles in the standard Martin shape, whereas the special Ditson mini-dreadnought models were sold only through the New York City store. Proof of this can be seen in a letter that Martin received from the Oliver Ditson store asking about the "new shape of ukulele No. O, you must have sent us some that were intended for Mr. Hunt." The writer continues: "our salesman did not like the new shape," and requested the standard shape instead.

While the Chas. H. Ditson Co. was probably the customer that prompted Martin to start ukulele production in 1915, the Oliver Ditson Co. didn't purchase its first ukuleles from Martin until July of 1918. The ukuleles purchased by the store were standard Martin models, sometimes with the Ditson stamp and sometimes with the standard Martin markings. When Martin started offering Customer Models to many of their bigger accounts in 1922 there is no indication that Oliver Ditson was made any such offer. This is not surprising, as the Boston Ditson store already was able to have its goods marked with their own stamp. After Martin phased out their Customer Model lines around the beginning of 1923, they began to put their name back on all of the instruments they were making. From this time on the ukuleles made for Ditson had the Ditson stamp on the back of the headstock and the Martin stamp inside the soundhole.

Oliver Ditson (Boston Store)

Martin Style	1918	1919	1920	1921	1922	1923	1924	1925	1926	Total
0	0	0	0	0	144	111	150	50	0	255
1	12	67	0	0	108	25	125	0	0	212
2	0	24	0	0	12	33	75	25	12	81
3	0	0	0	0	6	14	10	12	12	32
1 Taropatch	0	0	0	0	0	4	6	6	6	10
2 Taropatch	0	0	0	0	0	1	3	3	0	1
3 Taropatch	0	0	0	0	0	1	2	2	0	1
Totals	12	91	0	0	270	189	371	98	30	592

Wm. J. Dyer & Bro. (Stetson)

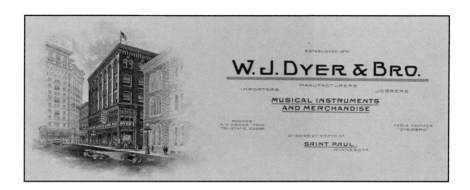

In April of 1922 Martin sent a letter to W. J. Dyer & Bro., a large musical instrument jobber based in St. Paul, Minnesota. The letter mentioned a request from Dyer to sell Martin goods "throughout the northwest." Martin explains that they can make a special "Customers' or 'C' Line; designs differing from our regular designs in inlaying and ornamentation. Styles and prices are the same as our regular line, discount is 50%." They explain that the goods will not bear the Martin name, but can be stamped with "whatever name you wish." In May of the same year Dyer sent Martin a "Stetson" die for stamping the sample instruments that they had ordered. Martin sent Dyer three guitars marked with the Stetson stamp, one 2-17-C, one 0-18-C, and one 0-21-C. They also sent a single Stetson-stamped Style 0-C ukulele. They sent a Style 5K ukulele also, but with a standard Martin stamp. The correspondence notes that the Stetson die was returned with the instrument shipment. There is no sign that Dyer ever ordered any more Customer Models from Martin, although they did continue to order standard Martin stamped instruments.

Wm. J. Dyer & Bro.	
Martin Style	1922
0	1

Grinnell Brothers (Wolverine)

Grinnell Brothers was a retail music chain with its headquarters in Detroit, Michigan. Besides the Detroit store, they also had Michigan branches in Jackson, Pontiac, Flint, Saginaw, Lansing, and Grand Rapids. Grinnell sold instruments under the "Wolverine" brand name, so when Martin suggested a Customer Line to the company, Grinnell chose to stamp the backs of the headstock "Wolverine." Unlike other companies that may have wanted to make customers believe that they were manufacturing their own ukuleles, Grinnell wanted to make sure that buyers would know they were really getting a Martin. Unable to use the Martin name on goods that they might sell in regions that were the sole agency of another retailer, Grinnell chose to have Martin stamp their ukuleles "Made Especially for Grinnell Bros. at Nazareth, PA."

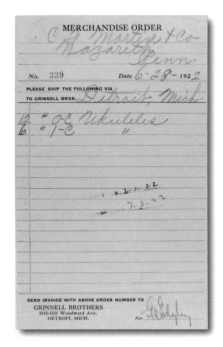

Order from Grinnell Brothers for Customer Model Wolverine ukuleles, 1922

Grinnell Brothers				
Martin Style	1922	1923	1924	Total*
0	30	60	50	90
1	21	36	50	57
2K	0	6	0	6
3K	0	2	0	2
5K	1	2	0	3
Totals	52	106	100	158

J. W. Jenkins Sons' Music Co.

J. W. Jenkins Sons' was a musical instrument retailer and catalog house in Kansas City, Missouri. Although they bought a good number of ukuleles from Martin, there is no indication in any of the sales records that the ukuleles they purchased were anything other than standard Martin instruments. Unlike many other dealers, Jenkins did not take up a special Customer Line of Martin goods.

Montgomery Ward

Montgomery Ward does not really fit in this section, as Martin never made ukuleles that were marked with the Montgomery Ward name. However, Martin did make ukuleles for Ward that were different than their standard instruments. In 1931 Ward ordered a special line of instruments from Martin that included special Martin 0-17S and 2-17 guitars, Style A mandolins, Style 0 soprano ukuleles, as well as special Style 0 concert ukuleles. Before the Montgomery Ward order, Martin had made just one Style 0 concert ukulele back in 1925, the year that the concert ukulele was introduced. Martin made a total of fifty-two Style 0 concert ukuleles for Montgomery Ward in 1931–1932.

MONTGOMERY WARD SALES--1931--1932					Feb 9,1932
	UKE 0	UKE 0-C	GTR 2-17	GTR 0-17S	MAND A
ALBANY	8	4	14	5	3
BALTIMORE	6-4	5	4	12	7-1
CHICAGO	11-7	14-2	13-7	17	2-5
DENVER	5	3	5	5	4
FORT WORTH	2-1	1	2-1	3	2-1
KANSAS CITY	15-12	6	10	6	3
OAKLAND	5	3	3	9	3
PORTLAND	5	3	3	2	5
ST. PAUL	20	8	15-7	11-6	5-5
	77	47	69	70	34
RETURNS:	24	2	15	5	12
	53	45	54	65	22
NET VALUE:	265.00	303.75	675.00	1098.50	275.00 $2617.25

Perlberg & Halpin (Beltone)

Perlberg & Halpin was a New York City based musical instrument importer and wholesale dealer. They sold some instruments under their "Beltone" brand (The Beltone brand name of P&H, though misspelled "Belltone" in Mike Longworth's *Martin Guitars: A History*, has only one "L". "Belltone" with two "L"s was a brand that later became a registered trademark of George Mossman, a Hawaiian ukulele maker, in 1928). When Martin offered P&H a Customer Line, they had Martin order them a Beltone Stamp. The stamp was used only briefly, for about a five month period in 1922. Like other ukuleles produced for the Customer Line, Beltone ukuleles had small differences in their specifications from the standard Martin line. Martin sent P&H some Beltone ukuleles with maple nuts instead of the standard ebony, but P&H wrote back asking them to stain the nuts so as to match the color of the ukuleles. An existing example of a Martin Beltone Style 0 appears identical to a standard Martin Style 0 with the exception of a slight variation in the soundhole rosette.

Perlberg & Halpin	
Martin Style	1922
0	53
0 (stained)	27
1	26
2	12
3	12
2K	12
3K	12
Totals	154

H. & A. Selmer, Inc.

H. & A. Selmer, Inc., with offices in New York City and Paris, was, and still is, best known for their woodwind instruments, but in the 1920s their New York City branch dealt in all sorts of musical instruments. In December of 1921 they wrote to Martin asking to be granted an agency for Martin instruments, but were turned away due to the fact that Chas. H. Ditson and Wm. J. Smith were the sole agents for the New York City territory. Just a month later though Martin wrote back offering Selmer a "Customers' Line of goods, similar in price but differing somewhat in design from our regular line." In January of 1923 Selmer purchased one dozen Style 0-C ukuleles from Martin. These were likely stamped with the Selmer stamp, but any changes to the Style 0 specifications that the Selmer ukuleles may have had are unknown.

H. & A. Selmer, Inc.	
Martin Style	1922
0	12

Wm. J. Smith & Co.

With the exception of the Chas. H. Ditson Co., Wm. J. Smith purchased more of Martin's early ukuleles than any other retailer. On some of these very early ukuleles, Smith added a small paper label on the inside of the body near the Martin stamp. One such label can be seen on the Martin ukulele with serial number 105. Smith was one of the first companies after Ditson to have their own stamp made and used on the ukuleles Martin was making for them. Martin ordered steel stamps for Smith and for Southern California Music Co. in August of 1916. Beginning in February of 1917 Smith began to order some of its ukuleles with their own stamp and some with the standard Martin stamp. They continued to order a small number of their ukuleles with the Smith stamp for the remainder of the year, but apparently felt ukuleles with the Martin name were better sellers. No more signs of ukuleles with the Smith stamp are seen in the sales ledgers after December of 1917.

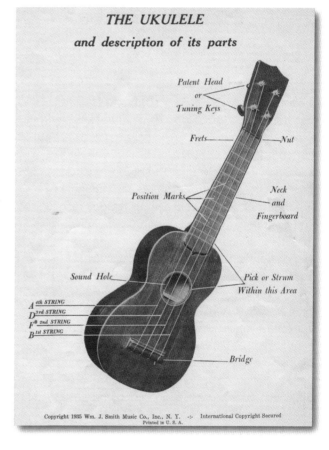

THE UKULELE
and description of its parts

Wm. J. Smith			
Martin Style	1917	1918	Total
1	110	14	124
2	27	0	27
3	2	0	2
Totals	139	14	153

Southern California Music Co.

The very first koa ukuleles Martin made were made by the request of Frank J. Hart's Southern California Music Company. Martin had a special stamp made for the koa guitars they supplied to the company starting in 1916. The same stamp was later used on the first koa wood Martin ukuleles, also made at the request of the company. The first six koa wood ukuleles were sold to SoCal in October of 1917. Noted in the sales ledger, three of the koa ukuleles were made like Styles 1, 2, and 3, and three were "Special Styles" with no further specifications mentioned. In 1919 SoCal ordered fifty Style 1, fifty Style 2, and twenty-five Style 3 ukuleles, as well as one of each style of taropatch all in "Full Koa" (the K designation for koa wood was not yet in use). No other references to ukuleles marked with the Southern California stamp could be found in the Martin archive, but at least one example exists of a mahogany Style 1 marked with their stamp.

Southern California Music Company

Martin Style	1917	1918	1919	Total
1K	1	0	50	51
2K	1	0	50	51
3K	1	0	25	26
1K Taropatch	0	0	1	1
2K Taropatch	0	0	1	1
3K Taropatch	0	0	1	1
Special Models	3	0	0	3
Totals	6	0	128	134

John Wanamaker

John Wanamaker was a department store with branches in New York City, Philadelphia, London, and Paris. Wanamaker ordered two Style 0 Customer Model ukuleles as a trial in August of 1922. These were stamped Martin, as the Wanamaker ukulele stamp was not received yet. In October Wanamaker received another twenty-five of these Style 0-C ukuleles, with the Wanamaker stamp on the back of the headstock but not inside the body. Martin explained the stamping to Wanamaker, noting that they had not received the metal stamp before the tops were glued on, making it impossible to place the stamp inside the body. They promised to stamp future orders in both locations, but as it happened no further orders were placed.

John Wanamaker	
Martin Style	1922
0	27

Wurlitzer

Beginning in 1922, Martin began manufacturing a large number of ukuleles for the The Rudolph Wurlitzer Company of Cincinnati, Ohio. Founded in Cincinnati in 1856, Wurlitzer had branches in many major cities by the early 1920s, including Chicago, New York City, Pittsburgh, Buffalo, San Francisco, Oakland, and Los Angeles. Wurlitzer's move into many cities in which Martin already had sole agents helped to spawn the idea of the specially-branded Customer Line of instruments. In 1922 Martin made special versions of five of its ukuleles and two of its taropatches for Wurlitzer. Most models had only minor differences from Martin-labeled models, but the Wurlitzer no. 839 was an exception. Based on a Martin Style 3K, the Wurlitzer model did not have the ornament below the bridge or the stripe down the center of the fretboard. Instead it had fancy fretboard inlays

Detail from Wurlitzer Model no. 839 ukulele

like those used on a Martin 5K. By 1923 Martin was selling its standard line to Wurlitzer, but they were marked with both the Wurlitzer stamp and the Martin stamp on the headstock, and only the Martin stamp inside of the body. In total Martin made well over 1000 ukuleles with the Wurlitzer stamp, all between 1922 and 1926.

Rudolph Wurlitzer

Martin Style	Wurlitzer Model Number	1922	1923	1924	1925	1926	Total
0	835	355	10	389	170	62	986
1	836	77	61	178	143	27	486
1K	837	90	34	67	45	0	236
2K	838	63	18	53	43	12	189
3K	839	62	12	28	25	0	127
2K Taropatch	841	19	1	43	32	0	95
3K Taropatch	844	0	12	0	0	0	12
Totals		666	148	758	458	101	2131

H. A. Weymann & Son

By their own description H. A. Weymann & Son was a "Musical Instrument Manufacturer, Wholesaler, and Jobber of Everything Musical" based in Philadelphia, Pennsylvania. Weymann made their own line of banjos, mandolins, guitars, and ukuleles. From 1923 to 1925 Weymann ordered Style 0 ukuleles from Martin to be made with "No Stamp." Weymann-made ukuleles are quite similar in construction to Martin ukuleles, causing some to mistake them for Martin-made instruments.

Decal from the headstock of a Weymann-made ukulele. Weymann may have placed similar decals on the ukuleles they obtained from Martin

H. A. Weymann & Son (No Stamp)

Martin Style	1922	1923	1924	1925	Total*
0	0	90	80	900	1070
1	0	0	0	200	200
Style 1 Taropatch	0	0	0	18	18
Totals	0	90	80	1118	1288

Production Totals

The production totals on the following pages were produced from a variety of sources. For ukuleles produced between 1915 and 1924, Martin sales books were used. These books recorded the sale of every individual instrument until 1924 when the method of logging the individual sales was changed. For the period of 1924–1927 Martin order books were used. These books record each individual instrument ordered by music stores and jobbers. The orders, obviously, come in before the sales, so when the company fell far behind on production, the orders and sales figures can look quite different. For example, 1925 and 1926 were Martin's two biggest years of ukulele production. 1925 was the biggest year for orders, with about 15,000. However, at the end of 1925, Martin had outstanding orders for about 4,000 instruments. Therefore, its sales for the year were closer to 11,000. In 1926, orders slowed and production was able to catch up. The sales records show about 14,000 ukuleles sold that year, but only about 10,000 of those were ordered that year. This is the main reason for discrepancies between these tables and the production totals found in *Martin Guitars: A Technical Reference*, by Johnson, Boak, and Longworth. Starting in late 1927 Martin began using production record sheets that are kept in their archives. These sheets show the actual batches of instruments that were being built, along with the dates that they reached various stages of production. These production record sheets were used to obtain production numbers from 1927 to 1973. Between 1974 and 1994 production record sheets were used as well, however these sheets were not as complete as the earlier sheets. All numbers in these tables are as accurate as they could be made. However, when working with this sort of data there are bound to be some mistakes and omissions.

Soprano Ukuleles

Year	Style 0	Style 1	Style 2	Style 3	Style 5	Style 1K	Style 2K	Style 3K	Style 5K	Total
1907	0	6[a]	0	0	0	0	0	0	0	6
1915	0	12	0	0	0	0	0	0	0	12
1916	0	759	313	149	0	0	0	0	0	1221
1917	0	1432	304	185	0	1	1	1	0	1924
1918	0	1168	225	66	0	0	0	0	0	1459
1919	0	2454	618	149	0	150	50	25	0	3446
1920	0	1571	522	299	0	200	251	224	0	3067
1921	0	851	262	83	0	296	82	38	0	1612
1922	2490	1049	389	143	0	236	135	137	44	4623
1923	2374	930	492	197	0	298	159	138	48	4636
1924	4165	1931	778	285	0	395	273	136	38	8001
1925	7032	3172	1433	640	1	1091	780	294	89	14532
1926	3197	2656	1244	437	0	908	705	436	166	9749
1927	2607	857	610	300	0	227	240	191	92	5124
1928	2000	300	400	300	0	200	50	75	75	3400
1929	1700	300	0	50	2	100	50	100	75	2377
1930	2800	400	0	125	0	100	75	150	50	3700
1931	1800	350	50	25	0	200	50	50	25	2550
1932	500	100	0	0	0	0	0	0	0	600
1933	194	50	25	0	0	0	0	25	0	294
1934	450	50	100	25	0	0	0	25	0	650
1935	550	100	75	50	0	50	0	25	0	850
1936	550	75	125	25	0	25	0	0	12	812
1937	800	150	175	75	1	125	0	36	0	1362
1938	450	150	100	50	0	100	0	25	12	887
1939	400	100	100	25	0	75	0	0	0	700
1940	500	75	75	50	0	100	0	0	0	800
1941	550	175	200	75	12	125	2	0	0	1139
1942	850	250	150	100	8	175	0	0	0	1533
1943	1138	375	300	175	0	375	0	0	0	2363
1944	900	425	300	150	0	160	0	0	0	1935
1945	1000	500	275	125	0	0	0	0	0	1900
Total 1915–1945	38997	22773	9640	4358	24	5712	2903	2131	726	87264

Soprano Ukuleles (continued)

Year	Style 0	Style 1	Style 2	Style 3	Style 5	Style 1K	Style 2K	Style 3K	Style 5K	Total
1915–1945	38997	22773	9640	4358	24	5712	2903	2131	726	87264
1946	1500	775	500	175	0	0	0	0	0	2950
1947	1250	900	450	325	0	0	0	0	0	2925
1948	950	625	475	275	0	0	0	0	0	2325
1949	2700	1447	950	575	0	0	0	0	0	5672
1950	3450	2000	1150	475	0	0	0	0	0	7075
1951	3500	1750	875	500	0	0	0	0	0	6625
1952	3048	1350	600	100	0	0	0	0	0	5098
1953	2900	850	325	125	0	0	0	0	0	4200
1954	2550	850	350	50	0	0	0	0	0	3800
1955	1550	400	125	100	0	0	0	0	0	2175
1956	2050	650	175	75	0	0	0	0	0	2950
1957	2500	200	175	100	0	0	0	0	0	2975
1958	2750	250	100	50	0	0	0	0	0	3150
1959	2950	350	175	50	0	0	0	0	0	3525
1960	2550	150	50	50	0	0	0	0	0	2800
1961	2450	299	150	50	0	0	0	0	0	2949
1962	2300	250	150	75	0	0	0	0	0	2775
1963	2450	400	100	25	0	0	0	0	0	2975
1964	1992	250	100	75	0	0	0	0	0	2417
1965	1246	149	100	50	0	0	0	0	0	1545
1966	699	0	0	25	0	0	0	0	0	724
1967	550	0	0	0	0	0	0	0	0	550
1968	400	0	0	60	0	0	0	0	0	460
1969	50	0	0	36	0	0	0	0	0	86
1970	0	0	0	60	0	0	0	0	0	60
1971	50	0	0	25	0	0	0	0	0	75
1972	150	0	0	75	0	0	0	0	0	225
1973	75	0	0	0	0	0	0	0	0	75
1974	0	0	0	0	0	0	0	0	0	0[b]
1975	50	0	0	0	0	0	0	0	0	50
1976	0	0	0	0	0	0	0	0	0	0
1977	24	0	0	13	0	0	0	0	0	37
1978	0	0	0	0	0	0	0	0	0	0
1979	35	0	0	15	0	0	0	0	0	50
1980	6	0	0	12	0	0	0	0	0	18
1981	18	0	0	0	0	0	0	3	0	21
1982	5	0	0	10	0	0	0	0	0	15
1983	0	0	0	6	0	0	0	0	0	6
1984	3	0	0	11	0	0	0	0	0	14
1985	2	0	0	4	0	0	0	0	0	6
1986	0	0	0	4	0	0	0	1	0	5
1987	2	0	0	6	0	0	0	1	0	9
1988	0	0	0	0	0	0	0	1	1	2
1989	4	0	0	8	0	0	0	6	0	18
1990	2	0	0	0	0	0	0	0	0	2
1991	6	0	0	6	0	0	0	2	0	14
1992	16	0	0	12	0	0	0	1	0	29
1993	0	0	0	4	0	0	0	0	0	4
1994	11	0	0	15	0	0	0	0	0	26
Total 1915–1994	87791	36668	16715	8065	24	5712	2903	2146	727	160749

Footnotes for Soprano Ukuleles

[a] Although listed here as Style 1, the specifications of the six ukuleles made in 1907 are not known.

[b] In some years during the 1970s no ukulele production records could be located, so it is unclear how many were made in these years.

Concert Ukuleles

Year	Style 0	Style 1	Style 2	Style 3	Style 1K	Style 2K	Style 3K	Style 5K	Total
1925	1	91	0	0	0	0	0	0	92
1926	0	311	0	1	0	0	1	1	314
1927	0	294	2	7	1	0	8	1	313
1928	0	150	0	3	2	0	16	1	172
1929	0	50	0	0	1	2	7	0	60
1930	0	175	0	0	0	0	0	1	176
1931	52	125	0	0	1	0	0	0	178
1932	0	0	0	0	0	0	0	0	0
1933	0	0	0	0	0	0	0	0	0
1934	0	25	0	0	0	0	0	0	25
1935	0	25	0	0	0	0	1	0	26
1936	0	50	0	0	1	2	0	0	53
1937	0	75	0	0	0	1	0	0	76
1938	0	50	0	0	0	0	0	0	50
1939	0	50	0	1	0	0	0	0	51
1940	0	100	0	0	0	0	0	0	100
1941	0	100	0	0	0	0	0	0	100
1942	0	75	0	0	0	0	0	0	75
1943	0	125	0	0	0	0	0	0	125
1944	0	100	0	0	0	0	0	0	100
1945	0	175	0	0	0	0	0	0	175
1946	0	225	0	0	0	0	0	0	225
1947	0	275	0	0	0	0	0	0	275
1948	0	225	0	0	0	0	0	0	225
1949	0	550	0	0	0	0	0	0	550
1950	0	550	0	0	0	0	0	0	550
1951	0	650	0	0	0	0	0	0	650
1952	0	650	0	0	0	0	0	0	650
1953	0	425	0	0	0	8	0	0	433
1954	0	350	0	3	0	0	0	0	353
1955	0	150	0	0	0	0	0	0	150
1956	0	325	0	0	0	0	0	0	325
1957	0	250	0	0	0	0	0	0	250
1958	0	325	0	0	0	0	0	0	325
1959	0	350	0	0	0	0	0	0	350
1960	0	150	0	0	0	0	0	0	150
1961	0	475	0	0	0	0	0	0	475
1962	0	125	0	0	0	0	0	0	125
1963	0	350	0	0	0	0	0	0	350
1964	0	250	0	0	0	0	0	0	250
1965	0	125	0	0	0	0	0	0	125
1966	0	0	0	0	0	0	0	0	0
1967	0	0	0	0	0	0	0	0	0
1968	0	1	0	0	0	0	0	0	1
1969	0	0	0	0	0	0	0	0	0
1970	0	2	0	0	0	0	0	0	2
1971	0	0	0	0	0	0	0	0	0
1972	0	0	0	0	0	0	0	0	0
1973	0	0	0	0	0	0	0	0	0
1974	0	0	0	0	0	0	0	0	0
1975	0	0	0	0	0	0	0	0	0
1976	0	0	0	0	0	0	0	0	0
1977	0	0	0	0	0	0	0	0	0
1978	0	0	0	0	0	0	0	0	0
1979	0	0	0	0	0	0	0	0	0
1980	0	0	0	0	0	0	0	0	0
1981	0	0	0	0	0	0	0	0	0
1982	0	5	0	0	0	0	0	0	5
1983	0	2	0	0	0	0	0	0	2
1984	0	1	0	0	0	0	0	0	1
1985	0	0	0	0	0	0	0	0	0
1986	0	2	0	0	0	0	0	0	2
1987	0	2	0	0	0	0	0	0	2
1988	0	0	0	0	6	0	0	0	6
1989	0	2	0	0	6	0	0	0	2
1990	0	0	0	0	0	0	0	0	0
1991	0	1	0	0	0	0	0	0	1
1992	0	8	0	0	5	0	0	0	13
1993	0	0	0	0	0	0	0	0	0
1994	0	12	0	0	0	0	0	0	12
Total	53	8959	2	15	23	13	33	4	9102

Tenor & Baritone Ukuleles

Year	Style 1 Tenor	Style 2 Tenor	Style 3 Tenor	Style 1K Tenor	Style 2K Tenor	Style 3K Tenor	Style 5K Tenor	Tenor Totals	Style 51 Baritone	Unusual Baritone
1928	181	0	0	0	0	0	0	181	0	0
1929	225	0	4	0	3	0	6	238	0	0
1930	150	0	2	0	1	0	3	156	0	0
1931	125	0	2	0	0	0	0	127	0	0
1932	50	0	0	0	0	0	0	50	0	0
1933	25	0	0	0	0	0	0	25	0	0
1934	104	0	0	0	0	0	0	104	0	0
1935	78	0	0	0	0	0	0	78	0	0
1936	78	0	0	1	0	0	0	79	0	0
1937	125	0	1	0	1	0	0	127	0	0
1938	75	0	0	0	0	0	0	75	0	0
1939	100	0	0	0	0	0	0	100	0	0
1940	75	0	0	0	0	0	0	75	0	0
1941	125	0	0	0	0	0	0	125	0	0
1942	100	0	0	0	0	0	0	100	0	0
1943	175	0	0	0	0	0	0	175	0	0
1944	100	0	0	0	0	0	0	100	0	0
1945	175	0	0	0	0	0	0	175	0	0
1946	175	0	0	0	0	0	0	175	0	0
1947	300	0	0	0	0	0	0	300	0	0
1948	225	0	0	0	0	0	0	225	0	0
1949	600	0	0	0	0	0	0	600	0	0
1950	775	0	0	0	0	0	0	775	0	0
1951	1125	0	0	0	0	0	0	1125	0	0
1952	1025	0	0	0	0	0	0	1025	0	0
1953	1200	0	0	0	0	0	0	1200	0	0
1954	625	0	0	0	0	0	0	625	0	0
1955	700	0	0	0	0	0	0	700	0	0
1956	525	0	0	0	0	0	0	525	0	0
1957	725	0	0	0	0	0	0	725	0	0
1958	650	0	0	0	0	0	0	650	0	0
1959	875	0	0	0	0	0	0	875	0	0
1960	700	0	0	0	0	0	0	700	630	0
1961	625	1	0	0	0	0	0	626	625	0
1962	450	0	0	0	0	0	0	450	775	0
1963	525	0	0	0	0	0	0	525	650	0
1964	475	0	0	0	0	0	0	475	549	0
1965	425	0	0	0	0	0	0	425	0	0
1966	175	0	0	0	0	0	0	175	250	0
1967	175	0	0	0	0	0	0	175	150	0
1968	25	0	0	0	0	0	0	25	300	0
1969	25	0	0	0	0	0	0	25	75	0
1970	161	0	0	0	0	0	0	161	137	0
1971	225	0	0	0	0	0	0	225	275	0
1972	100	0	0	0	0	0	0	100	150	0
1973	50	0	0	0	0	0	0	50	25	0
1974	0	0	0	0	0	0	0	0	0	0
1975	75	0	0	0	0	0	0	75	76	0
1976	0	0	0	0	0	0	0	0	0	0
1977	82	0	0	0	0	0	0	82	27	0
1978	0	0	0	0	0	0	0	0	0	0
1979	18	0	0	0	0	0	0	18	18	0
1980	16	0	0	0	0	0	0	16	20	2 (5K)
1981	6	0	0	3	0	0	0	9	5	7 (1K)
1982	0	0	0	0	0	0	0	0	3	1 (1K)
1983	14	0	0	0	0	0	0	14	16	0
1984	3	0	0	0	0	0	0	3	11	1 (1K)
1985	3	0	0	0	0	0	0	3	6	2 (1K)
1986	0	0	0	0	0	0	0	0	5	1 (1K)
1987	6	0	0	0	0	0	0	6	11	0
1988	6	0	0	1	0	0	0	7	13	0
1989	2	0	0	1	0	0	0	3	7	1*
1990	6	0	0	0	0	0	0	6	4	2 (1K)
1991	6	0	0	2	0	0	0	8	0	0
1992	16	0	0	0	0	0	0	16	16	0
1993	0	0	0	0	0	0	0	0	0	0
1994	0	0	0	0	0	0	0	0	0	0
Total	15986	1	9	8	5	0	9	16018	4829	17

*The baritone ukulele made in 1989 was noted as a "special" koa baritone.

Taropatches: Eight & Four String

Year	Eight String						Four String						Total
	Style 1	Style 2	Style 3	Style 1K	Style 2K	Style 3K	Style 1	Style 2	Style 3	Style 1K	Style 2K	Style 3K	
1916	60	26	32	0	0	0	16	7	9	0	0	0	150
1917	61	31	34	0	0	0	5	0	0	0	0	0	131
1918	17	8	1	0	0	0	0	0	0	0	0	0	26
1919	62	26	13	1	1	2	4	1	0	0	0	0	110
1920	34	20	10	13	11	12	0	0	0	0	0	0	100
1921	34	10	2	7	1	1	0	0	1	0	0	0	56
1922	56	23	9	14	27	7	3	2	0	0	0	0	141
1923	55	25	8	6	24	29	3	3	0	0	0	0	153
1924	171	38	20	33	84	8	11	0	0	1	0	3	369
1925	319	106	20	61	102	15	7	3	1	0	1	0	635
1926	177	54	17	60	50	12	0	0	0	0	0	0	370
1927	60	20	6	22	7	6	0	0	0	0	0	0	121
1928	0	0	0	0	0	0	0	0	0	0	0	0	0
1929	0	0	0	0	0	0	0	0	0	0	0	0	0
1930	0	0	0	0	0	0	0	0	0	0	0	0	0
1931	1	0	0	0	0	1	0	0	0	0	0	0	2
1932	0	0	0	0	0	0	0	0	0	0	0	0	0
1933	1	0	0	0	0	0	0	0	0	0	0	0	1
1934	0	0	1	0	0	0	0	0	0	0	0	0	1
1935	1	0	0	0	0	0	0	0	0	0	0	0	1
Total	1109	387	173	217	307	93	49	16	11	1	1	3	2367

Modern Martin Ukuleles: 2005–2011

Year	Style 5K	Style 5 Daisy	Style 3	Style 3K	Style 3 Cherry	Style 2	Style 2K	Style 2 Concert	Style 2K Concert	Style 2 Tenor	Style 2K Tenor	Total
2005	4	0	0	0	0	0	0	0	0	0	0	4
2006	139	2	0	0	0	0	0	0	0	0	0	141
2007	88	47	1	1	1	0	0	0	0	0	0	138
2008	3	19	56	80	36	0	0	0	0	0	0	194
2009	2	0	37	0	20	0	0	0	0	0	0	59
2010	5	2	30	33	35	0	0	0	0	0	0	105
2011	12	2	54	46	31	85	95	91	96	86	102	700
Total	253	72	178	160	123	85	95	91	96	86	102	1341

Photo Credits

All images are courtesy of **C. F. Martin Archives** and **C. F. Martin Museum,** unless noted below. Studio photography of the more current instruments by John Sterling Ruth Photography (www.johnsterlingruth.com).

Preface

Page ix: photo by Tom Walsh; **Page xi:** photo by Tom Walsh.

Chapter 2

Page 4: photo of archive books by Tom Walsh; **Page 5:** photo of machete by Tom Walsh, machete from author's collection; **Page 6:** postcard and photograph from author's collection; **Page 7:** drawing from *One Summer In Hawaii,* by Helen Mather, from author's collection; postcard from author's collection; five-string taropatch photo by Tom Walsh, taropatch from author's collection.

Chapter 3

Page 9: photo of Anthony Zablan courtesy Hawaii State Archives; photo of Cyclorama building from author's collection; **Page 10:** harp guitar photo by Tom Walsh; **Page 11:** materials from author's collection; **Page 12:** Bergstrom Ukulele Method courtesy of Paul Weber; **Page 13:** photo by Tom Walsh, ukuleles from author's collection; **Page 14:** photos by Tom Walsh, ukulele from author's collection; **Page 15:** Ditson ad and ukulele method books from author's collection.

Chapter 4

Page 16: sheet music from author's collection; **Page 17:** sheet music from author's collection; **Page 18:** ukulele photos by Tom Walsh, ukulele courtesy of Roger Phillips; Wm. Smith photo from author's collection; **Page 19:** photos by Tom Walsh, ukuleles courtesy of Stan Werbin; **Page 21:** taropatch photo courtesy of Andrew Roth; **Page 22:** advertising from author's collection; **Page 26:** ukulele photo courtesy of Frederik Goossens; **Page 27:** ukulele photo courtesy of Frederik Goossens; **Page 28:** postcard from author's collection; **Page 29:** ukulele photos by Tom Walsh, (left) courtesy of Stan Werbin, (right) from author's collection.

Chapter 5

Page 33: photo by Tom Walsh, tiple courtesy of Warren Dovel; **Page 35:** catalog from author's collection; **Page 36:** photo by Tom Walsh, ukulele courtesy of Stan Werbin; **Page 37:** method book photos from author's collection; **Page 38:** ukulele photo courtesy of Frederik Goossens; **Page 39:** ukulele photos by Tom Walsh, ukulele courtesy of Dave Wasser; **Page 40:** photos by Tom Walsh, ukuleles from author's collection; **Page 42:** photos by Tom Walsh, ukulele courtesy of Dave Wasser; **Page 43:** photos by Tom Walsh, stamps owned by C. F. Martin Archives; **Page 44:** catalog image from author's collection; ukulele photo by Tom Walsh, ukulele courtesy of Dave Pasant; **Page 45:** soundhole photo by Tom Walsh; ukulele photo courtesy of Frederik Goossens; **Page 46:** photo courtesy of Frederik Goossens; **Page 47:** photo from author's collection; **Page 48:** photo by Tom Walsh, ukulele from author's collection; **Page 49:** image from author's collection; **Page 50:** Wendell Hall and Johnny Marvin sheet music photos from author's collection; Cliff Edwards photo courtesy of Jerry Murbach; **Page 51:** graph created by Tom Walsh; **Page 52:** photo from author's collection; **Page 53:** sheet music from author's collection.

Chapter 6

Page 59: postcard from author's collection; **Page 61:** ukulele photo by Tom Walsh, ukulele from author's collection; **Page 62:** photo courtesy of Bill Watson; **Page 66:** instructional book photo and Christmas card photo from author's collection; **Page 67:** ukulele headstock photo by Tom Walsh, ukulele from author's collection;

Page 71: ad from author's collection; **Page 74:** photo by Tom Walsh, ukulele courtesy of Stan Werbin; **Page 75:** photo by Tom Walsh, ukulele courtesy of Stan Werbin; **Page 76:** pamphlet from author's collection; **Page 77:** photos by Tom Walsh, ukuleles courtesy of Stan Werbin.

Chapter 7

Page 80: method book from author's collection; **Page 81:** method book from author's collection; **Page 82:** images courtesy of the Ukulele Hall of Fame Museum; **Page 83:** photo by Tom Walsh, ukulele courtesy of Dave Pasant; **Page 84:** images from author's collection; **Page 85:** graph created by Tom Walsh; **Page 87:** photo courtesy of Bill Watson; inset photo by Tom Walsh, ukulele courtesy of Stan Werbin.

Chapter 8

Page 89: photo from author's collection; **Page 90:** photos by Tom Walsh, ukuleles courtesy of Stan Werbin (Harold Teen, Lyon & Healy Shrine, Martin Style 2), other ukuleles from author's collection; **Page 94:** photo from author's collection; **Page 95:** postcard and method book from author's collection; **Page 96:** sheet music and music book from author's collection; **Page 97:** Eddie Kamae photo courtesy of Eddie and Myrna Kamae; other photos from author's collection; **Page 99:** albums from author's collection.

Chapter 9

Page 100: photo from author's collection; **Page 103:** ad from author's collection; **Page 104:** ukulele soundhole photo by Tom Walsh, ukulele from author's collection.

Chapter 10

Page 111: color photo of Mike Longworth by Donelle Nunes Sawyer; ukulele photo by Tom Walsh, ukulele courtesy of Dave Pasant.

Chapter 11

Page 113: photo by Tom Walsh; **Page 119:** photo of Israel Kamakawiwoʻole courtesy of Mountain Apple Company, Hawaii (www.mountainapplecompany.com).

Appendix A

Page 121: ukulele photo courtesy of Mark Brown; **Page 122:** photos by Tom Walsh, ukuleles from author's collection; **Page 123:** ukuleles courtesy of Frederik Goossens, Stan Werbin, Dave Pasant, Warren Dovel, C. F. Martin Museum, and author's collection; **Page 125:** photos by Tom Walsh, ukuleles from author's collection; **Pages 125–129:** photos by Tom Walsh, tuning pegs from author's collection.

Appendix B

Page 132: photos by Tom Walsh, ukulele from author's collection; **Page 133:** photos by Tom Walsh, ukuleles from author's collection; **Page 135:** photo by Tom Walsh, ukulele courtesy of Roger Phillips; **Page 136:** (left) photo by Tom Walsh, ukulele from author's collection; **Page 137:** (left) photo by Tom Walsh, ukulele courtesy of Warren Dovel; (right) photo by Tom Walsh, ukulele from author's collection; **Page 139:** (left) photo by Tom Walsh, ukulele courtesy of Stan Werbin; (right) photo by Tom Walsh, ukulele from author's collection; **Page 140:** ukulele headstock photo by Tom Walsh, ukulele courtesy of Stan Werbin; **Page 143:** (left) photo by Tom Walsh, ukulele courtesy of Stan Werbin; (right) photo by Tom Walsh, ukulele from author's collection; **Page 144:** (left) photo by Tom Walsh, ukulele courtesy the Ukulele Hall of Fame Museum; (right) photo by Tom Walsh, ukulele courtesy of Stan Werbin; **Page 145:** (left) photo by Tom Walsh, ukulele from author's collection; **Page 146:** ukulele photo courtesy of Frederik Goossens; **Page 148:** photos by Tom Walsh, ukuleles courtesy of Stan Werbin; **Page 151:** photo by Tom Walsh, taropatch courtesy of Warren Dovel; **Page 152:** (right) photo by Tom Walsh, taropatch courtesy of Warren Dovel; **Page 153:** photos by Tom Walsh, taropatches courtesy of

Appendix B (continued)

Warren Dovel; **Page 154:** photos by Tom Walsh, taropatches courtesy of Warren Dovel; **Page 155:** (left) photo by Leo Coulson, taropatch courtesy of Intermountain Guitar and Banjo; (right) taropatch photo courtesy of Andrew Roth; **Page 158:** (left) photo by Leo Coulson, ukulele courtesy of Intermountain Guitar and Banjo; (right) photo by Tom Walsh, ukulele from author's collection; **Page 159:** (left) ukulele photo courtesy of Andy Roth; (right) photo by Tom Walsh, ukulele courtesy of Dave Pasant; **Page 160:** (left) photo by Tom Walsh, ukulele courtesy of Dave Pasant; (right) ukulele photo courtesy of Andy Roth; **Page 161:** photos by Tom Walsh, ukuleles courtesy of Dave Pasant; **Page 164:** (left) photo by Tom Walsh, ukulele from author's collection; (right) photo by Tom Walsh, ukulele courtesy of Dave Pasant; **Page 165:** photos by Tom Walsh, ukuleles courtesy of Dave Pasant; **Page 167:** ukulele photo by Tom Walsh, ukulele courtesy of Warren Dovel; **Page 168:** (left) photo by Tom Walsh, ukulele from author's collection; (right) photo by Tom Walsh, ukulele courtesy of Warren Dovel; **Page 169:** (left) photo by Tom Walsh, ukulele courtesy of Warren Dovel; (right) photo by Tom Walsh, ukulele courtesy of Dave Pasant.

Appendix C

Page 171: photos by Tom Walsh, ukuleles from author's collection; **Page 172:** photo by Tom Walsh, ukulele courtesy of Stan Werbin; **Page 173:** photo by Tom Walsh, ukulele from author's collection; **Page 174:** ukulele photo courtesy of William Bunch; **Page 176:** Johnie Dunn ukulele photo courtesy Bill Watson; **Page 177:** ukulele photos courtesy of Steve Farr; **Page 178:** photos by Tom Walsh, ukulele courtesy of Stan Werbin; **Page 179:** photos by Billy Voiers and Julia D. St. Clair, ukulele courtesy of the William D. Voiers collection; **Page 180:** photos by Tom Walsh, ukulele courtesy of Dave Pasant; **Page 181:** photos by Tom Walsh, taropatch courtesy of Dave Pasant; **Page 182:** photos by Tom Walsh, ukulele courtesy of Dave Pasant; **Page 183:** photos by Tom Walsh, ukulele courtesy of Dave Pasant.

Appendix D

Page 186: ukulele label photo by Tom Walsh, ukulele from author's collection; **Page 187:** ukulele soundhole photo courtesy of Frederik Goossens; **Page 190:** ukulele photos courtesy of Frederik Goossens; **Page 191:** (left) photo by Tom Walsh, ukulele from author's collection; (right) ukulele photo courtesy of Frederik Goossens; **Page 192:** (left) photo by Tom Walsh, ukulele courtesy of Stan Werbin; (right) photo by Tom Walsh, ukulele from author's collection; **Page 193:** (left) ukulele photo courtesy of Frederik Goossens; (right) taropatch photo courtesy of Andy Roth; **Page 194:** ukulele stamp photo by Tom Walsh, ukulele from author's collection; **Page 197:** ukulele and ukulele stamp photos by Tom Walsh, ukulele courtesy of Dave Wasser; **Page 199:** method book image from author's collection; **Page 200:** ukulele photo courtesy of Frederik Goossens; **Page 201:** ukulele photos by Tom Walsh, ukulele courtesy of Dave Wasser; **Page 202:** ukulele photo by Tom Walsh, ukulele courtesy of Dave Pasant; **Page 203:** ukulele decal photo by Tom Walsh, ukulele courtesy of Ukulele Hall of Fame Museum.

Index

Note: page numbers in *italics* refer to illustrations and captions.